KU-341-048

Foundations German

1

Second Edition

Tom Carty
Formerly Principal Lecturer in German
and Languages Programme Leader
at Staffordshire University
and the University of Wolverhampton

Ilse Wührer
Teaching Fellow in German, Keele University

Series Editor
Tom Carty

Review Panel for the Second Edition

Stefan Manz, Senior Lecturer, School of Languages
and Social Sciences, Aston University, Birmingham

Hanna Ostermann, Senior Lecturer, Department of Languages,
Northumbria University, Newcastle upon Tyne

Caroline Hill, Visiting Tutor, Modern Languages Teaching Centre,
University of Sheffield

Meike Reintjes, German Language Tutor,
Modern Languages, University of Southampton

Elisabeth Ruggles, Part-time Tutor, Modern Languages,
University of Southampton

palgrave
macmillan

© Tom Carty and Ilse Wührer 2003, 2011

All rights reserved. No reproduction, copy or transmission of this
publication may be made without written permission.

No portion of this publication may be reproduced, copied or transmitted
save with written permission or in accordance with the provisions of the
Copyright, Designs and Patents Act 1988, or under the terms of any licence
permitting limited copying issued by the Copyright Licensing Agency,
Saffron House, 6-10 Kirby Street, London EC1N 8TS.

Any person who does any unauthorized act in relation to this publication
may be liable to criminal prosecution and civil claims for damages.

The authors have asserted their rights to be identified as the authors of this
work in accordance with the Copyright, Designs and Patents Act 1988.

First edition 2003
Reissued with CDs 2010
Second edition 2011
Published by
PALGRAVE MACMILLAN

Palgrave Macmillan in the UK is an imprint of Macmillan Publishers Limited,
registered in England, company number 785998, of Houndmills, Basingstoke,
Hampshire RG21 6XS.

Palgrave Macmillan in the US is a division of St Martin's Press LLC,
175 Fifth Avenue, New York, NY 10010.

Palgrave Macmillan is the global academic imprint of the above companies
and has companies and representatives throughout the world.

Palgrave® and Macmillan® are registered trademarks in the United States,
the United Kingdom, Europe and other countries

ISBN 978-0-230-28474-6

This book is printed on paper suitable for recycling and made from fully
managed and sustained forest sources. Logging, pulping and manufacturing
processes are expected to conform to the environmental regulations of the
country of origin.

A catalogue record for this book is available from the British Library.

A catalog record for this book is available from the Library of Congress.

Audio Production: University of Brighton Media Centre
Produced by Brian Hill
Voices: Monika Lind, Ulla Spittler, Gerd Knischewski, Andreas Hoecht, Ilse Wührer

10 9 8 7 6 5 4 3
20 19 18 17 16 15 14

Printed and bound in China

CONTENTS

Acknowledgements

The authors would like to thank Ed Doragh for documents and information on his year at a German university.

All photographic illustrations were supplied by Ilse and Bernd Wührer, except for those by: Colette Carty p.1 (Anne) and p.3 (Kirsty); Simone Hapel pp. 12, 24, 36, 64, 119, 122; iStock International Inc. pp. 13, 38, 81, 83, 85, 86, 93, 95, 97, 98; Jennifer Schmidt pp. 52 (photos d and e), 71.

The authors would like to thank everyone who helped by posing for photographs.

Every effort has been made to trace all copyright holders, but if any have inadvertently been overlooked the publishers will be pleased to make the necessary arrangements at the first opportunity.

Ein herzliches Dankeschön an meinen Bruder, Bernd G. Wührer. Bernd und seine Freunde haben viel Zeit damit verbracht, Fotos für dieses Buch zu machen – und es war kalt in Darmstadt!

Ilse Wührer

INTRODUCTION

Mainly for the tutor

Level

Foundations German 1 is a course for beginners, designed specifically for ab initio optional or elective programmes in higher education and similar provision. The authors have many years' experience of teaching beginners' and intermediate courses in universities and of administrative responsibility for such provision. The Foundations Languages team keeps in close touch with languages departments and language centres, and this revised second edition is informed by the experience of a review panel of tutors.

The course is designed to fit the university teaching year and assumes two or three hours of contact per week. Intensive courses with more contact hours will take commensurately less time, although the flexible structure permits tutors to extend and supplement core work as they see fit.

In terms of the Common European Framework, the course delivers level A2 plus, with several competences at level B1. There are 10 units, each structured in the same way. Extension work, pairwork and a separate private study strand provide the flexibility noted above. Grammar and vocabulary are fully supported within each unit as well as in the reference pages. Answers to all exercises are given at the back of the book.

Unit structure

Element	Pages	Function	Skills
Core	6/8	Introduces, practises new material.	LSRW
Extra!	1	Extension work (e.g. unscripted dialogues, more demanding reading).	LR
Grammar	2	One page exposition, one page exercises.	
Vocabulary	1	German–English, listed by exercise.	
Partnerarbeit	2	Consolidation, in or out of class.	S
Weitere Übungen	2	Consolidation, private study.	LRW(S)

Skills – L = Listening, S = Speaking, R = Reading, W = Writing

Approach

Various approaches are taken to the introduction of new material, but most involve listening. Of these the commonest is **Hören und Lesen**, with the student listening to the dialogue while following the script before tackling input exercises, with further exercises then developing and applying the new material.

Introduction

To facilitate the use of German in the classroom, exercises are marked with an icon indicating the linguistic activity or activities: see **Im Unterricht** on page xiv.

Audio material

Two CDs to accompany the course come with each book. A track list can be found on pages xii and xiii. Digital licences for the download and use of MP3 files are also available. Visit http://www.palgrave.com/modernlanguages/license.asp#Digital. You can also download the transcript for the audio as a Word document at http://www.palgrave.com/modernlanguages/tapescripts.asp. You will need to register with www.palgrave.com and request access to do this. The webpage explains how.

Mainly for the student

Unit content

The 10 **units** all have the same clear, consistent structure. Each focuses on one or more topics or situations in which the language is used. A short **summary** at the start of the unit tells you what you will be able to do once you have completed it.

Unit core

The six or eight pages that follow are the **core** of the unit. This contains the inputs (new language) for the unit and various tasks designed to help you master it and make it your own. For ease of reference, each unit is divided into numbered items, each with an icon or icons indicating the language skills you will be using and developing (see the table of icons on page xiv).

The input exercises in the core are carefully designed to introduce new vocabulary and/or structures. They take various forms including *presentation*, such as when you are given numbers, days of the week or how to tell the time; and *matching exercises*, where you are introduced to new words or structures by matching up the German with its English equivalent or a picture; but most are *listening* items in the form of dialogues.

In some you will be asked to listen and repeat or to listen first and fill in gaps, checking the script afterwards. In most, however, you will listen and read, following the script in the book. Then there may be questions to answer in German, true/false statements or comprehension exercises with questions in English or German. Whatever form the input takes, it is absolutely vital to spend time and effort on this material. The exercises that follow enable you to practise and master the aspects of language introduced and then to apply them, in particular to produce your own German in speech and writing.

Extra!

The unit core is followed by a page headed **Extra!** As the heading implies, this material makes extra demands. It is that bit more challenging and gives you the opportunity to develop your listening and reading skills beyond the confines of the core input material while staying on related topics. Vocabulary from this page is given in the overall vocabulary lists at the end of the book.

Grammar and vocabulary

Two pages are then devoted to the new **grammatical structures** introduced in the unit. On the left-hand page you will find a clear overview of the grammar, while the opposite page provides a set of short exercises so that you can test yourself (answers at the back of the book). The **vocabulary** page gives the new words occurring in the unit core, exercise by exercise.

Partnerwork

Each unit closes with two pages of **partnerwork** giving prompts for each partner in a structured dialogue. This material can be used in or out of the classroom to develop communication skills. The scenarios are always based on the material in the unit core, so that you are securely in a familiar context. The challenge is to use language you have learned to communicate information your partner needs and then to respond to what he or she says.

Weitere Übungen

The strand of **supplementary exercises** beginning on page 123 gives further practice on a unit-by-unit basis and is designed to be used in private study, although it may be used in class. No new material is introduced in these pages.

Reference

Answers to all exercises are included at the back of the book along with material on **spelling** and **pronunciation**, an overall **grammar summary** supported by **definitions of grammatical terms**, and an overall **alphabetical vocabulary list** or **glossary**.

LEARNING A LANGUAGE

A language-learning programme is essentially workshop-based rather than lecture-based. It involves active classroom sessions and a variety of social interactions, including working with a partner, small-group activity and role-play, as well as answering questions and working through exercises. Feeding into the classroom sessions and flowing from them is what is called directed study, set by your tutor but allowing you a lot of flexibility in organising your work in ways that suit you. Beyond that there is private study, where you determine the priorities.

Apart from competence in the language itself, successful language learning is also recognised as rich in skills particularly valued by employers, such as communication and self-management.

How to make sure you get maximum benefit from your language course

1 A practical point first. Check the course module guide and/or **syllabus** to see what exactly is required of you. In particular, find out how the course or module is assessed. The course guide and assessment information will probably be expressed in terms of the four language skills of listening, speaking, reading and writing.

2 **Your tutor** is your guide. Using the material in the book, he or she will introduce new structures, ensure you practise them in class and then enable you to produce similar language until you develop the capacity to work independently.

3 While a tutor can show you the way, **only you can do the learning**. This means hard work both in the classroom and outside the timetabled hours.

4 **Regular attendance** at the language classes is vital. This isn't like a lecture-based course, where you can miss one session and then catch up from a friend's notes or even live with the fact that there is going to be a gap in your knowledge. A language class is a workshop in which one thing builds on another. You do things. Or, to put it more formally, you take part in structured activities designed to develop your linguistic competence.

5 But being there isn't the same as learning. You have to **participate**. This means being an active member of the class, listening carefully, working through the exercises, answering questions, taking part in dialogues, contributing to group work, taking the risk of speaking without the certainty of being right. It also means preparing before classes and following up afterwards …

6 … because what you do **outside the classroom** is vital, too. While new topics will normally be introduced in class, the tutor will also set tasks that feed into what you'll be doing in the next session. If you don't do the preparation, you can't benefit from the classroom activity, or the tutor will have to spend valuable time going over the preparation in class for the benefit of those who haven't done it in advance. Similarly, the

tutor will sometimes ask you to follow up work done in class with tasks designed to consolidate and develop what you have done there.

7 You should also take time to **review** and reflect on what you've been doing, regularly going over what you have done in class. This will also enable you to decide your priorities for private study, working on areas you find difficult or which are particularly important or interesting to you.

8 This assumes you are **organised**: keep a file or notebook in which you jot down what you have done and what you plan to do. It's a good idea to work for several shortish bursts a week rather than for a long time once a week.

9 While a lot of out-of-class work will be done at home, the university or college will probably have a learning centre, **Language Centre** or similar facility. Use this whenever you can to reinforce and supplement what you're doing in class. Make sure any material you use is suitable for your level: it will probably be classified or labelled using broad categories such as beginners, intermediate and advanced. The tutor may set specific work to be done in the Language Centre or you may be expected to spend a certain amount of time there, otherwise you should find times when you can drop in. The course assessment schedule may well include a **portfolio** for which you choose coursework items according to guidelines set by the tutor or the course.

10 Don't be afraid of **grammar.** This is simply the term for how we describe the way language works. Learn it and revise it as you go along: there are boxes with grammar points throughout each of the units of this book, and a grammar summary at the end of each unit as well as a grammar overview for the whole book. You probably feel hesitant about grammatical terms such as *direct object* or *definite article* but they are useful labels and easily learnt. There is a guide to such terms towards the end of the book.

11 In addition to listening-based work in class, you should regularly work in your own time on the accompanying audio material. Try to reproduce the **pronunciation** and intonation of the native speakers on the recording. It is much easier if you work at this from the start and establish good habits than if you approximate to the sounds of the language and have to correct them later. It's important to speak out loud rather than in your head. Why not work with a friend?

12 Always bear in mind that, in learning a language, you can normally understand (listening and reading) more than you can express (speaking and writing). Above all, relax when listening or reading: remember **you don't have to be sure of every word** to get the message and you don't need to translate into your native language.

13 Regular **practice** is the key. Remember *fluency* comes from the Latin for 'to flow': it means speaking flowingly, not necessarily getting everything perfectly right. It is also a good idea to dip back into early units in the book and test yourself.

14 Universities and colleges are international institutions and you will almost certainly be able to make contact with **native speakers**. Try out your German with German-speakers, get them to correct your pronunciation, and find out about their countries and cultures.

Tom Carty, Series Editor

OVERVIEW

	Communication	Vocabulary	Grammar
1	Introducing and giving information about oneself Understanding information about others Asking questions (formal and informal) to elicit such information	Countries; nationalities; jobs	Pronouns **ich**, **du**, **er**, **sie**, **Sie**; present tense of weak verbs and **sein** (**ich-**, **du-**, **Sie-**, **er-**, **sie-**forms); forming questions; **w**-words (question words) **was**, **wie**, **wo**, **wer**, **woher**, **warum**
2	Talking about daily routine Frequency Numbers 24-hour clock	Campus locations and activities, evening leisure activities; mealtimes, food and drink; numbers 1–99; adverbs of frequency, time of day	Gender; prepositions (**in**, **an** + accusative); **haben**; separable verbs; **essen** as example of strong verb; definite and indefinite articles, word order: position of main verb, and adverbs
3	Understanding information about the family circumstances of others Talking about your family Talking about what you own and need Healthy and unhealthy lifestyles	Family relationships; everyday objects; food and drink: healthy diet	Accusative of indefinite article; **kein**; possessives in nominative and accusative; pronouns **wir**, **sie** ('they'); plurals of nouns
4	Saying what you like and don't like doing/eating/drinking Stating preferences (i) Making and responding to suggestions, invitations Understanding information about leisure activities Ordering a meal Telling the time ('five to')	Days of the week; leisure activities, food and drink: preferences, eating out	**Gern**, **lieber**, **am liebsten**; modal verbs – **müssen**, **können**, **wollen**; **man kann** …; accusative of definite article; strong verbs **lesen** and **fahren**
5	Saying where you are or where someone/something is Giving and understanding information/opinions about where you and others live	Rooms; furniture/equipment; adjectives describing rooms and furniture	Recap articles and possessives: introduction of label 'nominative'; dative (articles and possessives) after prepositions; pronoun **ihr**; possessive **euer**; **es gibt** … ; adjectival endings in the accusative; adjectival endings before plural nouns

	Communication	Vocabulary	Grammar
6	Asking for and understanding directions Describing locations in a town centre Stating likes and dislikes Shopping	Shops, public buildings; clothes; colours	Imperative; prepositions with the dative/with the accusative; **gefallen**; **dieser**, **welcher**, **jeder**
7	Trying to fix a date Saying when your birthday is Understanding information about accommodation Making travel enquiries Buying a ticket at the station Buying a ticket from a machine Arriving at reception Booking a hotel room	Months; rail travel; about a ticket machine; hotel accommodation; student residence	**Um ... zu**; subordinate clauses: **wenn**, **dass**, **weil**; dative plural; ordinal numbers; dative pronouns; **seit**; indirect object
8	Talking about the recent past Describing how you feel	Food and drink: shopping and cooking; states of mind and emotions; aches and pains, parts of the body	Perfect tense; simple past tense used for **sein**, **haben**, modals; accusative pronouns
9	Brief lives of famous people Talking about your life, education and experience and those of others Saying what sort of job you would like Understanding CVs, information and advertisements about jobs Constructing a CV Applying for a job	Years and numbers over 100 Language needed to write a CV/job application; qualities needed for a job	Perfect tense (verbs in **-ieren**, verbs with an inseparable prefix, mixed verbs); reflexive verbs; **würde gern/möchte gern**; subordinate clauses: **als**, **obwohl**
10	Expressing wishes and hopes Contrasting then and now Making holiday arrangements Stating preferences (ii) Understanding a magazine article	Qualities of a potential partner; holiday activities and locations; living abroad	Genitive; adjectival endings; comparative of adjectives; modal verb **dürfen**

CD TRACK LIST

Two CDs are supplied with this book. They contain all the audio material to accompany the exercises.

- Where there is an audio element for an exercise it is marked with a 🎧 icon or a 🎧 icon.

- Every exercise has its own track, which will help you locate the material very easily.
- All the audio for the **Weitere Übungen** section is on CD2.
- Tutors who require digital licences for this audio material should visit http://www.palgrave.com/modernlanguages/license.asp#digital.

CD1

Track	**Unit 1 – Studenten**
01	Exercise 1a
02	Exercise 1b
03	Exercise 3a
04	Exercise 3b
05	Exercise 6
06	Exercise 7
07	Exercise 9a
08	Exercise 9b
09	Exercise 10
10	Exercise 12a
11	Extra! Exercise 18

	Unit 2 – Bibliothek oder Diskothek?
12	Exercise 1a
13	Aufgabe 1b
14	Aufgabe 1c
15	Aufgabe 2
16	Aufgabe 3c
17	Aufgabe 4
18	Aufgabe 5
19	Aufgabe 7
20	Aufgabe 11
21	Extra! Aufgabe 17

	Einheit 3 – Familie
22	Aufgabe 1 u. 2

23	Aufgabe 3 – Caroline
24	Aufgabe 3 – Andreas
25	Aufgabe 4a
26	Aufgabe 4b
27	Aufgabe 7
28	Aufgabe 11a
29	Aufgabe 11b
30	Extra! Aufgabe 13 – Annelie
31	Extra! Aufgabe 13 – Markus
32	Extra! Aufgabe 13 – Hanna
33	Grammatikübung 3 – Karin
34	Grammatikübung 3 – Klaus

	Einheit 4 – Am Wochenende
35	Aufgabe 1
36	Aufgabe 4
37	Aufgabe 7
38	Aufgabe 8a
39	Aufgabe 8b
40	Aufgabe 9
41	Aufgabe 10a
42	Aufgabe 11
43	Aufgabe 13
44	Extra! Aufgabe 14

	Einheit 5 – Zu Hause
45	Aufgabe 1a
46	Aufgabe 1b
47	Aufgabe 2a

48 Aufgabe 5
49 Aufgabe 8
50 Extra! Aufgabe 10 – Volker
51 Extra! Aufgabe 10 – Silvia
52 Extra! Aufgabe 10 – Oliver

Einheit 6 – In der Stadt

53 Aufgabe 1
54 Aufgabe 3 – U-Bahn-Station
55 Aufgabe 3 – Goethehaus
56 Aufgabe 4 – a
57 Aufgabe 4 – b
58 Aufgabe 7 – a
59 Aufgabe 7 – b
60 Aufgabe 9a – 1
61 Aufgabe 9a – 2
62 Aufgabe 9a – 3
63 Aufgabe 12
64 Extra! Aufgabe 15 – a
65 Extra! Aufgabe 15 – b
66 Extra! Aufgabe 15 – c
67 Extra! Aufgabe 16

Einheit 7 – Fahren

68 Aufgabe 1
69 Aufgabe 2
70 Aufgabe 3c
71 Aufgabe 4
72 Aufgabe 6a
73 Aufgabe 6b
74 Aufgabe 7
75 Aufgabe 8
76 Extra! Aufgabe 10

CD2

Einheit 8 – Gestern

01 Aufgabe 1
02 Aufgabe 2
03 Aufgabe 4
04 Aufgabe 5a
05 Aufgabe 5b
06 Aufgabe 7
07 Extra! Aufgabe 10 – Paloma
08 Extra! Aufgabe 10 – Jean-Paul

Einheit 9 – Lebensläufe

09 Aufgabe 2c

10 Aufgabe 3
11 Aufgabe 6
12 Aufgabe 7
13 Extra! Aufgabe 11

Einheit 10 – Zukunftspläne

14 Aufgabe 2
15 Aufgabe 4
16 Aufgabe 8
17 Aufgabe 11
18 Aufgabe 12
19 Extra! Aufgabe 15 – Helga
20 Extra! Aufgabe 15 – Benjamin
21 Extra! Aufgabe 15 – Renate
22 Extra! Aufgabe 15 – Dietmar

Weitere Übungen

23 Unit 1 Exercise 3
24 Unit 1 Exercise 4
25 Einheit 2 Übung 1
26 Einheit 2 Übung 2
27 Einheit 2 Übung 3
28 Einheit 2 Übung 5
29 Einheit 3 Übung 3
30 Einheit 3 Übung 6
31 Einheit 4 Übung 1
32 Einheit 4 Übung 4
33 Einheit 4 Übung 5
34 Einheit 5 Übung 2
35 Einheit 5 Übung 3
36 Einheit 6 Übung 1
37 Einheit 6 Übung 2
38 Einheit 6 Übung 3
39 Einheit 6 Übung 4
40 Einheit 6 Übung 5
41 Einheit 7 Übung 1b
42 Einheit 7 Übung 2
43 Einheit 7 Übung 4
44 Einheit 7 Übung 5
45 Einheit 8 Übung 4
46 Einheit 9 Übung 1
47 Einheit 9 Übung 3
48 Einheit 9 Übung 5
49 Einheit 10 Übung 2

Reference

50 Das Alphabet
51 Spelling and pronunciation
52 Using numbers

Im Unterricht / IN CLASS

These symbols appear next to exercises and indicate the skill or activity involved.

 Hören (listening)

 Sprechen (speaking)

 Lesen (reading)

 Partnerarbeit (pairwork)

 Wortsuche (wordsearch)

 Schreiben (writing)

 Hören und wiederholen (listening and repeating)

 Sprechen und/oder schreiben (speaking and/or writing)

 Gruppenarbeit (group or class work)

 Lückentext (filling in the gaps)

Here are some key words and phrases.

das Buch book
die Einheit unit
die Seite page
die Aufgabe/Übung exercise

der Satz sentence
das Wort word
die Vorbereitung preparation
der Test/die Arbeit test

die Deutschstunde German class
die Stunde lesson, hour
der Klassenraum classroom

die Antwort answer
die Frage question
das Beispiel example
die Lücke gap

zum Lernen! to be learnt!
richtig oder falsch? true or false?
beantworten Sie die Fragen answer the questions
schriftlich/mündlich in writing/orally
machen Sie Notizen/notieren Sie take notes
arbeiten Sie in Paaren/in Kleingruppen work in pairs/in small groups
mit einem Partner/einer Partnerin with a partner (m/f)
die Gruppe/Gruppenarbeit group/group work
zusammen/allein together/alone
das Rollenspiel role-play
wer weiß? who knows?

1 Studenten

The focus of this unit is on information about yourself and others. You will learn to give such information and to ask basic questions in formal and informal situations. You will also learn how to understand information about individuals.

1 Anne und Marc

a „Guten Tag. Ich heiße Anne Phillips. Ich komme aus Leeds. Ich lerne Deutsch."

Wie heißt du?	Ich heiße Anne.
Woher kommst du?	Ich komme aus Leeds.
Was lernst du?	Ich lerne Deutsch.

b „Hallo. Ich heiße Marc Berlande. Ich komme aus Marseille. Ich lerne Deutsch."

Heißt du Patrick?	Nein. Ich heiße Marc.
Kommst du aus Paris?	Nein. Ich komme aus Marseille.
Lernst du Spanisch?	Nein. Ich lerne Deutsch.

Grammatik

| I | ich heiße | ich komme | ich lerne |
| you? | heißt du? | kommst du? | lernst du? |

2 Und du? Interview

Introduce yourselves and ask/answer questions.

3 Wo wohnst du?

Grammatik

Gender (masculine/feminine):
Student/Studentin
Deutscher/Deutsche

Ich bin Student.
= I am *a* student.

a „Ich heiße Anke Christiansen. Ich bin Deutsche. Ich komme aus Flensburg, aber ich wohne in Birmingham in England. Ich bin Studentin."

Wie heißt du?	Ich heiße Anke.
Bist du Deutsche?	Ja.
Woher kommst du?	Ich komme aus Flensburg.
Wo wohnst du?	Ich wohne in Birmingham.

b „Ich heiße Peter Fiedler. Ich bin Österreicher. Ich komme aus Wien, aber ich wohne in New York. Ich bin Student."

Wie heißt du?	Ich heiße Peter.
Bist du Deutscher?	Nein. Ich bin Österreicher.
Woher kommst du?	Ich komme aus Wien.
Wo wohnst du?	Ich wohne in New York.

4 Rollenspiel/Role-play

With a partner, take on the roles of an interviewer and Anke or Peter, asking and answering as many questions as you can. Then swap roles.

5 Welches Land?/Which country?

Beispiel/Example:

a = *Deutschland*

Nationalitäten (m/f)

a Deutscher/Deutsche
b Österreicher/Österreicherin
c Engländer/Engländerin
d Grieche/Griechin
e Franzose/Französin
f Schotte/Schottin

g Belgier/Belgierin
h Ire/Irin
i Spanier/Spanierin
j Däne/Dänin
k Waliser/Waliserin
l Italiener/Italienerin

Länder					
Griechenland	Wales	Österreich	Schottland	Spanien	England
Dänemark	Frankreich	Irland	Deutschland	Italien	Belgien

6 Welche Länder?/Which countries?

You will hear five of the countries from exercise 5: write down which.

a _____   b _____   c _____

d _____   e _____

7 Marianne Möller

Without consulting the script below, listen to the interview. What do you notice about the questions? After looking at the script, compare it with exercise 3!

Wie heißen Sie?   Ich heiße Marianne Möller.
Woher kommen Sie?   Ich komme aus Hamburg. Ich bin Deutsche.
Wo wohnen Sie?   Ich wohne in Manchester.
Sind Sie Studentin?   Nein. Ich bin Lehrerin.

For help with spelling out names and with sound–spelling links in German, see 'The Sounds of German' on page 146, and CD2 tracks 50 and 51.

Grammatik

In all languages we speak differently according to the situation and the person we're talking to: a job interview is not like a chat with your best friend. German, like many other languages, has different words for 'you', familiar and formal. The questions in exercises 1 and 3 use **du**, the *familiar* word for 'you' and the questions in exercise 7 use **Sie**, the *formal* alternative.

Note the verb endings:	*familiar*	*formal*
	kom<u>st</u> du?	**komm<u>en</u> Sie?**
	wohn<u>st</u> du?	**wohn<u>en</u> Sie?**
The verb **sein** (to be) is *irregular*:	**bist du?**	**sind Sie?**

Students among themselves use the familiar **du**. You also use it with friends, family members and children. Otherwise the more formal **Sie** is used. Learn to use both.

8 **Fragen**/Questions

Fill in the questions, then interview a member of the class.

		familiar		*formal*
Ask	his/her name	**a** _____ ?	**b**	*Wie heißen Sie?*
	where she/he is from	**c** _____ ?	**d**	_____ ?
	where he/she lives	**e** _____ ?	**f**	_____ ?
	whether she/he is English	**g** _____ ?	**h**	_____ ?
	whether he/she is a student	**i** *Bist du Student(in)?*	**j**	_____ ?

9 **Kirsty und Tom**

Read the remarks made by Kirsty and Tom, then fill in the gaps in the questions put to them in the interview. Finally, check what you have written by listening to the two interview extracts on the recording.

Ich bin Deutscher. Ich komme aus Berlin und wohne in London. Ich bin Lehrer.

Ich wohne in Frankfurt, aber ich komme aus Glasgow. Ich bin Schottin und lerne Deutsch.

a *Aus dem Interview mit Tom:*

i _____ Sie Engländer?   Nein, ich bin Deutscher.

ii Wo _____ Sie?   Ich wohne in London.

iii Kommen Sie _____ Frankfurt?   Nein.

b *Aus dem Interview mit Kirsty:*

i _____ ?   In Frankfurt.

ii _____ ?   Nein, ich bin Schottin.

iii _____ ?   Ja, ich bin Studentin.

10 Wer ist das?

a Das ist Marianne Möller. Sie ist Lehrerin.

Sie wohnt in Manchester, aber sie kommt aus Hamburg.

Sie ist Deutsche.

b Das ist Tom Paschke. Er ist Lehrer.

Er kommt aus Berlin und wohnt in London.

Er ist Deutscher.

c Das ist Marc Berlande. Er ist Student in Glasgow.

Er kommt aus Marseille. Er ist Franzose.

d Das ist Sue Edwards aus Birmingham.

Sie ist Studentin in Leipzig.

Sie ist Engländerin. Sie lernt Deutsch.

Grammatik

Verbs

I	**ich heiße**	**ich wohne**	**ich komme**	**ich bin**
he	**er heißt**	**er wohnt**	**er kommt**	**er ist**
she	**sie heißt**	**sie wohnt**	**sie kommt**	**sie ist**

The first three verbs follow the *regular* pattern. Remember the last one, the verb **sein** (to be), is *irregular*.

11 Fragen

a
  i Wer ist das?
  ii Ist sie Sekretärin?
  iii Wo wohnt sie?
  iv Woher kommt sie?
  v Ist sie Amerikanerin?

b
  i Wie heißt er?
  ii Ist er Polizist?
  iii Wohnt er in Manchester?
  iv Kommt er aus Köln?
  v Ist er Deutscher?

c
  i Heißt er Adham Sawfik?
  ii Ist er Lehrer?
  iii Wo wohnt er?
  iv Woher kommt er?
  v Ist er Schotte?

d
  i Wer ist das?
  ii Woher kommt sie?
  iii Wo wohnt sie?
  iv Lernt sie Spanisch?
  v Ist sie Deutsche?

Grammatik

Don't confuse: **wer** = 'who' **wo** = 'where'!

12 Verben/Verbs

a You should be able to work out what the missing verbs are in the following statements. Check your decisions by listening to the recording.

i Ich _____ Deutsche. Ich _____ Silke und
_____ aus Stuttgart. Ich studiere Sport und Englisch.

ii Ich _____ Eva. Ich _____ Spanierin, aber ich
studiere in England. Ich studiere Literatur und _____
Englisch – und Deutsch!

iii Ich _____ Michael. Ich _____ aus Cork in Irland.
Ich _____ Student in Birmingham. Ich studiere Biologie. Ich
_____ auch Deutsch.

iv Guten Tag. Ich _____ Yannis und ich _____
aus Griechenland. Ich _____ Student hier in England. Ich
_____ in Brighton und studiere Psychologie.

b Now turn the students' statements beginning with **ich** (I) into statements beginning **er** (he) or **sie** (she) as appropriate.

Beispiel: Ich heiße Karl → Er heißt Karl; Ich bin Studentin → Sie ist Studentin

13 Vorstellungen/Introductions

Introduce yourself to your classmates using exercise 12 as a model. Your tutor will then ask another member of the class to report what you said. (Check the academic subjects in the unit vocabulary on page 10: if yours is not there, use a dictionary or ask your tutor for help.)

14 Rollenspiel: Was sind Sie von Beruf?/What's your job?

Take on the role of a character from the first column, choosing an item from each of the other columns. Make sure the words for nationality and job are the correct gender for the person you are playing! Introduce yourself to a partner.

Beispiel: *Guten Tag. Ich heiße Paul Dawson. Ich bin Engländer und ich komme aus Birmingham.
Ich bin Automechaniker von Beruf.*

Name	aus ...	Land	Beruf
Paul Dawson	Paris	Deutsche(r)	Busfahrerin
Anne Doyle	Rom	Franzose/Französin	Student
Javed Siddiqi	München	Ire/Irin	Journalistin
Richard Barrow	Liverpool	Engländer(in)	Automechaniker
Petra Walters	Birmingham	Italiener(in)	Lehrerin
Colette Petit	Glasgow	Schotte/Schottin	Kellner
Paolo Zinetti	Galway		Polizist
Anke Herrmann	Sheffield		Sekretärin

15 Wer ist das?

a Martin Heine ist Deutscher und kommt aus Leipzig. Er ist Student in Marburg. Er studiert Geschichte. Martins Freundin heißt Cristina. Sie kommt aus Rom und ist Sekretärin. Sie arbeitet in Frankfurt. Martin lernt Italienisch.

Fragen:
i Woher kommt Martin?
ii Studiert er in Leipzig?
iii Wer ist Cristina?
iv Ist sie Deutsche?

v Was ist sie von Beruf?
vi Wo arbeitet sie?

b Isabelle Bruneau ist Studentin in England und arbeitet als Kellnerin. Sie kommt aus Lyon in Frankreich. Sie lernt Englisch und Deutsch. Sie wohnt in London.

Fragen:
i Arbeitet Isabelle?
ii Ist sie Engländerin?
iii Wo ist Lyon?
iv Wo wohnt sie?

c „Hallo. Mein Name ist Bernd Voigt. Ich komme aus Bremen in Deutschland, aber ich wohne und arbeite in Salzburg in Österreich. Ich bin Journalist."

Fragen:
i Wie heißt er?
ii Wo ist Bremen?
iii Ist er Österreicher?
iv Was ist er von Beruf?

16 Rollenspiel: Guten Tag, Herr Heine

One of you takes on the role of Martin from exercise 15, the other is an interviewer. The interviewer should ask him: what he's called, where he's from, what he is studying, where he is studying, where Cristina is from, where she works and what her job is. This is a formal interview, so use **Sie** for 'you'. (Remember it takes a different verb ending from **sie** 'she'!)

17 Hallo, Silke!

Draft the text of an email introducing yourself to Silke. Ask her some questions as well, using the familiar **du**. (You will often find it written with a capital D in letters.)

> ## Am Ende der Stunde/At the end of the class
> „Auf Wiedersehen!"/„Tschüss!"
> „Bis nächste Woche!"

Extra!

18 Was macht er/sie?/What does he/she do?

Listen to the three speakers talking about themselves. You are not expected to understand everything they say but you ought to be able to note the information requested in the table and report back on it in German to the class/your partner.

Name	studiert?	aus?	wohnt in …?	arbeitet?
Annie				
Jürgen				
Padma				

19 Ursula ist Automechanikerin

Read this short article right through. Don't reach for your dictionary: you will probably not understand every word but you don't need to.

> Ursula Eggebrecht wohnt in Bremen. Die junge Amerikanerin (23 Jahre alt) kommt aus New York, aber sie studiert in Europa. Sie ist Psychologiestudentin an der Universität Bremen. Warum studiert sie nicht in New York oder Boston? „Mein Vater ist Deutscher und meine Mutter kommt aus Amsterdam", antwortet Ursula. „Ich bin Amerikanerin und Europäerin. Ich studiere hier in Deutschland und nächstes Jahr bin ich in Holland." Aber das kostet Geld und Ursula arbeitet auch. „Ja, ich habe einen interessanten Job – ich bin Automechanikerin!" Ursula repariert Autos.

a Once you've got the gist of the article, summarise it in English in two or three sentences.

b Now try to answer the questions in German.

   i Wo wohnt Ursula? _____

   ii Woher kommt sie? _____

   iii Was studiert sie? _____

   iv Studiert Ursula in Holland? _____

   v Arbeitet Ursula? _____

Grammatik

The Grammatik pages explain and summarise the grammar points from the unit. You may like also to look at the Guide to Grammatical Terms on pages 144–5 and the overall Grammar Summary starting on page 147. References such as ▶**G12** below point to the relevant section of the Grammar Summary. Remember, though, that the entry in the Grammar Summary will probably include more detail than you need, certainly in the early units.

～ Nouns

1 All nouns begin with a *capital letter*: **Lehrer**, **Studentin**.

2 All nouns have a *gender*: so far you have met *masculine* nouns
   e.g. **Student, Engländer, Deutscher, Journalist,**
   and their *feminine* equivalents
   e.g. **Studentin, Engländerin, Deutsche, Journalistin**

   These nouns refer to people but, as you will see later, all German nouns have a gender.

3 No word for 'a' is used with professions and nationality:
   Ich bin Deutscher. Sie ist Lehrerin. I am <u>a</u> German. She is <u>a</u> teacher.

～ Pronouns ▶**G12**

So far you've met **ich** (I), **er** (he) and **sie** (she), as well as **du** (informal/familiar you) and **Sie** (formal you).

～ Verbs ▶**G14.1, G14.6**

1 The present tense of regular verbs follows a pattern.
   The infinitive (basic form) ends in **-en**: e.g. **wohnen** (to live).
   The **Sie**-form is the same as the infinitive.

ich wohne	I live	**er/sie wohnt**	he/she lives
du wohnst	you live (informal)	**Sie wohnen**	you live (formal)

   Other regular verbs: **heißen*, kommen, lernen, studieren, arbeiten***
   (* **heißen** has the form **du heißt**, with no extra **s**; **arbeiten** has the forms **du arbeit<u>e</u>st** and **er/sie arbeit<u>e</u>t**.)

2 Irregular verb **sein** (to be)

ich bin	I am	**er/sie ist**	he/she is
du bist	you are (informal)	**Sie sind**	you are (formal)

～ Forming questions ▶**G19.2**

1 Invert the subject-verb order used in statements:

Statement:	**Er wohnt in Berlin.**	Question:	**Wohnt er in Berlin?**
	subject – verb		verb – subject

2 Note the 'W-words' introducing questions:
   <u>Was</u> studieren Sie?   <u>Wer</u> ist das?   <u>Wie</u> heißt er?
   <u>Wo</u> wohnst du?   <u>Woher</u> kommt sie?   <u>Warum</u> studierst du hier?

Grammatikübungen

1 Find nouns from the list to fill the gaps.

a Monika ist _____. Sie studiert Musik. Sie ist _____ – sie kommt aus Dresden.

b Martin ist _____ an der Universität. Er kommt aus Köln – er ist _____.

c Eva kommt aus Madrid – sie ist _____ . Sie arbeitet – sie ist _____.

d Paolo kommt aus Rom – er ist _____. Er arbeitet – er ist _____.

Journalist	Deutsche	Spanierin	Student
Italiener	Lehrerin	Studentin	Deutscher

2 Fill the gaps with a pronoun.

Peter ist Amerikaner. **a** _____ kommt aus New York. „Wohnen **b** _____ in New York, Peter?" – „Nein, **c** _____ wohne in Los Angeles und

d _____ arbeite in Hollywood."

Interessant, **e** _____ arbeitet in Hollywood! „Susi, arbeitest **f** _____ auch in Hollywood?" – „Nein. **g** _____ bin Studentin in San Francisco."

3 Complete the sentences with an appropriate form of a verb.

Der Lehrer **a** _____ Karl. Er **b** _____ in Hannover, er **c** _____ aus Graz. „Woher **d** _____ Sie?" – „Ich **e** _____ aus Graz." – „ **f** _____ das in Deutschland?" – „Nein, in Österreich. Ich **g** _____ Österreicher." – „Sie **h** _____ Österreicher!"

4 Reconstruct the questions to which the following are the answers. (There could be more than one possibility.)

a Sie heißt Marianne.

b Ich wohne in Liverpool.

c Ja, ich bin Student.

d Er arbeitet in Hamburg.

e Ich komme aus München.

f Nein, ich bin Deutscher.

g Er ist Kellner.

h Sie lernt Deutsch.

5 W-questions. Insert **was/wer/wie/wo/woher** as appropriate.

„ **a** _____ ist das?" – „Das ist Martin." – „ **b** _____ wohnt er?" – „In Berlin." – „ **c** _____ heißt er? – „Braun. Martin Braun." – „ **d** _____ kommt er? – „Aus Berlin." – „ **e** _____ ist er von Beruf?" – „Er ist Student." – „ **f** _____ studiert er?" – „Biologie."

Vokabeln

Exercise 1

und	and
Guten Tag	hello, good day
ich	I
heißen	to be called
kommen (aus)	to come (from)
lernen	to learn
Deutsch	German (language)
wie heißt du?	what's your name?
du	you (informal)
wo(her)	where (from)
was	what
hallo	hello (informal)
nein	no

Exercise 3

ich bin	I am
Deutsche(r)	German (f/m)
aber	but
wohnen	to live
in	in
bist du?	are you?
ja	yes
Österreicher(in)	Austrian (m/f)
Wien	Vienna

Exercise 5

Engländer(in)	Englishman/-woman
Grieche/Griechin	Greek (m/f)
Franzose/Französin	Frenchman/-woman
Schotte/Schottin	Scot (m/f)
Belgier(in)	Belgian (m/f)
Ire/Irin	Irishman/-woman
Spanier(in)	Spaniard (m/f)
Däne/Dänin	Dane (m/f)
Waliser(in)	Welshman/-woman
Italiener(in)	Italian (m/f)
Griechenland	Greece
Österreich	Austria
Schottland	Scotland
Spanien	Spain
Dänemark	Denmark
Frankreich	France
Irland	Ireland
Deutschland	Germany
Italien	Italy
Belgien	Belgium

Exercise 7

Sie	you (formal)
sind Sie?	are you (formal)?
Lehrer(in)	teacher (m/f)

Exercise 10

wer	who
wer ist das?	who is that?
ist	is
er/sie	he/she

Exercise 11

Sekretärin	secretary (f)
Amerikaner(in)	American (m/f)
Polizist(in)	policeman/-woman
Spanisch	Spanish (language)
Köln	Cologne

Exercise 12

studieren	to study
Sport	sport
Englisch	English (language)
Literatur	literature
Biologie	biology
auch	also, as well
hier	here
Psychologie	psychology

Exercise 14

Was sind Sie von Beruf?	What's your job?
Rom	Rome
München	Munich
Busfahrer(in)	bus driver (m/f)
Journalist(in)	journalist (m/f)
Automechaniker(in)	car mechanic (m/f)
Kellner(in)	waiter/waitress

Exercise 15

Geschichte	history
Freundin	(girl)friend
Freund	(boy)friend
arbeiten	to work
als	as
mein Name	my name

Extra/Grammatik/Weitere Übungen

warum	why
mit	with

Partnerarbeit

1 Vorstellungen

Introduce yourself to your partner. After an initial greeting, tell him/her:

- your name
- the town or city you're from
- your nationality
- where you live

- that you're a student
- what you're studying
- that you work (if you do)
- … and what your job is

When you've got all the information across, your partner will check it back with you by making a series of statements about you e.g. **Sie heißen Martin** ('Your name is Martin'): tell her/him whether she/he is right and correct her/him where necessary (**Nein, ich heiße Mark!**).

richtig right, correct	
falsch wrong	
Können Sie das bitte wiederholen? Please could you repeat that?	

2 Rollenspiel

Your partner will take on up to four roles. Ask questions to obtain the information needed to fill in the form relating to each 'person' he/she plays. Their first names are Alex, Bernie, Chris and Sam. Use **du** or **Sie** but be consistent.

Name: _____ _____ _____ _____

Nationalität: _____ _____ _____ _____

Wohnort: _____ _____ _____ _____

Beruf: _____ _____ _____ _____

Arbeitet in: _____ _____ _____ _____

Partnerarbeit

B

1 Vorstellungen

Greet your partner in German, then listen carefully to what he or she tells you, jotting down key words when it helps. You can ask for any information again but remember to stick to German!

When you are ready, check back on the information with your partner by making a series of statements. Use the formal **Sie** e.g. **Sie kommen aus Manchester**. He/She will then tell you whether or not you are correct.

richtig	right, correct
falsch	wrong
Können Sie das bitte wiederholen?	Please could you repeat that?

2 Rollenspiel

Your partner has a form to fill in about the roles you are to play, which are outlined below. Answer her/his questions so that he or she can get the information right. The names have been chosen so that they can apply to a male or female but remember to use the correct gender for nationality and job. Speak only German!

> Your name is Alex Andrews. You're English and you come from Liverpool but you live and work in New York as a journalist.

> You are Chris Bradley. You're a teacher. You live and work in Denmark. You are Irish from Limerick.

> You are Bernie Lyons. You are a bus driver in Glasgow. You live in Paisley and originally come from Motherwell.

> Your name is Sam Humphreys. You work as a waiter/waitress and study literature. You come from Brighton and live in London, where you study and work.

2 Bibliothek oder Diskothek?

In this unit you will learn to talk about your daily routine.
You will also learn the numbers 1–99 and start using
the 24-hour clock.

 1 Zahlen 1–19

a Listen and repeat:

0	null	6	sechs	11	elf	16	se<u>ch</u>zehn
1	eins	7	sieben	12	zwölf	17	sie<u>b</u>zehn
2	zwei	8	acht	13	dreizehn	18	achtzehn
3	drei	9	neun	14	vierzehn	19	neunzehn
4	vier	10	zehn	15	fünfzehn		
5	fünf						

 b Circle the numbers you hear.

3   5   6   9   12   14   17   18

c Write the numbers you hear (use figures).

_____   _____   _____   _____   _____   _____   _____   _____

 d Write down a number and see if your partner can say it, then swap roles.

For more about using
numbers, see 'The Sounds
of German' on page 146,
and CD2 track 52.

 2 Zahlen 20–29

20	zwanzig	25	fünfundzwanzig
21	einundzwanzig	26	sechsundzwanzig
22	zweiundzwanzig	27	siebenundzwanzig
23	dreiundzwanzig	28	achtundzwanzig
24	vierundzwanzig	29	neunundzwanzig

3 Logik! 30–99

See if you can work out the pattern:

a Match the figures to the correct words.

73 einundachtzig
54 siebenundvierzig
66 dreiundsiebzig
47 achtunddreißig
95 vierundfünfzig
81 sechsundsechzig
38 fünfundneunzig

b Write in the words.

30 _____
40 _____
50 _____
60 _____
70 _____
80 _____
90 _____

What is surprising about the word for 30?

c Welche Zahlen hören Sie?

i 34/43? **ii** 45/54? **iii** 56/65? **iv** 78/87? **v** 89/98?

d Say out loud:

92 44 79 31 63 57 85

4 Die Uhrzeit/The time

Once you are familiar with numbers you can start telling the time. The 24-hour clock is used more in German-speaking countries than it is in the English-speaking world.

9:00	9:10	9:15	9:25	9:30	9:45
9:59	21:05	21:20	21:35	21:50	

Grammatik

9 **Uhr** 9 o'clock   9.05 Uhr = **neun Uhr fünf**

– **Wie viel Uhr ist es?/Wie spät ist es?**
What's the time?
– **Es ist 9.45 Uhr (neun Uhr fünfundvierzig).**

– **Um wie viel Uhr?** At what time?
– **Um 9.15 Uhr (um neun Uhr fünfzehn).**
At nine fifteen.

Grammatik

Definite article ('the')
der (masculine)
die (feminine)
das (neuter)

der Morgen/der Vormittag morning	am Morgen/am Vormittag
	morgens/vormittags
der Nachmittag afternoon	am Nachmittag nachmittags
der Abend evening	am Abend abends

5 Um wie viel Uhr?

a Listen to Ralf talking about his morning routine, then fill in the times he gives. (Use figures.)

i

„Ich stehe um

_____ auf."

ii

„Ich frühstücke um

_____."

iii

„Ich gehe um

_____ an
die Universität."

iv

„Die Vorlesung
beginnt um

_____."

v

„Ich trinke um

_____ Kaffee."

vi

„Ich gehe um

_____ in die
Bibliothek."

b Fragen:
   i Steht Ralf um 8 Uhr auf?
   ii Wann frühstückt er?
   iii Um wie viel Uhr geht er an die Universität?
   iv Was beginnt um 9 Uhr?
   v Trinkt er um 10.15 Uhr Cola?
   vi Wohin geht er um 11 Uhr?

Grammatik

wann? when?
was? what?
wohin? where (to)?

Aufstehen is a *separable verb*: its prefix
(**auf**) goes to the end of the sentence:
ich stehe früh <u>auf</u> I get up early

6 Partnerübung: Interview

Um wie viel Uhr …   stehen Sie auf?/frühstücken Sie?/gehen Sie an die Uni?
                          stehst du auf?/frühstückst du?/gehst du an die Uni?

7 Am Nachmittag

„Was machen Sie nachmittags?"

„Ich gehe oft in die Bibliothek. Manchmal gehe ich in das Sportzentrum."

„Und heute?"

„Heute Nachmittag habe ich um 15 Uhr eine Vorlesung. Um 16 Uhr spiele ich Basketball."

Grammatik

Ich gehe oft in die Bibliothek. Oft gehe ich in die Bibliothek.
(See the item on word order in the unit Grammar section on page 20.)

Indefinite article ('a')
ein Student (masculine
eine Vorlesung (feminine)
ein Sportzentrum (neuter)

Haben (to have) is *irregular*:
ich habe
du hast   Sie haben
er/sie hat

  8 Und was machen Sie nachmittags?

Describe your afternoons to the rest of the class.

| Ich gehe … | in die Bibliothek
in die Mensa/Kantine
in das Sportzentrum
in die Stadt
an die Universität
nach Hause
zur Arbeit
schwimmen | Ich spiele … | Basketball
Fußball
Tischtennis
Gitarre |
| | | Ich habe… | eine Vorlesung
ein Seminar
eine Deutschstunde |

Stadtbibliothek
Volkshochschule
Kommunale Galerie

9 **Heute Nachmittag**

Was macht Tony heute Nachmittag?

13.30	library
14.30	into town
16.00	German class
17.10	sports centre: football
18.45	home

 10 **Was machen Sie abends?**

Match the German verbs correctly with their English equivalents.

Ich …
1 bleibe zu Hause
2 gehe aus
3 sehe fern (*separable*)
4 höre Musik
5 lese ein Buch
6 schreibe E-Mails
7 tanze
8 trinke Bier

I …
a listen to music
b drink beer
c stay at home
d dance
e go out
f watch TV
g read a book
h write emails

  11 **Abends**

 a Listen to the recording and see if you can complete the script by noting down what Bernd says.

 b Then give the information in English: how often do the four students do the various things they mention?

Petra: „Abends gehe ich selten aus. Ich sehe oft fern oder höre Musik. Manchmal lese ich."

Ralf: „Ich bleibe nie zu Hause. Ich gehe in die Kneipe oder die Diskothek."

Jasmin: „Ich bleibe immer zu Hause. Ich schreibe E-Mails, aber ich sehe selten fern. Ich gehe um 23 Uhr ins Bett."

Bernd: „_____

_____"

immer	**oft**	**manchmal**	**selten**	**nie**
always	often	sometimes	rarely	never

12 Ihr Tagesablauf/Your daily routine

Fragen:

a Um wie viel Uhr stehen Sie auf?

b Gehen Sie abends aus?

c Wann frühstücken Sie?

d Was machen Sie abends zu Hause?

e Wann gehen Sie an die Universität?

f Wann gehen Sie ins Bett?

g Was machen Sie nachmittags?

h Um wie viel Uhr ist die Deutschstunde?

i Was machen Sie um 8.30 Uhr, 11 Uhr, 15 Uhr, 21 Uhr?

  13 Partnerübung: Interview

Now ask a fellow student the questions from exercise 12, using the informal **du**-form.

  14 Annas Mahlzeiten/Anna's meals

Anna ist Studentin. Zum Frühstück isst sie Toast oder Joghurt. Sie trinkt eine Tasse Kaffee. Um 13 Uhr geht sie immer in die Mensa. Zum Mittagessen isst sie normalerweise ein Käsebrot oder ein Schinkenbrot und sie trinkt eine Cola. Das Abendessen ist um 18 Uhr. Sie isst Nudeln mit Fisch oder Salat. Sie trinkt ein Glas Orangensaft. Sehr gesund!

das Frühstück	**zum Frühstück**	for breakfast
das Mittagessen	**zum Mittagessen**	for lunch
das Abendessen	**zum Abendessen**	for dinner

Fragen:

a Was trinkt Anna morgens?

b Geht sie oft in die Mensa?

c Wann isst sie ein Käsebrot?

d Trinkt sie abends eine Cola?

e Was isst sie zum Abendessen?

f Und was trinkt sie?

Grammatik

Learn the genders of nouns (see unit vocabulary page 22).

e.g.	*masculine*	*feminine*	*neuter*
'the'	**der Fisch**	**die Tasse**	**das Glas**
'a/an'	**ein**	**eine**	**ein**

The verb **essen** (to eat) is a *strong verb*:

ich esse (vowel change)	**du isst**
Sie essen	**er/sie isst**

  15 Rollenspiel: Konversation mit Anna

With a partner, role-play a conversation with Anna. Ask her as many questions as possible, using the information in exercise 14. Use the informal **du**-form.

Extra!

16 Kontraste: die Tagesabläufe von zwei Studenten

Vera

11.00: aufstehen
12.30: fernsehen
14.00: Kaffee trinken mit Susanne (Café Bauer)
16.00: Vorlesung (Literatur)
19.00: Abendessen (Pizza und Cola)
20.30: Kino (Film: Moulin Rouge)
23.00: ausgehen und Wein trinken (Bar „Bei Joe")
1.00: nach Hause gehen

Walter

7.00: aufstehen
7.15: Frühstück (Orangensaft und Müsli)
7.45: schwimmen gehen
9.00: Vorlesung (Chemie)
12.00: Bibliothek
13.00: Mittagessen (Mensa)
15.00: Seminar (Politik)
19.00: Abendessen (Salat) und Buch lesen - zu Hause bleiben

in die Bar	to the bar
ins Kino	to the cinema

Fragen:

a Trinkt Vera mit Paul Kaffee?
b Beginnt Veras Vorlesung um 14 Uhr?
c Was macht sie am Abend?
d Wann geht Vera ins Kino?
e Um wie viel Uhr steht Walter auf?
f Was macht er am Vormittag?
g Wohin geht Walter um 12 Uhr?
h Geht er abends aus?

17 Konversationen im Café

Listen to the two conversations at a cafe in Heidelberg. Although there will be some words you have not come across yet, you will be able to get the gist of the exchanges. See if you can tell when a conversation is formal and when it is more informal.

Collect as much information as you can about:
Annette   Klaus   Herr Wolf   Frau Petri

Grammatik

～ Articles ▶G1, G4

	masculine	feminine	neuter
definite ('the'):	**der**	**die**	**das**
indefinite ('a'/'an'):	**ein**	**eine**	**ein**

All nouns have a gender. To make sure you remember the gender of a noun, always learn it with its definite article:

<u>der</u> Morgen   **<u>die</u> Vorlesung**   **<u>das</u> Frühstück**

～ Verbs ▶G14.2, 14.3, 14.6

1 The infinitive of separable verbs has a prefix:

<u>auf</u>stehen, <u>aus</u>gehen, <u>fern</u>sehen.

In the present tense, this prefix goes to the end of the sentence:

Ich <u>stehe</u> um 8 Uhr <u>auf</u>.   <u>Gehen</u> Sie oft <u>aus</u>?

Separable verbs are formed by adding a prefix to an existing verb: the three above are formed from **stehen** (to stand), **gehen** (to go) and **sehen** (to see).

2 Strong verbs often have a change of vowel-sound in the **du**-form and the **er/sie**-form:

lesen (to read)	**fernsehen** (to watch TV)
ich lese du l<u>ie</u>st Sie lesen er/sie l<u>ie</u>st	ich sehe fern du s<u>ie</u>hst fern Sie sehen fern er/sie s<u>ie</u>ht fern (The verb **fernsehen** is separable and strong!)

3 **haben** (to have) is irregular:

ich habe	
du hast	Sie haben
er/sie hat	

～ Word order ▶G19.1, G19.2

1 Adverbs come immediately after the verb: **Ich bleibe <u>immer</u> zu Hause.**
Compare with: I *always* stay at home.

2 The verb has second place in the sentence:

Take the statement   **Sie <u>geht</u> um neun Uhr an die Uni(versität).**

You can start with the time expression but, unlike in English, the subject (**sie**) is put after the verb, which keeps its position.

Um neun Uhr <u>geht</u> sie an die Universität.

3 Note questions: **<u>Gehst</u> du heute in die Bibliothek?**
Wann <u>gehst</u> du in die Bibliothek?

Grammatikübungen

1 Test yourself on the genders of the nouns you have met so far by putting them into masculine, feminine and neuter columns in your notebook.

Then check the answers on page 174 to see whether you were right.

Orangensaft	Kneipe
Diskothek	Lehrer
Bier	Kaffee
Tasse	E-Mail
Abend	Sportzentrum
Fisch	Glas
Toast	Studentin
Käsebrot	Deutschstunde

2 Complete the following sentences with an appropriate form of a verb from the list. Make sure you know which are irregular, separable and strong!

a Wann _____ die Vorlesung?

b Um 11 Uhr _____ ich Kaffee.

c Er _____ nachmittags in die Bibliothek.

d Abends _____ sie ein Buch.

e Was _____ Sie zum Frühstück?

f Ich _____ selten _____ . Ich _____ zu Hause.

g _____ du heute ein Seminar?

h Um wie viel Uhr _____ er _____ ?

essen aufstehen bleiben trinken beginnen gehen ausgehen haben lesen

3 Insert a time/frequency expression into each of the sentences **(i)** after the verb and **(ii)** at the start of the sentence. Make any necessary adjustments to the word order.

Example:

Sie geht an die Universität. (in the morning)

Sie geht _morgens_ an die Universität.   _Morgens_ geht sie an die Universität.

a Eva geht in die Bibliothek.   (in the afternoon)

b Ich esse Toast.   (sometimes)

c Er sieht fern.   (always)

d Ich gehe nach Hause.   (at 5 pm)

e Sie spielt Tischtennis.   (often)

f Ich habe eine Deutschstunde.   (today)

Vokabeln

Aufgabe 1

Zahlen *pl*	numbers

Aufgabe 5

um	(before a time) at
aufstehen *sep*	to get up
frühstücken	to have breakfast
gehen	to go
an die Universität	to the university
die Vorlesung	lecture
beginnen	to begin
trinken	to drink
der Kaffee	coffee
in die Bibliothek	to the library
wann?	when?
um wie viel Uhr?	what time?
wohin?	where to?

Aufgabe 7

machen	to do
nachmittags	in the afternoon
oft	often
manchmal	sometimes
in das Sportzentrum	to the sports centre
heute	today
heute Nachmittag	this afternoon
spielen	to play
der Basketball	basketball

Aufgabe 8

die Mensa	canteen
die Kantine	canteen
die Stadt	town
nach Hause (gehen)	(to go) home
zur Arbeit (gehen)	(to go) to work
schwimmen	to swim
Fußball	football
Tischtennis	table tennis
Gitarre	guitar
das Seminar	seminar
die Deutschstunde	German lesson

Aufgabe 10

abends	in the evening
bleiben	to stay, remain
zu Hause	at home
ausgehen *sep*	to go out
fernsehen* *sep*	to watch TV
Musik hören	to listen to music

lesen*	to read
das Buch	book
schreiben	to write
die E-Mail	email
tanzen	to dance
das Bier	beer

Aufgabe 11

selten	seldom, rarely
oder	or
nie	never
die Kneipe	pub
die Diskothek	discotheque
immer	always
ins Bett gehen	to go to bed
ins = in das	into the

Aufgabe 14

die Mahlzeit	meal
Mahlzeiten *pl*	meals
das Frühstück	breakfast
zum Frühstück	for breakfast
essen*	to eat
isst	eats
der Toast	toast
der/das Joghurt	yoghurt
die Tasse	cup
eine Tasse Kaffee	a cup of coffee
das Mittagessen	lunch
zum Mittagessen	for lunch
normalerweise	normally
das Käsebrot	cheese sandwich
das Schinkenbrot	ham sandwich
die Cola	cola
das Abendessen	evening meal, dinner
zum Abendessen	for dinner
Nudeln *pl*	pasta
der Fisch	fish
der Salat	salad
das Glas	glass
der Orangensaft	orange juice
ein Glas Orangensaft	a glass of orange juice
sehr	very
gesund	healthy

* Verb strong in present tense ▶ **G14.2**

Partnerarbeit

A

1 Morgen/Tomorrow

A friend phones and wants to arrange a time when he/she can meet you.
Greet your partner and tell him/her that

11:00   you have a lecture

13:00   you're going to the canteen for a cheese sandwich

14:30   you're going to the library

17:00   you have an Italian class

19:30   you play table tennis

Remember to use the 24-hour clock!

Your partner will then ask some questions to make sure that he/she has got the correct information.

2 Wann?

Ask your partner when he/she does things during the day and make a note of the information. Ask about ...

getting up	going into town
breakfast	playing football
lecture	watching television
drinking coffee	drinking beer

Do this exercise first using the informal, then using the formal 'you'.

Fahrräder auf dem Campus

23

Partnerarbeit

B

1 Morgen/Tomorrow

You phone a friend in order to arrange a time when the two of you can meet up. After the initial greeting, ask your friend what he or she is doing tomorrow. Form questions beginning **was** or **wann**. Use the familiar **du**-form.

... am Morgen?   *... am Nachmittag?*
... in die Mensa?   *... Tischtennis?*

2 Wann?

Your partner asks you a number of questions about your activities in the course of a day. Answer the questions using the information below.

7.45	aufstehen	12.00	Stadt
8.00	Frühstück	15.15	Fußball spielen
10.00	Vorlesung	17.20	fernsehen
11.30	Kaffee	19.00	Bier

Die Zentralbibliothek der Humboldt-Universität zu Berlin

3 Familie

In this unit you will learn to talk about family and about everyday objects. You will greatly expand your vocabulary and also find out about making nouns plural.

 1 Stephanies Fotoalbum

Stephanie spricht über ihre Familie.

meine Eltern

meine Mutter
Martina (51)

mein Vater
Christian (53)

ich **Stephanie** (19)
(ledig)

mein Freund
Alex (21)

meine Schwester **Caroline** (25) (verheiratet),
ihr Mann **Heinz** (29), ihre Kinder **Jessica** (3),
Michael (2)

mein Bruder **Andreas** (22) (ledig),
seine Freundin **Tina** (23)

 2 Stephanies Familie

 a Fragen:

i	Wie alt ist Stephanie?	**v**	Wo arbeitet ihr Vater?
ii	Ist sie verheiratet?	**vi**	Wie heißt Carolines Mann?
iii	Was studiert Stephanie?	**vii**	Hat Caroline Kinder?
iv	Was ist ihre Mutter von Beruf?	**viii**	Hat Andreas eine Freundin?

 b Rollenspiel: Use the family album as a prompt to take on the role of Stephanie talking about her family.

Beispiel: *Ich heiße Stephanie. Ich bin 19 Jahre alt. Meine Mutter heißt …*

Grammatik

Possessives	'my'	'her'	'his'
masculine	**mein Bruder**	**ihr Bruder**	**sein Bruder**
feminine	**mein<u>e</u> Schwester**	**ihr<u>e</u> Schwester**	**sein<u>e</u> Schwester**
neuter	**mein Auto**	**ihr Auto**	**sein Auto**
plural	**mein<u>e</u> Eltern**	**ihr<u>e</u> Eltern**	**sein<u>e</u> Eltern**

3 Caroline und Andreas

Here are some details about Caroline and Andreas. Fill in the missing possessive adjectives: **sein(e)** or **ihr(e)**. Check your answers on the recording.

Das ist Caroline. Sie ist verheiratet und **a** _____ Mann heißt Heinz. Er ist Bibliothekar von Beruf und er arbeitet in Gießen. Caroline hat zwei Kinder. **b** _____ Kinder heißen Jessica und Michael. Sie sind drei und zwei Jahre alt. Die Kinder sind noch klein und Caroline arbeitet im Moment nicht. Sie hat ein Auto – **c** _____ Auto ist sehr alt. Caroline hat auch einen Bruder – Andreas. **d** _____ Bruder ist nicht verheiratet.
e _____ Schwester Stephanie studiert in Marburg. Sie ist neunzehn Jahre alt und ledig.
f _____ Freund heißt Alex. Carolines Eltern heißen Martina und Christian. **g** _____ Eltern wohnen in Frankfurt.

Das ist Andreas. Er ist nicht verheiratet, aber er hat eine Freundin. **h** _____ Freundin heißt Tina. Sie ist sehr nett. Andreas wohnt auch in Frankfurt und er studiert noch.
i _____ Eltern wohnen in der Beethovenstraße. Andreas hat ein Moped. **j** _____ Moped ist neu und fährt gut. **k** _____ Freund Ali studiert Biologie in Darmstadt. Nachmittags fahren Andreas und Ali oft zum Schwimmbad. Andreas hat viele Hobbys.
l _____ Hobbys sind Schwimmen, Musik und Filme.

4 Interviews

a Interview mit Andreas

- Wie heißen Sie?
- Wie alt sind Sie?
- Sind Sie verheiratet?
- Haben Sie eine Freundin?
- Wie heißt Ihre Freundin?
- Haben Sie Geschwister?

- Was ist Ihr Vater von Beruf?
- Wie alt ist Ihre Mutter?

- **i** _____ Name ist Andreas.
- **ii** Ich bin _____ Jahre alt.
- **iii** Nein, ich bin _____.
- Ja.
- **iv** _____ Freundin heißt Tina.
- **v** Ja. Ich habe _____ Schwestern, aber keinen Bruder.
- **vi** Mein Vater ist _____ bei Siemens.
- **vii** Meine Mutter ist _____ Jahre alt.

b Interview mit Caroline

i	_____ ?	– Ich bin 25.
ii	_____ ?	– Nein, ich bin verheiratet.
iii	_____ ?	– Mein Mann heißt Heinz.
iv	Haben Sie Kinder?	– Ich habe einen Sohn und eine Tochter.
v	_____ ?	– Meine Tochter ist 3 Jahre alt.
vi	_____ ?	– Ja, ich habe eine Schwester und einen Bruder.
vii	_____ ?	– Meine Mutter ist Architektin.

Grammatik

The indefinite article ('a')

ein Sohn (masculine), **eine** Tochter (feminine), **ein** Kind (neuter)

When a <u>masculine</u> noun is the object of a sentence **ein** becomes **einen**:

	masculine	*feminine*	*neuter*	*plural*
Sie hat ...	**ein<u>en</u> Sohn**	**eine Tochter**	**ein Kind**	**Kinder**

<u>NB:</u> The feminine **eine** and neuter **ein** stay the same.

The negative of **ein** is **kein**. It follows the same pattern as **ein**.

Ich habe ...	**kein<u>en</u> Bruder**	**keine Schwester**	**kein Kind**	**keine Kinder**

Possessives

Ihr 'your' (formal) begins with a capital letter. This distinguishes it from **ihr** 'her'.
Like the other possessives, it follows the same pattern as **mein** and **ein**:

Ihr Sohn	**Ihre Tochter**	**Ihr Kind**	**Ihre Eltern**

5 Das ist meine Familie

Describe your family to a partner who sketches out your family tree on the basis of what you say. Check it afterwards, using only German to correct any errors. Reverse roles.

Beispiel: *Ich habe einen Bruder und zwei Schwestern. Mein Bruder ist ...*

6 Und das ist seine/ihre Familie

Using the family tree drawn up in exercise 5, describe your partner's family to a third party/the class. Remember to use **er/sie** and the possessives **sein(e)/ihr(e)** as appropriate.

7 Großvaters Katze/Grandfather's cat

Herr Baumann ist Stephanies Großvater.

– Großvater, du hast kein Auto.
– Hast du einen Fernseher?
– Hast du einen Computer?
– Und ein Handy?
– Was hast du denn?

– Nein. Ich habe ein Fahrrad.
– Nein. Ich habe ein Radio.
– Ich brauche keinen Computer!
– Nein. Ich habe ein Telefon.
– Eine Katze.

Make a list of what the grandfather does and doesn't own, using the correct form of **ein** or **kein**:

Stephanies Großvater hat ein(e/en): _____ , *er hat kein(e/en)* _____ *etc.*

8 Was hast du?

a Link the words below to the correct drawing.

b Note down the gender of the objects (*m*, *f* or *n*). If in doubt, use a dictionary.

c Take turns with your partner to ask and answer questions.
Choose either informal or formal 'you' and be consistent.

| Hast du Haben Sie | einen eine ein | MP3-Player *m* Brieftasche *f* Radio *n* Fernseher Handy Computer Kugelschreiber Handtasche Wörterbuch Kreditkarte Auto Fahrrad Katze | ? | Ja, ich habe | einen ... eine ... ein ... |
| | | | | Nein, ich habe | keinen ... keine ... kein ... |

1 2 3 4 5 6 7 8 9 10 11 12 13

9 Was brauchst du?/What do you need?

With a partner, take turns to choose statements from the following list and say which objects from exercise 8 you need, using **mein**, **meine** or **meinen** as appropriate. In most cases, there is more than one possibility. Use your imagination!

Beispiel: Ich *telefoniere oft … Ich brauche mein Handy.*

Ich schreibe heute einen Test.
Ich höre oft Musik.
Meine Eltern wohnen in Frankfurt.
Ich bin Fußball-Fan.

Ich gehe abends in die Stadt.
Heute kaufe ich ein.
Ich telefoniere oft.

Grammatik

Remember the possessives follow the pattern of the indefinite article **ein**, so there is a special masculine object form: **meinen** 'my' (similarly, **seinen** 'his', **ihren** 'her' etc.)

 10 Bleiben sie fit?

Read the information about the Baumanns and the Schmidts and answer the true/false questions below. Correct any false statements.

> Herr und Frau Baumann wohnen in Mannheim. Sie sind Rentner. Er ist 76 Jahre alt, sie ist 74. Sie bleiben fit und gesund. Sie essen viel Obst und Gemüse und gehen schwimmen. Sie fahren oft Rad und haben kein Auto. Sie lesen viel und hören Radio.
> Herr Baumann sagt: Unser Hobby ist Fitnesstraining!
>
> Herr und Frau Schmidt wohnen in München. Sie sind auch Rentner. Beide sind 80 Jahre alt. Sie rauchen viel und sehen immer fern. Sie haben ein Auto und sie essen oft Wurst und Pizza. Sie trinken auch manchmal Bier und gehen nie in das Sportzentrum. Ihr Hobby ist Fernsehen!

Richtig oder falsch?

Familie Baumann		Familie Schmidt	
a Sie wohnen in München.	r/f	**f** Sie sind 79 und 80 Jahre alt.	r/f
b Sie arbeiten nicht.	r/f	**g** Sie haben kein Auto.	r/f
c Sie sind gesund.	r/f	**h** Sie essen oft Wurst.	r/f
d Sie essen Pizza.	r/f	**i** Sie trinken Bier.	r/f
e Sie haben ein Auto.	r/f	**j** Sie gehen oft ins Sportzentrum.	r/f

Grammatik

sie 'they':   **sie wohnen** *regular verb.*
            sie sind 'they are' (from **sein** 'to be') *irregular verb.*
(Distinguish from **Sie** 'you' and **sie** 'she'.)

Possessives: **unser** (our), **ihr** (their)

11 **Wir essen gesund …**/We eat healthily …

Listen to the interviews with Herr Baumann and Frau Schmidt. The following summaries each contain one inaccurate point: which is it?

a He is 76. They are healthy. They eat lots of fruit and vegetables. They go swimming and cycling. They often watch TV. They listen to the radio.

b She is 80. They often eat pizza. They drink beer. They sometimes drink wine. They never cycle.

Grammatik

wir 'we':	**wir wohnen** *regular verb*
	wir sind 'we are' (from **sein** 'to be') *irregular verb*

 12 **Partnerübung**

Q Hast du/Haben Sie …   einen Freund/eine Freundin?
einen Bruder/eine Schwester?
Kinder/einen Sohn/eine Tochter?
einen Hund/eine Katze?

A Ja/Nein, ich habe   einen/keinen Bruder/zwei Brüder *etc.*

<u>Plurals:</u> **Brüder, Schwestern, Söhne, Töchter, Hunde, Katzen**

Q Wie heißt dein(e)/Ihr(e) …   Freund(in)?
Mutter/Vater/Schwester/Bruder/Tochter/Sohn?
Katze/Hund?

A Mein(e) Vater/Mutter heißt …

Q Wie heißen deine/Ihre …   Eltern/Kinder/Geschwister?
A Meine Eltern heißen …

Q Wie alt ist   dein/Ihr Freund?
deine/Ihre Freundin? etc.

Grammatik

<u>Possessive:</u> **dein** 'your' (informal):
dein Vater (m)   **deine Mutter** (f)   **dein Kind** (n)   **deine Eltern** (pl)

Extra!

13 Familie, Freunde und Hobbys

a You will hear three people talking about their respective families, friends and hobbies. Draw up a grid like the one below. Jot down in it in German keywords as much relevant information as possible.

Name	Familie	Freunde	Hobbys
Annelie			
Markus			
Hanna			

b With the help of your notes, write a summary in German. Use whole sentences.

14 Kinder lesen nicht?

You won't understand every single word at first reading, but don't worry – you are not being asked to translate the passage.

a Through attentive reading, work out the German equivalents of:

- **i** no surprise
- **ii** young people
- **iii** to own
- **iv** connection (2 different words!)
- **v** investigation
- **vi** availability
- **vii** reading ability
- **viii** grades
- **ix** to benefit from

b Summarise the content of the article in English in three or four sentences.

> Die Kinder von heute leben online. Es ist also keine Überraschung, dass Kinder und Jugendliche eher ein Handy als ein Buch besitzen. Das geht aus einer interessanten Studie der britischen National Literacy Trust (NLT) hervor. 17.000 Kinder zwischen sieben und 16 Jahren nahmen an der Studie teil – 86 Prozent besitzen ein Handy, aber nur 73 Prozent haben ein Buch zu Hause.
>
> Es gibt einen klaren Zusammenhang zwischen der Verfügbarkeit von Büchern und der Lesefähigkeit der Kinder. „Unsere Untersuchung zeigt, dass diese Verbindung existiert", so NLT-Direktor Jonathan Douglas.
>
> Bücher zu Hause bedeuten bessere Noten in der Schule. So war es immer. Aber Kinder können auch vom Lesen auf iPhones und Computern profitieren; wichtig ist, dass Schüler lesen und schreiben. Wie sie das lernen ist nicht wichtig.

Grammatik

～ Indefinite article ('a'/'an') ▶ G4.1, G4.2

ein Computer	eine Kreditkarte	ein Auto
(masculine)	(feminine)	(neuter)

1 When a masculine noun is the object of a sentence, the indefinite article is **einen**. The feminine and neuter indefinite articles remain unchanged.

Ein Computer   kostet   1600 Euro.   Peter   braucht   ein<u>en</u> Computer.
— subject —   verb   subj   verb   —— object ——

Peter braucht eine Kreditkarte/ein Auto.

2 **Kein** is the negative of **ein** and follows the same pattern:

Kein Computer kostet 50 Euro!   **Peter braucht kein<u>en</u> Computer.**
No computer costs 50 euros!   Peter doesn't need a computer
                                         (literally *Peter needs no computer*.)

3 This special form of the indefinite article or **kein** is called the accusative.

～ Plurals ▶ G2

There is no single way of forming the plural of a noun:

Freund – Freund<u>e</u>; Schwester – Schwester<u>n</u>; Sohn – S<u>ö</u>hne; Auto – Autos.

While there are patterns, it is easier and safer at this stage to learn the plural when you first come across a noun. The vocabulary beginning on page 160 gives the plural of each noun listed.

～ Pronouns and verbs ▶ G12, G14.1

Wir (we) and **sie** (they) are followed by a verb form which is the same as the infinitive:
Wir wohn<u>en</u> in Mannheim. Sie bleib<u>en</u> fit.

Exception: irregular verb **sein** (to be): **wir/sie sind** (we/they are)

～ Possessives ▶ G4.1

	masculine	feminine	neuter	plural
my	**mein**	**meine**	**mein**	**meine**
your (informal)	**dein**	**deine**	**dein**	**deine**
your (formal)	**Ihr**	**Ihre**	**Ihr**	**Ihre**
his/its	**sein**	**seine**	**sein**	**seine**
her/its	**ihr**	**ihre**	**ihr**	**ihre**
our	**unser**	**unsere**	**unser**	**unsere**
their	**ihr**	**ihre**	**ihr**	**ihre**

1 **Ihr** (your) is capitalised in the same way **Sie** (you) is capitalised.
  ihr (her/their) corresponds to **sie** (she/they).

2 **Mein** and the other possessives follow the pattern of the indefinite article **ein**:
  mein Computer, meine Kreditkarte, mein Auto.

Ich brauche mein<u>en</u> Computer.   **Er braucht sein<u>en</u> Computer.**
Brauchen Sie Ihr<u>en</u> Computer?   **Wir brauchen unser<u>en</u> Computer.**

Grammatikübungen

1 Give the correct form of **ein** or **kein**. Remember to check the genders of nouns!

   a Ich kaufe heute e____ Brieftasche.
   b Er trinkt abends e____ Bier und liest e____ Buch.
   c Sie hat e____ Computer, aber k____ Handy.
   d Ich habe e____ Hund und e____ Katze.
   e Morgens esse ich e____ Käsebrot.
   f Er hat e____ Tochter und e____ Sohn.
   g Ich habe k____ Geschwister.

2 The following plurals occur in Units 1 to 3. Give the singular and gender.

   a Länder **b** Studenten **c** Mahlzeiten **d** Töchter **e** Kinder

3 Give the correct form of an appropriate verb.

   Wir **a** _____ Studenten und **b** _____ in Heidelberg. Wir **c** _____ Fahrräder und
   d _____ fit. Wir **e** _____ viel Obst, aber wir **f** _____ manchmal viel Bier!

4 Karin or Claus? You will hear two people talking about themselves, a man and a woman. Listen to the recording and answer the questions. Note that they are mixed up, some refer to him and some to her!

   a Was ist ihre Mutter von Beruf?
   b Wie heißt sein Bruder?
   c Wo wohnt seine Freundin?
   d Wie heißt ihre Katze?
   e Was ist seine Mutter von Beruf?
   f Wie alt ist ihre Schwester?
   g Wie heißt ihre beste Freundin?
   h Wie heißt sein Hund?
   i Was ist sein Vater von Beruf?
   j Wie alt ist ihre Mutter?

5 Match the statements below with the sentences on the right and add the missing endings (if any!).

   1 Ich telefoniere oft.
   2 Er schreibt E-Mails.
   3 Sie lernt Deutsch.
   4 Er besucht seine Großeltern in Mannheim.
   5 Ich höre abends Musik.
   6 Sie kauft heute Nachmittag ein.

   a Ich brauche mein___ Radio.
   b Sie braucht ihr___ Kreditkarte.
   c Er braucht sein___ Auto.
   d Er braucht sein___ Computer.
   e Sie braucht ihr___ Wörterbuch.
   f Ich brauche mein___ Telefon.

Vokabeln

Aufgabe 1

sprechen*	to speak
– er/sie spricht	
über	about
Eltern *pl*	parents
Jahre alt	years old
ledig	single
die Mathematik	mathematics
die Informatik	computer science
die Mutter	mother
der/die Architekt(in)	architect (m/f)
der Vater	father
der/die Ingenieur(in)	engineer (m/f)
bei	at, for
die Schwester	sister
verheiratet	married
der Mann	husband; man
Kinder *pl*	children
noch	still
klein	small
der Bruder	brother

Aufgabe 2

wie alt?	how old?
das Auto	car

Aufgabe 3

der/die Bibliothekar(in)	librarian (m/f)
im Moment	at the moment
nicht	not
alt	old
nett	nice
das Moped	moped
neu	new
fahren*	to go/drive
– er/sie fährt	
gut	well
das Schwimmbad	swimming pool
viele	many
Hobbys *pl*	hobbies
das Schwimmen	swimming
Filme *pl*	films

Aufgabe 4

die Geschwister *pl*	brothers and sisters
der Sohn	son
die Tochter	daughter

Aufgabe 7

der Großvater	grandfather
das Fahrrad	bicycle
der Fernseher	TV set

das Radio	radio
der Computer	computer
brauchen	to need
das Handy	mobile phone
das Telefon	telephone
Was hast du denn?	What have you got, then?
die Katze	cat

Aufgabe 8

die Brieftasche	wallet
der Kugelschreiber	ballpoint pen
die Handtasche	handbag
das Wörterbuch	dictionary
die Kreditkarte	credit card

Aufgabe 9

der Test	test
einkaufen *sep*	to shop
telefonieren	to telephone
der Fan	fan

Aufgabe 10

der/die Rentner(in)	pensioner (m/f)
viel	a lot
das Obst	fruit
das Gemüse	vegetable(s)
Rad fahren*	to cycle
das Fitnesstraining	fitness training
beide	both
rauchen	to smoke
die Wurst	sausage

Aufgabe 12

der Hund	dog

Possessives

mein	my
dein	your *informal*
Ihr	your *formal*
sein	his
ihr	her/their
unser	our

**Extra/Grammatikübungen/Partnerarbeit/
Weitere Übungen**

der CD-Spieler	CD-player
kaufen	to buy
die Großeltern *pl*	grandparents
der Stammbaum	family tree
besuchen	to visit

For guidance on plurals ▶ **G2**

*Verb strong in present tense ▶ **G14.2**

Partnerarbeit

1 Stammbaum/Family tree

Describe the family presented in the family tree below to Partner B. He/She will draw up a diagram with the information you provide and then check the details by asking questions about individual family members. Start with Ulrike …

Hannelore (75) und **Gregor** (79) – ihre Großeltern

| **Gisela** (50) | | **Herbert** (53) |
| ihre Mutter | ihre Eltern | ihr Vater |

Ulrike (18)

ihr Bruder **Manfred** (21)   **Ulrike** (18)   ihr Bruder **Walter** (25)
seine Freundin **Vera** (20)   ihr Freund **Thomas** (21)   seine Frau **Sabine** (26)
sein Hund **Gomez**   ihre Katze **Mikesch**   ihre Kinder **Hanna** (2)
Benno (1)

2 Du brauchst …

Your partner will tell you what he/she is doing. You tell him/her what he/she needs for each activity, choosing items from the following list. He/She then responds by telling you whether he/she has those items or not. Use your imagination!

Check any genders you are not sure of.

Sie brauchen   ein(e/en) …
Du brauchst …

Handy	Kugelschreiber	Auto
Fernseher	Kreditkarte	Computer
Fahrrad	Katze	Bibliothek
Wörterbuch	Freund(in)	
｜DVD-Rekorder	MP3-Player	
Radio	Bier	

Partnerarbeit

1 Stammbaum/Family tree

Your partner will describe Ulrike's family in some detail, providing you with information on their names, ages and relation to Ulrike. Complete the diagram below and then check if your information is correct by asking your partner questions about each family member.

Hannelore (_75_) und _Gregor_ _69_) – ihre _Großeltern_

_Gisila_____ (_60_)
Ihre Mutter

_____ Ihre Eltern _____

Habbot (53)
ihr Vater

ihr _____ (_)
seine Freundin ____ (_)
_____ **Gomez**

Ulrike (_)
ihr _____ (_)
_____ Katze _____

_____ **Walter** (_)
seine _____ (_)
____ Kinder _____ (_)
_____ (1)

2 Was brauche ich?

Tell your partner what you're doing (the activities are listed below).
For each one, he/she will suggest what you need. You then respond by telling him/her whether you have what he/she suggests. Use your imagination!

Ich lerne Deutsch.　　Ich telefoniere viel.

Ich fahre in die Stadt.　　Ich tanze oft.

Ich kaufe ein Moped.　　Ich höre abends Musik.

Ich habe ein(e/en) …
Ich habe kein(e/en) …

Am Wochenende

In this unit you will learn how to talk about your leisure time, to express likes and preferences, to make suggestions and issue invitations. You will also learn the days of the week and the other way to tell the time.

1 Was machst du gern?/What do you like doing?

Listen to Silvia, Felix and Anna saying what they like doing, and fill in the gap in each of the sentences below.

a _____Felix_____ kocht gern.

b Silvia _____ gern spazieren.

c _____ kauft gern Kleider.

d Felix _____ gern.

e Silvia liest _____ Krimis.

f Anna fährt gern _____ .

Grammatik

Lesen 'to read' (**er/sie liest**) and fahren 'to drive/go' (**er/sie fährt**) are *strong verbs* ▶ **G14.2.**

ich koche <u>gern</u> 'I like cooking'
er/sie kocht <u>gern</u> 'he/she likes cooking'

2 Und du? Was machst du gern?

Beispiel: *Ich gehe gern ins Kino* etc.

- spazieren gehen
- rauchen
- lesen
- Auto fahren
- Kleider kaufen
- kochen
- schwimmen
- in die Kneipe gehen
- fernsehen
- Musik hören
- tanzen
- ins Kino gehen
- Fußball spielen

3 Umfrage/Survey

You will know most of the food and drink vocabulary in this exercise. Check the rest in the unit vocabulary. Take it in turns to ask the class. One student keeps count of the responses and gives the results at the end.

Wer trinkt gern …
Kaffee/Tee/Mineralwasser/Cola/Orangensaft/Bier/Wein?

Wer isst gern …
Pizza/Pommes frites/Obst/Gemüse/Salat/Fleisch/Fisch?

Wer geht gern …
ins Kino/in die Diskothek/ins Sportzentrum/einkaufen/
schwimmen/spazieren?

Beispiel: 15 *Personen trinken gern Kaffee, 17 trinken gern Tee … usw.*

 4 Richtig oder falsch?

Listen as Thomas and Karin are asked about their preferences. Which statements are true and which false?

a Thomas never drinks milk. t/f
b Thomas doesn't like beer. t/f
c Karin doesn't like wine. t/f

d Karin doesn't drink mineral water. t/f
e Karin prefers tea to cola. t/f

**Grammatik**

gern/lieber/am liebsten
Das ist Thomas. Was macht er gern? …

Thomas trinkt *gern* Kaffee.
Er trinkt *lieber* Apfelsaft.
Er trinkt *am liebsten* Rotwein.
Er trinkt *nicht gern* Milch.

 5 Sie trinkt gern Tee

Look at the following list of food and drink items. Make up sentences indicating the likes and dislikes of Gudrun, Frank und Gabi.

	Cola	Tee	Bier	Wein	Salat	Pizza	Käse	Fisch
Gudrun	👍👍	👍	👎	👍👍👍	👍👍	👎	👍	👍👍👍
Frank	👎	👍👍	👍👍👍	👍	👍	👍👍👍	👍👍	👎
Gabi	👍	👍👍👍	👎	👍👍	👎	👍	👍👍👍	👍👍

  6 Und was isst/trinkst du gern?

Get together with a partner and find out what he/she likes or does not like to eat and drink. Tell the class about your partner's likes and dislikes. (Use a dictionary where necessary.)

7 Was machst du am Wochenende?

Listen to the conversation on the phone between Astrid and Christoph and note down in English what they like (or don't like) doing at the weekend.

8 Die Uhrzeit

In addition to the 24-hour clock, which you have already met, there is another way of telling the time in German which is used in most everyday conversations just as in English.

a Listen to the times.

Viertel <u>nach</u> zehn

halb elf

Viertel <u>vor</u> elf

Note that **halb elf** means 10.30 not 11.30!

fünf (Minuten) <u>nach</u> zehn

zwanzig (Minuten) <u>nach</u> zehn

zwanzig (Minuten) <u>vor</u> elf

zwölf Uhr/Mittag

zwölf Uhr/Mitternacht

b Using the 12-hour clock, write down (in figures) the times you hear:

   i _____   ii _____   iii _____   iv _____   v _____

c Wie spät ist es?
Beispiel: *Viertel nach acht*
8.15   8.30   8.45   8.05   8.20   8.40   4.10   7.25   2.35   5.45   9.50   11.55

9 Die Wochentage

Zum Lernen!

Montag Dienstag Mittwoch Donnerstag Freitag Samstag/Sonnabend Sonntag
(**Samstag** heißt **Sonnabend** in Norddeutschland)

> **Samstag + Sonntag = das Wochenende**
> **am Montag**: 'on Monday' **montags**: '(on) Mondays' (regularly)

10 **Einladung**/Invitation

a Without reading the script, listen to the recording of Petra and Thomas: what do they agree to do? When you have answered that question, read the script:

Petra:	Hallo, Thomas. *Wie geht's?*
Thomas:	Gut, danke. Petra, was machst du denn heute Abend?
Petra:	Ich muss für mein Examen arbeiten. Warum?
Thomas:	Ich will essen gehen. *Kommst du mit?*
Petra:	Heute kann ich *leider* nicht ausgehen, *tut mir leid.*
Thomas:	Oh, aber *vielleicht* können wir am Mittwoch ins Restaurant gehen?
Petra:	Am Mittwoch … Ich gehe um halb acht mit Martin ins Kino.
Thomas:	*Schade.* Kannst du am Freitag ausgehen?
Petra:	*Ja, das geht.* Um wie viel Uhr?
Thomas:	Gegen neun Uhr, *ist das in Ordnung?*
Petra:	Ja, das ist OK. Wohin gehen wir?
Thomas:	Vielleicht ins „Buena Vista", das ist sehr gut. Isst du gern spanisch?
Petra:	Spanisch … ja, aber ich esse lieber italienisch.
Thomas:	Dann müssen wir ins „Bella Italia" gehen. Die Pizza ist dort fantastisch.
Petra:	Prima. *Wo treffen wir uns?*
Thomas:	Um Viertel vor neun am Stadttheater. Ich muss jetzt gehen – meine Gitarrenstunde *fängt* um drei Uhr *an.*
Petra:	*Tschüss* Thomas, *bis Freitag.*

b Which of the words or phrases in italics is the equivalent of:

i (That's a) pity **ii** Is that all right? **iii** I'm sorry **iv** Are you coming along?
v That's fine **vi** perhaps **vii** See you on Friday **viii** How are you? **ix** 'Bye
x Where shall we meet? **xi** starts/begins **xii** unfortunately

---

Grammatik

Können 'to be able to', 'can', **müssen** 'to have to', 'must', **wollen** 'to want to' are known as *modal verbs*. They are usually followed by a second verb in the *infinitive* form which comes at the end of the sentence. Modal verbs have a distinctive pattern:

können:	ich kann	du kannst	er/sie kann	wir/Sie/sie können
müssen:	ich muss	du musst	er/sie muss	wir/Sie/sie müssen
wollen:	ich will	du willst	er/sie will	wir/Sie/sie wollen

Example: **Ich <u>muss</u> in die Bibliothek <u>gehen</u> – ich <u>kann</u> heute nicht <u>ausgehen</u>.**
I have to go to the library – I can't go out today.

Note: **Er muss nicht gehen** means 'He doesn't have to go', <u>not</u> 'He must not go'.

---

c In the dialogue script, find the modal verbs and the infinitives with them.

d Role-play the dialogue. Change each shaded phrase. Swap roles.

11 Ich habe keine Zeit

Fragen:

a Warum hat Stefan morgen keine Zeit?

b Was will Anna machen?

c Hat Stefan am Mittwoch Zeit?

d Wann trifft Anna ihre Freundinnen?

e Wann können sie Tennis spielen?

f Warum muss Stefan zu Hause sein?

12 Was kann man machen?

a When there is a clear context, you can often understand written information including words you have not met before. Read the information without referring to the vocabulary list. Find in it the German for the English phrases listed below:

PIZZERIA „NAPOLI"
Italienische Küche
Täglich von 17 Uhr bis 23 Uhr.

Altdeutsche Bierstube
Biergarten Mittagstisch Weinkarte
kinderfreundlich
Öffnungszeiten: Mo-Fr 12.00-21.00
Sa 11.30-23.00 So 12.00-14.30

Stadttheater. „Cyrano de Bergerac" von Edmond de Rostand
Samstag 20 Uhr Eintritt 5 Euro.

Charly's Diskothek. Samstag ab 23 Uhr
Große Tanznacht mit DJ Benny Ahrens

Kino am Bahnhofsplatz. **„Herr der Ringe"** ab 12 Jahren
Mo-Fr 19.30 Sa/So 15.30, 19.30
Mo-Do €6,50 (Kinder €3,50) Fr-So €7,50 (Kinder €4,00).

i opening times

ii admission/entrance

iii Italian cuisine

iv from 11 pm

v daily

vi wine list

vii children welcome

Grammatik

Was kann man am Wochenende machen? – <u>Man kann</u> ins Restaurant gehen.
The handy pronoun **man** means 'one', 'you'. It is followed by the **er/sie** form of the verb.
Man kann *in die Kneipe/ins Theater/in die Diskothek/ins Kino* gehen.
(**ins = in das**)

b Fragen:

i Was kann man am Samstagnachmittag machen?

ii Was kann man samstags um 23 Uhr machen?

iii Was kann man am Sonntagabend machen?

iv Wann kann man am Sonntag ins Kino gehen?

v Wann kann man ins Restaurant gehen?

vi Wann kann man ins Theater gehen?

13 Im Restaurant

Petra:	Haben Sie einen Tisch für zwei Personen?
Kellner:	Ja, dort drüben am Fenster.
Thomas:	Gut, wir nehmen den Tisch.
Petra:	Wir möchten gern die Speisekarte.
Kellner:	Einen Moment bitte … Hier ist die Speisekarte.
Petra:	Vielen Dank. (*nach 5 Minuten …*)
Kellner:	Was möchten Sie, bitte?
Petra:	Ich nehme die Pizza Spezial. Kann ich auch einen Salat haben?
Kellner:	Ja natürlich … Tomatensalat oder Cäsarsalat?
Petra:	Ich nehme den Tomatensalat.
Kellner:	Einmal Pizza Spezial und Tomatensalat …Und für Sie?
Thomas:	Ich bekomme die Tomatensuppe und das Huhn mit Sahnesauce.
Kellner:	Und was möchten Sie trinken?
Thomas:	Kann ich die Weinkarte sehen, bitte? … Wir nehmen den Weißwein Nummer 12, bitte.
Kellner:	Einmal den Chardonnay, in Ordnung. Sonst noch etwas?
Petra:	Danke, das ist alles.

Ich nehme/bekomme/möchte … einen Salat/**eine** Pizza/**ein** Eis
den Tomatensalat/**die** Pizza Spezial/**das** Vanilleeis

Grammatik

Definite article ('the')
der Salat (masculine), **die** Pizza (feminine), **das** Eis (neuter).

Accusative form: When a masculine noun is the object of a sentence, **der** becomes **den**, while the feminine and neuter definite articles remain unchanged:
Ich nehme … den Salat   die Pizza   das Eis

Rollenspiel: im Restaurant. Nehmen Sie die Konversation als Modell. Hier ist die Speisekarte.

SPEISEKARTE

Tomatensuppe	€5,50
Gemüsesuppe	€6,00
Pizza Romano	€9,60
Pizza Salami	€10,00
Weißwein/Rotwein	€3,00
Mineralwasser	€1,70
Vanille-/Schokoladeneis	€3,80

Extra!

14 Manfreds Woche

A market research company is doing a survey about student lifestyles and Manfred is being asked about his activities during one particular week. Listen carefully to the interview and note down in German what he is doing on the days given. Use the 24-hour clock.

NB: There is information about the whole week – make sure you select what he says about the days in question.

 Montag

Donnerstag

 Samstag

15 Zusammen oder allein?/Together or alone?

Read below an account of what Sabine and Rolf like (and dislike!) as far as leisure activities and food are concerned. What can they do together? Find as many activities as possible that they can share, and also those they cannot share.

Sabine

Ich bin sehr sportlich und gehe oft ins Sportzentrum. Am liebsten spiele ich Tennis, aber ich mache auch gern Aerobic und manchmal gehe ich schwimmen. Fußball spiele ich nicht gern. Samstags gehe ich immer ins Kino - am liebsten sehe ich amerikanische und britische Filme. Ich gehe gern in die Kneipe, aber ich trinke nie Bier. Ich trinke lieber Wein oder Apfelwein. Ins Restaurant gehe ich nicht oft, denn das kostet viel Geld. Ich koche lieber mit Freunden zu Hause und wir essen zusammen. Spaghetti mit Sauce esse ich besonders gern! Ich höre gern Musik und gehe auch manchmal in die Diskothek, aber ich tanze lieber auf Partys. Das macht mehr Spaß. Am Wochenende gehe ich manchmal spazieren, aber am liebsten bleibe ich sonntags im Bett!

Rolf

Abends bleibe ich gern zu Hause und lese. Ich sehe auch gern fern und höre Musik - am liebsten höre ich Jazz und Soul. Freitags gehe ich oft in die Disko, denn ich tanze sehr gern. Ich fahre gern Auto und oft fahre ich nach München und gehe dort ins Kino. Ich sehe gern alte amerikanische Filme, aber am liebsten sehe ich Science-fiction Filme. In München kann man auch gut italienisch essen! Ich gehe fast nie in die Kneipe, denn ich rauche nicht und trinke nicht gern Bier. Am liebsten trinke ich im Sommer Apfelwein im Gartencafé. Ich gehe oft schwimmen und spiele manchmal Fußball mit Freunden, aber ins Sportzentrum gehe ich nie. Das ist langweilig. Am Wochenende besuche ich manchmal meine Eltern, aber ich gehe lieber mit meinen Freunden aus.

Beispiel: *Sabine und Rolf können zusammen Musik hören.*
Sie können nicht zusammen Bier trinken.

Grammatik

~ Liking and preference

1 The adverb **gern** indicates a liking. It comes directly after the verb:

Ich trinke <u>gern</u> Tee. I like drinking tea.

Ich gehe <u>gern</u> ins Kino. I like going to the cinema.

2 **Lieber** indicates preference:

Ich gehe gern ins Kino, ich gehe <u>lieber</u> ins Theater.

I like going to the cinema but I prefer (going to) the theatre.

3 **Am liebsten** expresses what you like most of all:

Ich trinke <u>am liebsten</u> Rotwein. Ich gehe <u>am liebsten</u> ins Restaurant.

~ Modal verbs ▶G14.4

> **können** 'to be able to'/'can'
> **ich kann   du kannst   er/sie kann**
> **wir/Sie/sie können**

> **müssen** 'to have to', 'must'
> **ich muss   du musst   er/sie muss**
> **wir/Sie/sie müssen**

> **wollen** 'to want to'
> **ich will   du willst   er/sie will**
> **wir/Sie/sie wollen**

These *irregular* verbs all follow the same distinctive pattern and are usually followed by a second verb in the infinitive form at the end of the sentence.

Ich <u>will</u> am Montag ins Restaurant <u>gehen</u>.   I want to go to the restaurant on Monday.
         1   2

~ man

This useful pronoun is used much more often than its English equivalent, 'one':

Am Wochenende kann <u>man</u> spät aufstehen.

At the weekend one/you can get up late.

~ Definite article: the accusative form ▶G4.2

In Unit 3 you saw the accusative form of the indefinite article before masculine nouns, used when the noun is the object of the sentence: **Er kauft ein<u>en</u> Computer.**

The definite article, too, has an accusative form: before masculine nouns it changes from **der** to **den** when the noun is the object of the sentence. The feminine (**die**), neuter (**das**) and plural (**die**) definite articles remain unchanged.

Der Rotwein kostet 3 Euro.   **Ich nehme <u>den</u> Rotwein.**
— subject —   verb   verb   — object —

Grammatikübungen

1 Express (1) liking/ (2) preference/ (3) 'like most of all'/ (4) 'don't like' for the following:

		1	2	3	4
a	Ich trinke ...	Mineralwasser	Cola	Orangensaft	Bier
b	Er isst ...	Pasta	Pizza	Pommes frites	Salat
c	Ich ...	lese	höre Musik	spiele Gitarre	gehe spazieren
d	Sie gehen ...	ins Kino	in die Stadt	ins Sportzentrum	in die Diskothek

2 Complete each sentence by choosing the correct form of an appropriate modal verb and an infinitive from the two sets of verbs below.

„**a** _____ du heute Abend ins Restaurant **b** _____?" „Es tut mir leid, ich
c _____ heute nicht **d** _____. Ich **e** _____ zu Hause
f _____." „Was **g** _____ Sie **h** _____?" „**i** _____ wir
bitte die Weinkarte **j** _____?"

Modals:	Infinitives:
können willst wollen kann muss	**bleiben ausgehen sehen gehen trinken**

3 Explain to a German-speaking friend what you can do in Stoke-on-Trent, where she/he will be an exchange student. Use the pronoun **man**.

Stoke-on-Trent, Staffordshire (240,000 inhabitants) has two local universities. Student social life is lively. There are many clubs and discos, good traditional pubs and two multi-screen cinemas. If eating out, try one of the excellent Balti restaurants. The New Victoria Theatre in neighbouring Newcastle-under-Lyme has a national reputation. The large Potteries Shopping Centre and the shopping and leisure complex at Festival Park cater for your retail needs. The beauty of the Peak District is a short drive away.

4 Max and Sabine have shared a flat but are now moving on. They have agreed to divide up their belongings by choosing one item at a time. Write out what happens, turn by turn.

Sabine nimmt den/die/das ...,
Max nimmt den/die/das ... etc.

Fernseher   Radio   DVD-Rekorder

MP3-Player   Handy   Katze

Hund   Wörterbuch   CDs

Moped   Computer

Vokabeln

See Appendix p. 190 for more vocabulary in exercise 13 and Extra!

Aufgabe 1

gern	(see grammar)
kochen	to cook
spazieren gehen	to go for a walk
die Kleider *pl*	clothes
Krimis *pl*	detective stories
Auto fahren*	to drive a car
– er/sie fährt	

Aufgabe 2

das Kino	cinema

Aufgabe 3

der Tee	tea
das Mineralwasser	mineral water
der Wein	wine
die Pommes frites *pl*	chips
das Fleisch	meat

Aufgabe 4

die Milch	milk

Aufgabe 8

Viertel	quarter
vor	before
nach	after
halb	half (to the next hour)

Aufgabe 9

die Woche	week
Montag	Monday
Dienstag	Tuesday
Mittwoch	Wednesday
Donnerstag	Thursday
Freitag	Friday
Samstag	Saturday
Sonnabend	Saturday (N. Germany)
Sonntag	Sunday
Norddeutschland	North Germany
das Wochenende	weekend
am Montag	on Monday
montags	on Mondays (regularly)

Aufgabe 10

die Einladung	invitation
wie geht's?	how are you?
gut, danke	fine, thanks
denn	(here =) then
für	for
das Examen	exam
mitkommen *sep*	to come along/come too
leider	unfortunately

(es) tut mir leid	I'm sorry
vielleicht	perhaps
schade	(that's a) pity
das geht	that's OK
gegen	(here =) about
in Ordnung	all right, OK
gut	good
die Pizza	pizza
dort	there
fantastisch	fantastic
prima!	great!
treffen*	to meet
– er/sie trifft	
wo treffen wir uns?	where shall we meet?
am Stadttheater	at the Stadttheater
jetzt	now
anfangen* *sep*	to begin, start
– er/sie fängt … an	
bis	until

Aufgabe 11

morgen	tomorrow
die Zeit	time

Aufgabe 12

italienische Küche	Italian cuisine
täglich	daily
von … bis …	from … until …
„Die Altdeutsche Bierstube"	name of pub
der Biergarten	beer garden
der Mittagstisch	lunchtime menu
die Weinkarte	wine-list
kinderfreundlich	welcoming to children
Öffnungszeiten *pl*	opening hours
der Eintritt	entrance, admission
ab	from
große Tanznacht	big dance night
das Theater	theatre

Aufgabe 13

der Tisch	table
Personen *pl*	persons
dort drüben	over there
am Fenster	by the window
möchte(n) *irreg*	would like
die Speisekarte	menu
vielen Dank	many thanks
bitte	please
nehmen*	to take (here = to have)
– er/sie nimmt	
natürlich	of course
einmal	once (here = one)

* Verb strong in present tense ▶ **G14.2**

Partnerarbeit

A

1 Suche Partner .../Lonely Hearts

a Partner B wants to put a Lonely Hearts ad in the local paper. Find out if he/she likes the following activities by asking the appropriate questions.

cinema swimming reading music pub shopping

sports centre Spanish cuisine watching TV writing emails

b On the basis of what emerged in exercise **a**, help Partner B to draft an ad describing himself/herself and his/her ideal partner. The two examples below will give you some ideas.

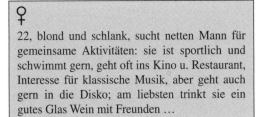

♀

22, blond und schlank, sucht netten Mann für gemeinsame Aktivitäten: sie ist sportlich und schwimmt gern, geht oft ins Kino u. Restaurant, Interesse für klassische Musik, aber geht auch gern in die Disko; am liebsten trinkt sie ein gutes Glas Wein mit Freunden ...

♂

Er ist 24 und groß (1,98m), Nichtraucher, aber trinkt gern Rotwein; Architekt; möchte gern zusammen mit einer interessanten jungen Frau Köln kennen lernen. Er interessiert sich für Theater, Kino und gutes Essen. Er kocht gut und gern, aber noch lieber geht er chinesisch essen. Wer möchte ihm Köln zeigen?

2 Einladung

Invite your partner to join you in a variety of activities. Unfortunately, he/she seems to be reluctant to do so and comes up with a string of excuses. You know that he/she cannot resist the temptation of pizza, though ... Keep your trump card until last!

The following vocabulary will come in handy:

Willst du ... Kannst du ...	heute Abend Samstagnachmittag morgen Abend	einkaufen/schwimmen gehen in die Kneipe gehen tanzen gehen ins Konzert gehen spazieren gehen Fußball spielen italienisch essen gehen

Partnerarbeit

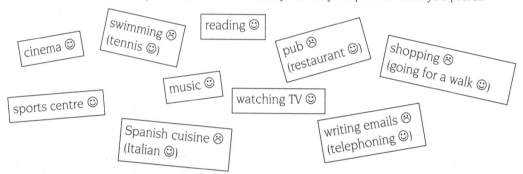

1 Suche Partner .../Lonely Hearts

a You want to put a Lonely Hearts ad in the local paper. Partner A will ask questions about your likes and dislikes in order to compile your profile. Answer the questions using the information below. If you do not like an activity ☹, tell your partner what you prefer.

cinema ☺

swimming ☹
(tennis ☺)

reading ☺

pub ☹
(restaurant ☺)

shopping ☹
(going for a walk ☺)

music ☺

watching TV ☺

sports centre ☺

Spanish cuisine ☹
(Italian ☺)

writing emails ☹
(telephoning ☺)

b On the basis of what emerged in exercise **a**, Partner A will help you to draft an ad describing you and your ideal partner. The two examples below will give you some ideas.

22, blond und schlank, sucht netten Mann für gemeinsame Aktivitäten: sie ist sportlich und schwimmt gern, geht oft ins Kino u. Restaurant, Interesse für klassische Musik, aber geht auch gern in die Disko; am liebsten trinkt sie ein gutes Glas Wein mit Freunden ...

Er ist 24 und groß (1,98m), Nichtraucher, aber trinkt gern Rotwein; Architekt; möchte gern zusammen mit einer interessanten jungen Frau Köln kennen lernen. Er interessiert sich für Theater, Kino und gutes Essen. Er kocht gut und gern, aber noch lieber geht er chinesisch essen. Wer möchte ihm Köln zeigen?

2 Einladung

Your partner invites you to join him/her in a variety of activities. You are a bit reluctant as you are not too keen on his/her company, so you think up a number of excuses. However, there is one proposition you cannot resist – a pizza washed down with a glass of red wine in your favourite Italian restaurant ....

The following vocabulary will come in handy:

Tut mir leid, ich kann	heute Abend morgen Abend Samstagnachmittag	leider nicht	einkaufen gehen, tanzen gehen, etc.
Ich muss	arbeiten/meine Mutter besuchen/kochen/E-Mails schreiben/einkaufen gehen etc.		

Oh ja, sehr gern! Yes, with pleasure.

5 Zu Hause

In this unit, you will learn to talk about where you and others live.

 1 Handygespräche/Conversations on a mobile

a *Tom und Astrid*

- Hallo?
- … Oh … Hallo, Tom … Ist Ute da?
- Ich glaube, sie ist noch im Bett … Moment …
  Nein, sie ist gerade unter der Dusche – sie sagt, sie ist in zwanzig Minuten fertig.
- Tom, ich bin jetzt im Unterricht! Ich rufe später an, um etwa Viertel nach zehn.
- OK. Tschüss.
- Tschüss.

b *Silvia und Markus*

- Hallo.
- Hallo, ich bin's … Was machst du?
- Ich arbeite.
- In der Bibliothek?
- Nein – in meinem Zimmer. Ich sitze am Computer …
- Schade … ich bin mit Anna und Jens im Eiscafé. Wann bist du fertig?
- Ich weiß nicht – ich hab' noch viel zu tun.
- OK, ich rufe später an. Tschüss.
- Tschüss.

> **ich bin's** = it's me!

 Fragen:

i Ist Ute noch im Bett?	**iii** Was macht Silvia?	**v** Wo ist Markus?
ii Wo ist Astrid?	**iv** Wo ist sie?	**vi** Was macht er später?

Grammatik

in: Up to now, you have met this preposition in contexts where it is telling us '*where to*' (**wohin**), involving a change of place:

Er geht in den Supermarkt/in die Diskothek/ins (= in das) Sportzentrum.
It is followed by an *accusative* form.

When it tells us simply '*where*' (**wo**), it is followed by the *dative* form of the article: masculine and neuter **dem/einem**, feminine **der/einer**:

Sie ist im Unterricht.   Ich arbeite in der Bibliothek.   Wir sind im Eiscafé.
    (masculine)   (feminine)   (neuter)
    (**im** = **in dem**)

Possessives follow the pattern of the indefinite article **ein**:
Ich arbeite in meinem Zimmer.

As you will see later, certain other prepositions are followed by the accusative or the dative depending on the context.

2 Wo seid ihr?

Yasmin und Paul

a Listen to the recording and fill in the missing locations.

– Hallo, Paul. Wir sind im **i** _____ . Wo seid ihr?

– In der **ii** _____ .

– Wann ist eure Deutschstunde?

– Um drei Uhr. Wir sind um fünf fertig. Wie lange bleibt ihr im
   iii _____?

– Bis halb fünf – dann gehen wir nach Hause.

– Geht ihr heute Abend aus?

– Vielleicht … Was wollt ihr machen?

– Wir sind ab neun Uhr in der **iv** _____ .

– Ja, OK … bis neun Uhr!

– Tschüss!

b Role-play the dialogue with a partner, changing the locations. Remember the gender of the noun determines whether it is preceded by **im** or **in der**.

Grammatik

The plural of **du**, the familiar 'you', is **ihr**. The verb ends in **-t**:
ihr bleibt, **ihr geht**, **ihr wollt**. Irregular verb **sein** 'to be': **ihr seid**.
The corresponding possessive 'your' is **euer** (masculine and neuter),
eure (feminine and plural) – **eure Deutschstunde**.

3 Welches Zimmer ist das?

das Wohnzimmer
die Küche
das Schlafzimmer
das Badezimmer
die Garage
der Balkon
das Esszimmer

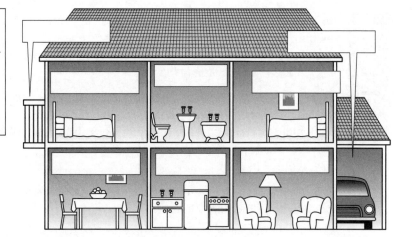

4 Das ist unsere Wohnung/This is our flat

Bernd schreibt über seine neue Wohnung.

> Das erste Zimmer links ist das Esszimmer. Es ist ziemlich klein. Es gibt nur einen Tisch und vier Stühle. Das zweite Zimmer links ist das Wohnzimmer. Es gibt ein Sofa, zwei Sessel, ein Bücherregal und einen Fernseher. In der Ecke steht eine Lampe. Rechts von dem Wohnzimmer ist die kleine Küche. Wir haben einen Elektroherd, einen Kühlschrank, eine Waschmaschine und eine Mikrowelle. Es gibt auch einige Schränke.
> Rechts von der Küche ist unser Schlafzimmer. Es gibt natürlich ein Bett und zwei Nachttische, auch einen Kleiderschrank und einen Stuhl. Das letzte Zimmer ist das Badezimmer/WC. Es ist sehr modern. Es gibt eine Dusche und eine Badewanne.
> Es gibt keinen Garten.

Grammatik

When the construction **es gibt** ('there is'/'there are') is followed by a masculine noun in the singular, the distinctive accusative form must be used, that is, **den/einen** rather than **der/ein**: **Es gibt einen Tisch**.

Remember, feminine and neuter articles do not have a distinctive accusative form and remain unchanged (**die/eine, das/ein**): **Es gibt eine Dusche, ein Bett** etc.

L

a Welches Zimmer ist das? Use Bernd's description above to help you label the rooms.

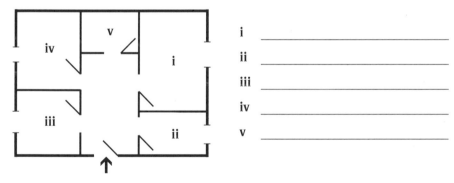

i _____

ii _____

iii _____

iv _____

v _____

b Without looking at the vocabulary, try to find in the text the German for these words. Then check to see whether you got them right!

lamp, wardrobe, electric cooker, bookshelves (singular in German!), washing machine, bed, bath, cupboards, sofa, fridge, bedside tables, armchairs, microwave, shower.

5 Möbel/Furniture

Write down what furniture there is in the hand-drawn living room directly below, before listening to the description on the recording. Then describe the other rooms (**a–e**).

6 Hier wohne ich ...

Give information about where you live.

Fragen:
- **a** Was gibt es in dem Wohnzimmer?
- **b** Gibt es einen Fernseher im Schlafzimmer?
- **c** Was gibt es in der Küche?
- **d** Wo sitzen Sie abends?
- **e** Wie viele Schlafzimmer gibt es?
- **f** Essen Sie in der Küche?
- **g** Gibt es eine Garage?

7 Peters Zimmer

Peters Zimmer ist klein und dunkel. Auf dem Fußboden liegen DVDs und Kleider. Es gibt Bücher und Papiere auf dem Stuhl, Tassen und Teller auf dem Schreibtisch. Zwei Gläser stehen auf seinem Bett. Unter dem Bett gibt es Bierflaschen. Peter putzt nicht, er kocht nicht, er räumt nie auf, er will nicht einkaufen oder abwaschen.

a Fragen:

i Wo sind die Bierflaschen?
ii Was gibt es auf dem Stuhl?
iii Wo sind die Gläser?
iv Was gibt es auf dem Schreibtisch?

 b Cover up the text and describe Peter's room to your partner, using the picture.

Grammatik

<u>Prepositions</u>
Like **in**, the prepositions **auf**, and **unter** are followed by the *dative* when they describe *location*, where something is: **DVDs liegen auf <u>dem</u> Fußboden**.
Contrast with **legen** 'to lay, put down': **Er legt das Buch auf <u>den</u> Stuhl.** (There's a change of place, so *accusative*.)

 8 Einladung

a In the text on the next page there are a number of adjectives. See if you can find the German equivalents of those listed here. Go for the more obvious ones first and then use your powers of deduction and a process of elimination to work out the rest.

1 bright/light	**7** comfortable	**13** new
2 cosy	**8** small	**14** kitschy
3 modern	**9** compact	**15** old-fashioned
4 wonderful	**10** big	**16** exclusive
5 dark	**11** great	**17** dear/expensive
6 cold	**12** warm	**18** delicious

b In the text, the German equivalents of the adjectives from 10 to 18 have an ending (**-en**, **-e** or **-es**), those 1 to 9 have none. From the text, can you work out in which circumstances an adjective has an ending and when it doesn't? Check your answer against the Grammar box on the next page.

Stefan und Monika haben eine schöne neue Wohnung. Ihre Freunde Andreas und Verena kommen zum Kaffeetrinken.

M Das ist unser Wohnzimmer … Es ist schön und hell, und es gibt einen großen Balkon. Wir haben noch keinen Fernseher, aber wir kaufen nächste Woche einen.

A Das ist wirklich gemütlich. Ihr habt tolle Sessel! Und der Balkon ist besonders praktisch. Im Sommer kann man auf dem Balkon grillen und Partys feiern.

S Hoffentlich gibt es einen warmen Sommer!

M … So, das ist unser Esszimmer. Die Stühle habe ich vom Sperrmüll.

V Wirklich? Die sind ja ganz modern. Habt ihr auch die Kissen vom Sperrmüll?

S Nein, Monika kann sehr gut nähen …

V Die Kissen sind wunderbar … Und das ist euer Schlafzimmer?

M Ja, es ist ein bisschen dunkel und kalt, aber das ist OK. Wir haben ein neues Bett, von Ikea. Es ist sehr bequem.

A Das ist ein großes Zimmer … Ihr braucht noch eine Lampe für das Bett!

S Ja, das stimmt. Monika hat eine kitschige, altmodische Lampe, aber …

M Moment mal! Das ist eine ganz exklusive, teure Lampe von meinem Ex-Freund …

S Und das ist die Küche … sehr klein, aber kompakt und gemütlich. Und hier gibt es jetzt Kaffee und Kuchen!

V Wo kauft ihr die Kuchen?

S Monika backt köstliche Kuchen – wir kaufen sehr selten beim Bäcker.

V Nächste Woche kommt ihr in die Felsingstraße, und ich backe einen Schokoladenkuchen – in Ordnung?

S Das ist eine fantastische Idee!

Grammatik

Note the endings on adjectives after the indefinite article in the accusative singular, and with no article in the accusative plural:

einen groß<u>en</u> Balkon **eine kitschige Lampe** **ein neu<u>es</u> Bett** **köstlich<u>e</u> Kuchen**
masculine   feminine   neuter   plural

If the adjective is not before the noun, there is no ending: **Das Bett ist sehr bequem.**

The prepositions **von**, **zu** and **bei** (and some others) are always followed by a dative form:
<u>zum</u> **Kaffeetrinken**, **von mein<u>em</u> Ex-Freund**, <u>beim</u> **Bäcker**.
(zum = zu dem, beim = bei dem, vom = von dem)

9 Was haben Monika und Stefan?

a On the basis of the conversation above, make up sentences about the couple's flat. Include an adjective with an appropriate ending.

Beispiel: Sie haben einen großen Balkon.

b Do the same for your own accommodation: Ich habe / Wir haben …

Extra!

10 Mein Haus

a You will hear three people talking about themselves and their accommodation. Listen carefully to Volker, Silvia and Oliver describing where they live and note down the relevant information using the headings below, and German key words. Don't worry if you don't understand everything – just note down as much as you can.

Name	Wohnort	Zimmer	Möbel
Volker			
Silvia			
Oliver			

b Using the information collected above, write a short description in German of where these three people live. Use whole sentences.

11 Im Studentenwohnheim/In the hall of residence

STUDENTENWOHNHEIM Gustav Heinemann Str. 54

Mietdauer   01-01 bis 31-07   **Monatliche Miete**   217,00 EURO
Mietzahlung   Gesamtmiete für den ersten Monat bitte vor dem Einzug zahlen.
Kaution   in Höhe von einer Monatsmiete

INVENTAR
Haustürschlüssel   Zimmerschlüssel   Briefkastenschlüssel
Schlüssel bekommen Sie vom Hausmeister werktags 8.00 bis 14.00.

Zimmereinrichtung
Schreibtisch 140 × 70 cm   Lampe 60 cm
Bürodrehstuhl   Sofa 2-Sitzer
Bücherregal 180 × 100 × 30 cm   Kleiderschrank 4 Türen 100 × 240 × 60 cm
Bett und Matratze 90 × 200 × 12 cm

Einrichtung Gemeinschaftsbereich 4 Personen
Esstisch   4 Stühle   Herd   Kühlschrank   4 Oberschränke
Badezimmer mit Badewanne und Dusche   WC

Draft an email in English telling family or friends about the accommodation you will have when in Germany.

Grammatik

～ Articles and possessives ▶ G4.1, G4.2, G4.3, G11

1 The basic form is used when the noun is the subject of a sentence. It is called the *nominative*.

The *definite article* shows number and gender:

> singular: masculine **der**, feminine **die**, neuter **das**; plural: **die**

The *indefinite article* has a simpler pattern:

> masculine and neuter **ein**, feminine **eine**. There is no plural.

The *possessives* and **kein** follow a pattern based on **ein/eine**:

masculine and neuter	**mein**	**dein**	**sein**	**ihr**	**unser**	**Ihr**	**euer**	**kein**
feminine and plural	**meine**	**deine**	**seine**	**ihre**	**unsere**	**Ihre**	**eure**	**keine**

2 You have seen earlier that when a masculine singular noun is the object of a sentence, the article preceding it changes from **der/ein/mein** etc. to **den/einen/meinen** etc. The feminine, neuter and plural forms remain as in the nominative: **Ich kaufe einen Tisch, eine Lampe und ein Sofa. Am Wochenende besuche ich meine Eltern.**

This form is called the *accusative*. As you've seen, the accusative is different from the nominative <u>only</u> in front of masculine nouns. The accusative is also used after **in** (and certain other prepositions) when they tell us 'where to' (**wohin**). It is also used after **es gibt** (there is/are): **Er geht oft in <u>den</u> Garten. Es gibt ein<u>en</u> Balkon.**

3 As you have seen in this unit, when **in** (and certain other prepositions such as **auf** and **unter**) tell us 'where' (**wo**), they are followed by a *dative* form:

> masculine/neuter: **dem/einem/meinem**   feminine: **der/einer/meiner**

Arbeitest du in dein<u>em</u> Zimmer? Helga ist in <u>der</u> Küche.

The dative must always be used after certain other prepositions, e.g. **bei**, **mit**, **von**, **zu**.

～ Adjectival endings ▶ G5

1 When adjectives occur before a noun, they have an ending. In this unit, you are introduced to the pattern <u>indefinite article + adjective + noun</u> in the *accusative*:

> Masculine: **Es gibt einen groß<u>en</u> Balkon.**
> Feminine: **Sie hat eine altmodisch<u>e</u> Lampe.**
> Neuter: **Wir haben ein neu<u>es</u> Bett.**

2 You've also met the pattern <u>adjective + plural noun</u>: **Ihr habt toll<u>e</u> Sessel!**

～ Informal 'you' ▶ G12, G14

The plural of **du** is **ihr**, verb ending **-t**: **Ihr hab<u>t</u> eine schöne Wohnung!**
The matching possessive is **euer**: **Ist das euer Schlafzimmer?**

Grammatikübungen

1 Complete ten sentences using in each case the correct (accusative) form of the indefinite article after **es gibt**. A tip: you will need to be sure of the gender of each noun!

In meinem Zimmer gibt es *einen/eine/ein*   … Radio … Computer … Lampe
                                            … Fernseher … Schreibtisch

In unserer Küche gibt es *einen/eine/ein*   … Kühlschrank … Elektroherd … Tisch
                                            … Waschmaschine … Mikrowelle

2 Accusative or dative? Which of the bracketed forms is correct?

  a Nachmittags arbeiten wir in (*die/der*) Bibliothek.
  b Geht ihr oft (*ins/im*) Kino?
  c Sie steht im Moment unter (*die/der*) Dusche.
  d Ich sitze an (*meinen/meinem*) Schreibtisch.
  e Er geht (*ins/im*) Zimmer und arbeitet.
  f Abends sehe ich (*ins/im*) Wohnzimmer fern.

3 Using the dative. Complete with the correct entry from the list at the end of the exercise.

  a Wir kaufen selten _____ Bäcker – Monika backt gern. Sie ist immer
    _____ Küche!
  b Ich habe die Lampe _____ Freund.
  c Die Lampe ist jetzt _____ Tisch _____ Schlafzimmer.
  d Er wohnt _____ Freundin zusammen.
  e Sie laden uns _____ Kaffeetrinken ein.

auf einem	in der	zum	mit seiner	beim	von einem	im

4 Add an ending to the adjective *where appropriate*.

  a Ihr habt eine schön____ Küche!
  b Meine neu____ Wohnung ist sehr modern____ .
  c Es gibt ein klein____ Esszimmer.
  d Unsere Sessel sind elegant____ und bequem____ .
  e Er hat einen klein____ Balkon, aber keinen Garten.
  f Ich kaufe morgen eine teur____ Lampe für mein Schlafzimmer.

5 How do you say …

  a Do you live here in Rostock? (To a middle-aged couple you have just met.)
  b You bake delicious cakes. (To your boyfriend/girlfriend.)
  c Do you have a flat with a garage? (To an estate agent.)
  d Do you have a shower or a bath? (To fellow students who have moved in together.)

Vokabeln

See Appendix p. 190 for more vocabulary from exercise 8, Extra!, Grammatikübungen and Partnerarbeit

Aufgabe 1

da	there
glauben	to think, believe
im Bett	in bed
gerade	just
unter	under
die Dusche	shower
sagen	to say
fertig	finished
im Unterricht	in a class
anrufen *sep*	to phone
später	later
etwa	about, roughly
ich bin's	it's me
das Zimmer	room
sitzen	to sit
das Eiscafé	ice-cream parlour
ich weiß nicht	I don't know
viel zu tun	a lot to do

Aufgabe 2

ihr seid	you are (pl, informal)
euer/eure etc.	your (pl, informal)
wie lange?	how long? (time)
das Wohnzimmer	living room
die Küche	kitchen
das Schlafzimmer	bedroom
das Badezimmer	bathroom
die Garage	garage
der Balkon	balcony
das Esszimmer	dining room

Aufgabe 4

die Wohnung	flat
der/die/das erste, zweite	the first, second
links	(on the) left
ziemlich	fairly
Stühle *pl*	chairs
der Stuhl	chair
das Sofa	couch
Sessel *pl*	armchairs
das Bücherregal	bookcase
die Ecke	corner
stehen	to stand
die Lampe	lamp
rechts von	to the right of
der Elektroherd	electric cooker

der Kühlschrank	refrigerator
die Waschmaschine	washing machine
die Mikrowelle	microwave
einige	some
Schränke *pl*	cupboards
Nachttische *pl*	bedside tables
der Kleiderschrank	wardrobe
letzt	last
die Badewanne	bath
der Garten	garden

Aufgabe 7

dunkel	dark
auf	on
der Fußboden	floor
liegen	to lie
Bücher *pl*	books
Papiere *pl*	papers
Tassen *pl*	cups
Teller *pl*	plates
der Schreibtisch	desk
Gläser *pl*	glasses
Bierflaschen *pl*	beer bottles
putzen	to clean
aufräumen *sep*	to tidy up
abwaschen* *sep*	to wash up

Aufgabe 8

schön	beautiful
hell	bright
groß	big
nächste Woche	next week
wirklich	really
gemütlich	cosy
toll	great
besonders	especially
praktisch	practical
der Sommer	summer
grillen	to barbecue
Partys feiern	have parties
hoffentlich	hopefully
warm	hot, warm
der Sperrmüll	bulky refuse
(often picked up by bargain-hunters)	
ganz	quite
modern	modern
Kissen *pl*	cushions
nähen	to sew
wunderbar	wonderful
ein bisschen	a bit
bequem	comfortable

*Verb strong in present tense ▶**G14.2**

Partnerarbeit

1 Wohnungsplan

Swap information with your partner in order to complete the plan of a flat below. Ask questions to find out about the rooms that are still blank on your plan. You will also tell him/her how the living room is furnished (couch, armchair, bookcase, two lamps, TV set).

He/She will then tell you about the furniture/equipment in one room. Sketch it in on the plan.

Compare notes afterwards. You ask the first question.

Example: **A** *Wo ist das Badezimmer?* **B** *Links/Rechts vom/von der …*
A *Im Wohnzimmer gibt es …*

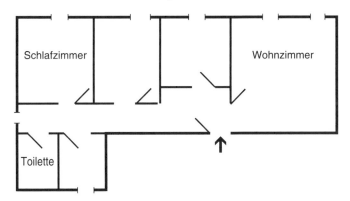

2 Wo ist Stefan?

Tell your partner what these men are doing at home. He/She responds by indicating which room the man is in. Use the pictures below, then try to think of other activities.

Example: 1 Stefan's listening to music
A *Stefan hört Musik.* **B** *Er ist im Wohnzimmer.*

2 Felix　　　3 Carsten　　　4 Ralf

3 Ulrike ist im Kino

Your partner tells you about Ulrike's leisure activities, and you respond by indicating where Ulrike pursues this activity.

Example: **B** *Ulrike sieht einen Film.* **A** *Sie ist im Kino.*

Partnerarbeit

B

1 Wohnungsplan

Swap information with your partner in order to complete the plan of a flat below.
Ask her/him questions to find out about the rooms that are still blank on your plan.
She/He will also give you details of the furniture in one room. Sketch it in on the plan.

You then tell her/him what there is in the kitchen (electric cooker, microwave, fridge, washing machine).

Compare notes afterwards. Your partner asks the first question.

Example: **B** *Wo ist die Toilette?*   **A** *Links/Rechts vom/von der …*
B *In der Küche gibt es …*

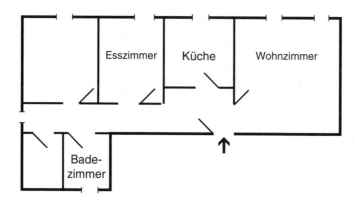

2 Stefan ist im Wohnzimmer

Your partner says what the men are doing, and you tell him/her which room each man is in.

Example: **A** *Stefan hört Musik.* **B** *Er ist im Wohnzimmer.*

3 Was macht Ulrike?

You tell your partner about Ulrike's leisure activities, and he/she tells you where Ulrike is.
Try to think of as many possibilities as you can.

Example: 1   She's eating a pizza.
B *Ulrike isst eine Pizza.* **A** *Sie ist im Restaurant.*

2
3
4

In der Stadt

In this unit you will learn how to ask for and understand directions and talk about locations in a town. You will also learn how to express likes and dislikes, particularly in relation to clothes.

1 Kennst du die Felsingstraße?/Do you know Felsingstraße?

- Kennst du die Felsingstraße?
- Das ist *nicht weit von dem Krankenhaus*, oder …?
- Genau – *wir sind um die Ecke*. Nimmst du den Bus?
- Ja, die Linie fünf.
- Es gibt eine Haltestelle in der Humboldtstraße. *Geh über die Straße* und dann rechts. *Die nächste Straße links* ist die Sankt-Johann-Straße. Es gibt eine Kirche *an der Ecke. Geh am Krankenhaus vorbei* und nimm die zweite Straße rechts: das ist die Felsingstraße. Die Nummer 72 ist *auf der linken Seite* – wir sind *im ersten Stock*.
- Gibt es nicht eine Schule dort *in der Nähe*?
- Ja, wir sind *direkt gegenüber der Schule*.

a Among the phrases in italics, find the German equivalents of:

i	on the left-hand side	**vi**	the next street on the left
ii	cross the street	**vii**	directly opposite the school
iii	go past the hospital	**viii**	not far from the hospital
iv	we are round the corner	**ix**	nearby
v	on the corner	**x**	on the first floor

Grammatik

The *imperative* is the form of the verb used for giving instructions:
<u>Geh</u> über die Straße. <u>Nimm</u> die zweite Straße rechts.
For the informal imperative singular, take the **du**-form of the verb and simply remove the **-st** ending: **geh(st) → geh, nimm(st) → nimm**.

Über, **an** and **auf** belong to the category of prepositions followed by the accusative or the dative. Here **über** indicates change of place ('where to') rather than location, so the article is in the accusative: **über <u>die</u> Straße**. **An** and **auf** indicate location in this text, so the articles following them are in the dative: **an <u>der</u> Ecke, auf <u>der</u> linken Seite**.

---

b On the basis of the instructions, draw a sketch-map showing how to get to the flat from the bus stop. Include all the locations mentioned. Compare your sketch with a partner's.

2 Es ist nicht weit

Referring to your sketch but not the text, describe how you get to the flat in exercise 1.
Use the **ich**-form: *Ich gehe über die Straße* …

> **Frankfurt am Main**
> In der Finanzhauptstadt
> Deutschlands sind auch viele
> historische Sehenswürdigkeiten. Der
> weltberühmte *Faust*-Autor Johann
> Wolfgang von Goethe (1749–1832)
> kam aus Frankfurt, und man kann
> sein Haus sehen. In der Frankfurter
> Paulskirche tagte 1848–49 das erste
> demokratische deutsche Parlament.
>
> *tagte = met, sat

 3 Wie komme ich zum Goethehaus?

a *Rafael ist in Frankfurt am Main und sucht das Goethehaus und die Paulskirche.*

An der U-Bahn-Station Willy-Brandt-Platz

– Entschuldigen Sie bitte, wie komme ich zum Goethehaus?
– Ah, das ist nicht **a** _____. Gehen Sie hier die *Friedensstraße*
geradeaus und nehmen Sie dann die erste Straße **b** _____.
Das ist die *Bethmannstraße*. Gehen Sie am **c** _____ vorbei bis
zur Kreuzung und dann links in die *Berliner Straße*. Nach etwa fünf Minuten gehen Sie
halblinks in den *Großen Hirschgraben*. Das Goethehaus ist dann gleich auf der linken
d _____.
– Vielen Dank für Ihre Hilfe. Auf Wiedersehen.
– Auf Wiedersehen!

Vor dem Goethehaus

– Entschuldigung, wie komme ich am besten zur Paulskirche?
– Da müssen Sie hier über die Straße gehen und dann die **e** _____
rechts rein – in die *Weißadlergasse*. Nehmen Sie dann die zweite Straße
f _____ und gehen Sie **g** _____ bis zur
Ampel. Dort gehen Sie **h** _____ die *Berliner Straße* und dann
sehen Sie die Paulskirche schon.
– Vielen Dank!

Grammatik

Gehen Sie! (Go!) **Nehmen Sie!** (Take!)
Imperative (formal): reverse the normal order. **Sie nehmen → nehmen Sie!**
For the *informal plural*, use the **ihr**-form without the pronoun: **Geht! Nehmt!**

b Now look at the map and try to follow the directions given on the previous page. Do you get to the right places?

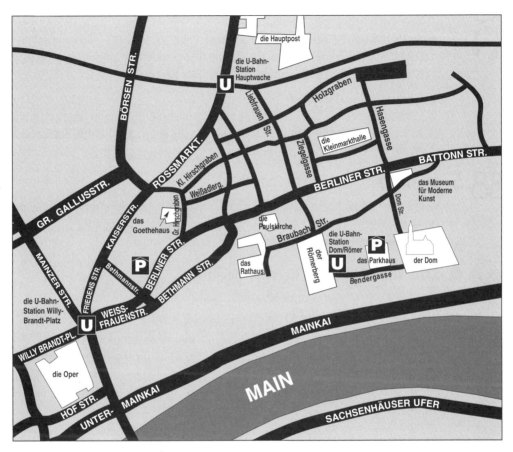

Frankfurt am Main, Innenstadt

Entschuldigen Sie, wie komme ich **zum** …	Paulsplatz? **zur** …	Post?
	Dom	Markthalle
	Parkhaus	U-Bahn-Station
	Goethehaus	
	Rathaus	
	Museum	

Gehen Sie geradeaus/links/rechts … bis zum/zur … am/an der … vorbei
Nehmen Sie die erste/zweite/dritte/vierte Straße rechts/links.
Der/Die/Das … ist … auf der rechten/linken Seite.

4 Entschuldigen Sie ...

Refer to the map of Frankfurt. Here are the answers, what were the questions? When you have decided, check by listening to the recording.

a *Sie sind an der U-Bahn-Station Willy-Brandt-Platz.*
„Es ist in der Berliner Straße. Gehen Sie hier geradeaus, an der Paulskirche vorbei. Es ist auf der rechten Seite, an der Ecke zur Domstraße."

b *Sie sind vor dem Goethehaus*
„Gehen Sie hier links in die Berliner Straße. Nehmen Sie dann die zweite Straße rechts, so kommen Sie zum Römerberg. Gehen Sie links, an der U-Bahn-Station vorbei, und es ist auf der linken Seite, vor dem Dom."

5 Wohin?

Working with a partner and referring to the map and question/answer guidelines on the previous page, role-play asking for and giving directions to locations in Frankfurt city centre. Remember to agree where you are starting from!

6 Die Innenstadt/The town centre

Match up the German words with their English equivalents. Check your decisions in the unit vocabulary on page 72.

1	die Bank	**a**	railway station
2	der Buchladen/die Buchhandlung	**b**	Karstadt department store
3	der Bahnhof	**c**	florist's
4	die Kirche	**d**	bank
5	der Supermarkt	**e**	petrol station
6	die Post	**f**	pharmacy
7	die U-Bahn-Station	**g**	bookshop
8	die Apotheke	**h**	baker's
9	das Kaufhaus „Karstadt"	**i**	chemist's, drug store
10	die Tankstelle	**j**	church
11	das Blumengeschäft	**k**	underground station
12	die Bäckerei	**l**	post office
13	die Drogerie	**m**	supermarket

7 In der Nähe

a *Sie sind am Bahnhof*

– Entschuldigen Sie, gibt es hier in der Nähe eine Apotheke?

– Eine Apotheke? … Ja. Gehen Sie hier **a** _____ und nehmen Sie die **b** _____ Straße links. Sie kommen dann zur Rheinstraße – gehen Sie rechts an der **c** _____ . Die Apotheke ist auf der linken Seite **d** _____ Karstadt.

– Danke.

– Bitte.

b *Im Goetheweg, auf dem Campus*

– Entschuldigen Sie, gibt es eine Bank in der Nähe?

– Ja, … gehen Sie hier rechts in den Goetheweg, **e** _____ um die Ecke und dann **f** _____ . An der Ampel gehen Sie wieder rechts: Die Bank ist auf der **g** _____ Seite.

– Vielen Dank.

entschuldigen Sie Excuse me	**bitte** it's a pleasure/no problem (also 'please')
danke thanks	**bitte?** Sorry? What did you say?
vielen Dank thanks a lot	

Now check the directions against the street plan below!

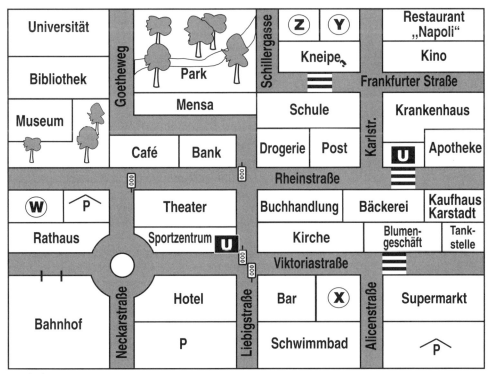

Stadtplan

8 Rollenspiel: Gibt es …?

With a partner, role-play asking if there is one of the following nearby and giving directions. Use the street plan. Remember **es gibt** is followed by the accusative!

Sie sind vor dem Bahnhof
ein Buchladen, ein Parkhaus, ein Restaurant

Sie sind im Goetheweg
eine Bäckerei, ein Supermarkt

9 Fragezeichen/Question marks

a You will hear a set of three directions given by passers-by. Trace these directions on the map on page 65 to find out which mystery locations they lead to. The locations are marked with letters in circles on the map. The point of departure in all cases is the exit from the station.

b There are no directions to the fourth mystery location. Once you have identified it, tell your partner how to get there.

10 Neben der Bank/Next to the bank

a Read this short text, referring to the street plan on page 65:

> Hier ist die Innenstadt.
> Die Post ist **gegenüber** einer Bäckerei und **neben** einer Drogerie.
> Die Bäckerei ist **zwischen** einem Buchladen und einem Kaufhaus.
> Das Krankenhaus ist **hinter** einer Apotheke.
> Das Museum ist **vor** der Bibliothek.

L **b i** Der Supermarkt ist _____ e_____ Tankstelle und
e_____ Blumengeschäft.
ii Die Tankstelle ist neben e_____ _____ .
iii Das Rathaus ist gegenüber d_____ Bahnhof.
iv Das Blumengeschäft ist _____ e_____
_____ und e_____ _____ .
v Der Supermarkt ist vor d_____ _____ .

c Wo ist …
i die Bar? **ii** das Kino? **iii** die Schule? **iv** die Bibliothek? **v** der Park?

11 In unserer Stadt

With a partner, agree on how you would give a German speaker directions for how to get between two locations in your town or a city you both know.

12 Im Kaufhaus

Claudia sucht ein Kleid.

In der Abteilung „Damenbekleidung"/In the ladieswear department
V = **Verkäuferin**/shop assistant

C: Schau mal, Monika, dieses Kleid – ist das nicht toll?

M: Mmmhh, ich weiß nicht … Die Farbe gefällt mir nicht. … Aber wie findest du dieses?

C: Ja doch, hübsch. Welche Größe ist es? … 38, das ist richtig.
Ich probiere das Kleid mal an … (*tries it on*)
Nein, dieses Kleid gefällt mir nicht – es ist zu lang. Vielleicht nehme ich diesen Rock
hier … eine neue schwarze Bluse habe ich zu Hause. Wie gefällt dir dieser Rock?

M: Sehr schick … und sexy! Hm … ist der Rock nicht zu kurz?

C: Nein, das ist in Ordnung … Du, dieser Rock gefällt mir! Und das ist auch die richtige
Größe.

M: Prima … wie teuer?

C: 45 Euro, das ist OK.

V: Kann ich Ihnen helfen? Gefällt Ihnen dieser Rock?

C: Ja danke, ich nehme den Rock …
Ich muss noch etwas für Michael kaufen, er braucht ein neues Hemd. Er hat eine
schicke Hose, eine neue Jacke, aber kein Hemd – nur alte T-Shirts … Furchtbar! Er
trägt nie einen Anzug …

M: Komm, da müssen wir in die Herrenabteilung. …
Schau mal, diese Krawatte *musst* du für Michael kaufen …

C: Krawatte mit Micky Maus … ich weiß ja nicht, ein bisschen bunt!

Fragen:

a Warum kauft Claudia das Kleid nicht?

b Was kauft sie?

c Was will sie für Michael kaufen?

Grammatik

D**ieser** Rock <u>gefällt</u> mir.	Ich kaufe *diesen* Rock.	Es gefällt **mir**.
D**iese** Bluse <u>gefällt</u> mir.	Ich kaufe *diese* Bluse.	Gefällt es <u>dir</u>?
D**ieses** Kleid <u>gefällt</u> mir.	Ich kaufe *dieses* Kleid.	<u>Ihnen</u>?
D**iese** T-Shirts <u>gefallen</u> mir.	Ich kaufe *diese* T-Shirts.	

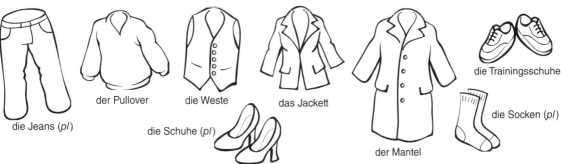

die Jeans (*pl*)

der Pullover

die Weste

die Schuhe (*pl*)

das Jackett

der Mantel

die Trainingsschuhe

die Socken (*pl*)

13 Das gefällt mir nicht

Ihr Partner/Ihre Partnerin ist sehr negativ.

Beispiel: Wie findest du _diesen Rock_? _Dieser Rock_ gefällt _mir_ nicht.

a Wie findest du …

i dieses T-Shirt?	**iv** diesen Pullover?	**vii** dieses Kleid?
ii diese Jacke?	**v** diese Socken?	**viii** dieses Jackett?
iii dieses Hemd?	**vi** diesen Rock?	**ix** diese Schuhe?

b Swap roles and take the conversation one step further: from the items below choose reasons for not liking particular items of clothing.

zu lang	zu kurz	zu teuer	zu klein	zu groß
zu modern	zu altmodisch	zu langweilig	zu bunt	

Beispiel: Wie findest du _diese Jacke_? _Die_ Jacke gefällt mir nicht. _Sie_ ist zu altmodisch.
Und _dieser Rock_? _Er_ ist zu lang.

Grammatik

<u>Demonstrative adjective</u>
Dieser follows the pattern of the definite article **der**, **die**, **das** etc.
nominative: **dies<u>er</u> Rock, dies<u>e</u> Jacke, dies<u>es</u> Hemd.**
accusative: **Ich nehme dies<u>en</u> Pullover.**
(Reminder: Feminine and neuter accusative remain as in the nominative.)

<u>Pronouns</u>
'it' = **er** for masculine nouns, **sie** for feminine, **es** for neuter

14 Du trägst/You are wearing …

a Get together with a partner and describe the clothes he/she is wearing. Swap roles.

b Now each partner takes it in turns to describe what another student in the class is wearing. See if your partner can guess who you are talking about. To help you to be more specific, here is a list of colours. You ought to be able to work out what most of them are …

blau	**rot**	**grün**	**gelb** (yellow)	**braun**	**weiß**	**schwarz** (black)	**beige**	

Beispiele: Sie trägt einen blau<u>en</u> Pullover (m.)
Sie trägt eine grün<u>e</u> Jacke. (f.)
Er trägt ein rot<u>es</u> Hemd. (n.)
Er trägt schwarz<u>e</u> Schuhe. (pl)

Extra!

Berlin Stadtmitte

Berlin ist die Hauptstadt von Deutschland. Es gibt viele wichtige und interessante Sehenswürdigkeiten in Berlin, zum Beispiel den *Reichstag* und das *Brandenburger Tor*. Hier ist ein Plan von der Stadtmitte.

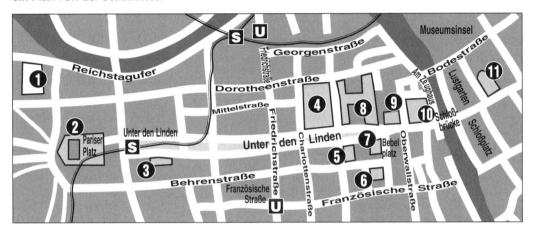

KEY			
1	Reichstag	6	St. Hedwigs-Kathedrale
2	Brandenburger Tor	7	Staatsoper
3	Russische Botschaft	8	Humboldt-Universität
4	Staatsbibliothek	9	Neue Wache
5	Königliche Bibliothek	10	Deutsches Historisches Museum
		11	Berliner Dom

U = Underground
S = Railway Station

 15 Wohin will der Tourist gehen?

A visitor to Berlin arrives at the *Bahnhof Friedrichstraße* and asks for directions to three tourist attractions in the city centre. Listen to the recording and follow the directions on the map above. Where does the tourist want to get to?

a _____ b _____ c _____.

 16 Stadttour

You are on a city centre sightseeing tour during a visit to Berlin. Listen to the tour guide's commentary as the bus drives through the streets shown above. Give three of the various places mentioned, plus an item of information about each of them. Remember you are not expected to understand everything!

Grammatik

～ The imperative ▶G15

The imperative is used to give instructions.

1 When addressing one or more people with whom you are on formal terms, reverse the order of the pronoun **Sie** and the verb: **Sie gehen → gehen Sie!**

2 When talking to someone with whom you are on informal terms, the imperative form is based on the **du**-form of the verb. Delete the **-st** ending: **du gehst → geh! du arbeitest → arbeite!**

3 If you are speaking informally to more than one person, you use the **ihr**-form of the verb but without the pronoun: **ihr geht → geht!**

～ Dieser (this), jeder (each, every), welcher? (which?) follow the pattern of the definite article. ▶G4

masculine (nominative)	feminine	neuter	plural
der	**die**	**das**	**die**
dieser, jeder, welcher	**diese** etc.	**dieses** etc.	**diese** etc.

Dieser Rock/Diese Jacke/Dieses Kleid ist schön. Diese Schuhe sind teuer.

As with the article, the accusative form is the same as the nominative, except for the masculine: **den/diesen**. Example: **Ich kaufe diesen Pullover.**

～ gefallen ▶G4.3, G12

1 This strong verb expresses liking for objects. (Use **gern** after the verb to express liking for activities: **Ich spiele gern Basketball.**) Because **gefallen** means literally 'to please', you have to be careful: **Die Jacke gefällt mir** 'I like the jacket' (literally 'The jacket pleases me').

2 **Gefallen** is always followed by a dative object. The dative pronoun corresponding to **ich** is **mir** (me), **du → dir** (you, informal singular), **Sie → Ihnen** (you, formal).

„Gefällt dir dieses Kleid?" – „Ja, es gefällt mir sehr."
"Gefallen dir diese Schuhe?" – „Nein, sie gefallen mir nicht."

～ Prepositions ▶G11

1 The prepositions you have met so far are mostly followed by the dative. Some always (such as **zu**, **von**, **mit**, **gegenüber**), some when they tell us 'where' (**wo**) (such as **in**, **auf**, **an**, **über**).

2 There are prepositions which are always followed by the accusative. Examples you have met are **für**, **um**, **durch** and **entlang**:

durch den Park (through the park), **um die Ecke** (round the corner),
die Straße entlang (along the street).

Note that **entlang** normally comes after the noun.

Grammatikübungen

1 Complete the sentences with an appropriate verb in the imperative from the list at the end. You are talking to (a) a stranger in the street; (b) a fellow-student; (c) friends of yours, a young couple. Note: there are two surplus verbs in the list!

i _____ nicht so viel Bier!   (b)   **iv** _____ eine Flasche Wein. (b)

ii _____ hier über die Straße. (a)   **v** _____ am Kino vorbei.   (c)

iii _____ nächsten Montag.   (c)   **vi** _____ in der Bibliothek. (b)

kommt	kommen Sie	bring	bringt
trink	geht	gehen Sie	arbeite

2 Complete each question with (**a**) the appropriate form of **gefallen**, and (**b**) the correct form of the demonstrative adjective, then (**c**) complete the reply. You must be sure of genders!

i   Gefällt/Gefallen dir   dies___ Kleid?   Ja, *es* gef_____ mir sehr.

ii _____   dies___ Jacke?   Nein, *sie* gef_____ mir nicht.

iii _____   dies___ Rock?   Ja, _____

iv _____   dies___ Krawatte?   Nein, _____

v   _____   dies___ Schuhe?   Nein, _____

vi _____   dies___ Pullover?   Ja, _____

3 Match up the correct halves of the sentences.

  1 Die Bank ist hier an …   **a** … dem Park.

  2 Ich gehe morgens durch …   **b** … die Ecke, in der Bahnhofstraße.

  3 Die Apotheke ist in …   **c** … die Adenauerstraße.

  4 An der Ampel gehen Sie über … **d** … der Brandtstraße.

  5 Er wohnt mit …   **e** … den Park.

  6 Die Kinder spielen Fußball in … **f** … der Ecke.

  7 Unsere Wohnung ist um …   **g** … seiner Freundin zusammen.

  8 Gehen Sie … entlang.   **h** … die Straße.

Berlin

6 In der Stadt

Vokabeln

See Appendix p. 190 for more vocabulary from exercises 12, 13 and 14.

Aufgabe 1

kennen	to know (be familiar with)
nicht weit von	not far from
das Krankenhaus	hospital
oder?	(here =) isn't it?
genau	exactly
um	round
der Bus	bus
die Linie	route
die Haltestelle	stop
über	over, across
die Straße	street
der/die/das nächste …	the next (also: nearest)
die Kirche	church
an der Ecke	on the corner
vorbeigehen *sep*	to go past
auf der linken Seite	on the left-hand side
im ersten Stock	on the first floor
die Schule	school
in der Nähe	nearby
(direkt) gegenüber	(directly) opposite

Aufgabe 3

das Goethehaus	Goethe's birthplace
suchen	to look for
entschuldigen Sie	excuse me
wie komme ich zu …	how do I get to …
geradeaus	straight on
das Parkhaus	multi-storey car park
die Kreuzung	crossroads
halblinks	fork left
gleich	immediately
die Hilfe	help
… rein	into …
bis zu	as far as
die Ampel	traffic lights
sehen*	to see
der Paulsplatz	square in Frankfurt
der Dom	cathedral
das Rathaus	town hall
das Museum	museum
die Post	post office
die Markthalle	market hall
die U-Bahn	underground
die Station	station (on underground)

Aufgabe 4

vor	in front of, before

Aufgabe 6

die Bank	bank
der Buchladen	bookshop
der Bahnhof	railway station
der Supermarkt	supermarket
die Apotheke	pharmacy
das Kaufhaus	department store
die Tankstelle	petrol station
das Blumengeschäft	flower shop
die Bäckerei	baker's/bakery
die Drogerie	chemist's, drug store

Aufgabe 7

wieder	again

Aufgabe 9

der Kreisverkehr	roundabout
durch	through

Aufgabe 10

die Innenstadt	the town centre
neben	next to
zwischen	between
hinter	behind

Aufgabe 12

schau mal	look!
das Kleid	dress
die Farbe	colour
gefallen*	lit. to please (but see Grammatik)
finden	to find, think of
hübsch	pretty
welche(r/s)	which
die Größe	size
richtig	right, correct
anprobieren *sep*	to try on
(zu) lang	(too) long
der Rock	skirt
schwarz	black
die Bluse	blouse
schick	elegant, chic
kurz	short
helfen*	to help
etwas	something
das Hemd	shirt
die Hose	trousers
die Jacke	jacket
das T-Shirt	T-shirt
furchtbar	terrible

*Verb strong in present tense ▶G14.2

Partnerarbeit

1 Was trägt Sophie?

Your partner describes what Sophie is wearing and you decide which of the three drawings below corresponds to this description. When you think you know, show your partner the drawing you think she/he is describing.

2 Lars trägt ...

Now you describe Lars' clothes in the drawing below. Your partner will show you which of the three pictures on the Partner B page he/she thinks you are describing. Tell him/her whether it's right (**richtig**).

Er trägt ...

3 Kleider

Once you've found which picture of Sophie was being described, look at all three pictures with your partner and discuss the differences. Do the same with the pictures of Lars.

Hier trägt er/sie (k)ein(e/en) ...

Partnerarbeit

B

1 Sophie trägt ...

Describe what Sophie is wearing in the picture below. Your partner will show you which one of the three drawings on the Partner A page he/she thinks you have described.

Tell him/her whether it's right (**richtig**).

Sie trägt ...

2 Was trägt Lars?

Now you have to decide which picture of Lars your partner is describing. When you think you know, show him/her.

3 Kleider

Once you've found which picture of Lars was being described, look at all three pictures with your partner and discuss the differences. Do the same with the pictures of Sophie.

Hier trägt er/sie (k)ein/e/n ...

7 Fahren

In this unit you will learn to talk about dates, travel and accommodation, make travel enquiries and buy tickets.

1 Die Monate: zum Lernen!

Januar	April	Juli	Oktober
Februar	Mai	August	November
März	Juni	September	Dezember

> **im März, am neunzehnten/zwanzigsten März, am 19./20. März**
> Note the point after the number.

2 Ich gebe auf!

Ute will ihre Eltern besuchen. Nach einer Konversation mit Hans schreibt sie eine E-Mail an ihre Schwester.

Hans sagt, dass er im **a** _____ keine Zeit hat. Am **b** _____ten verbringt er zwei **c** _____ bei seinen Freunden in Dresden. Er kommt also am

d _____sten zurück – am Abend. Am **e** _____sten hat er einen Termin beim Zahnarzt … und ab dem **f** _____sten arbeitet er, um Geld für die Sommerferien zu verdienen.

Ich gebe auf!

Grammatik

Word order
- **Dass** introduces a subordinate clause and sends the verb to the end.
  Du weißt, <u>dass</u> ich diese Woche keine Zeit <u>habe</u>.
- The construction **um … zu** (<u>um</u> Geld <u>zu</u> verdienen 'in order to earn money') also has the verb at the end (in the infinitive form).

Dative plural: possessive **-en** ending, noun **-n** ending: **bei sein<u>en</u> Freund<u>en</u>**.

3 Wann?

To give a date, you have to combine the month (see exercise 1) with an ordinal number ('first', 'twenty-fifth' etc.). You met some of these in Unit 6:
im <u>ersten</u> Stock, die <u>dritte</u> Straße rechts.

These two examples are irregular: the regular pattern is easy to learn:

der zwei<u>te</u>, der fünf<u>te</u>, der neunzehn<u>te</u>; der zwanzig<u>ste</u>, der einunddreißig<u>ste</u>
See the fuller list on the grammar page, p. 82.

> **Wann ist dein/Ihr Geburtstag?**
> **Mein Geburtstag ist <u>der</u> zwöl<u>fte</u> (12.) Februar** ('the 12th of February').
> **Wann hast du/haben Sie Geburtstag?**
> **Ich habe <u>am</u> 12. (zwölf<u>ten</u>) Februar Geburtstag** ('on the 12th of February').

a **i** Heute ist der _____ .
    ii Mein Geburtstag ist der _____ .
    iii Ich habe am _____ Geburtstag.

b Es ist der … **i** 24/1   **ii** 15/4   **iii** 9/6   **iv** 3/10   **v** 10/12

c Listen to the recording and write down (in figures) the five dates you hear:
    i _____   **ii** _____   **iii** _____
    iv _____   **v** _____

d Wann haben Sie/hast du Geburtstag?
    Wer hat im Februar Geburtstag?
    Wer hat heute/morgen/nächste Woche Geburtstag?

4 Ein Sprachkurs in Deutschland/A language course in Germany

Sie sind Vijay. Beantworten Sie die Fragen.

> Seit sechs Monaten lernt Vijay Basran Deutsch. Das macht Spaß und er bekommt sehr gute Noten. Um sein Deutsch zu verbessern, macht Vijay einen intensiven Sprachkurs. Der Kurs findet zu Ostern in Bonn statt und dauert 10 Tage. Vijay lernt Deutsch, weil er nach dem Studium im Ausland arbeiten möchte.

a Wie lange lernen Sie Deutsch?   **d** Wie lange dauert der Kurs?
b Was machen Sie zu Ostern?   **e** Warum lernen Sie Deutsch?
c Warum machen Sie diesen Kurs?

Grammatik

Word order
Um sein Deutsch zu verbessern, <u>macht</u> Vijay einen Sprachkurs.

◄──────────────►,

When a subordinate clause comes first, the main verb follows immediately, after a comma.
Weil (like **dass**) is a *subordinating conjunction* and sends the verb to the end.
Er lernt Deutsch, weil er im Ausland <u>arbeitet</u>.

Seit 6 Monaten/Seit Oktober lernt Vijay Deutsch.
Vijay has been learning German for 6 months/since October.
Note the present tense in German.

5 Bestätigungsschreiben/Letter of confirmation

Vijay receives this letter from the administrator of his Easter German course in Bonn. Summarise in English the information it contains.

Bonn, 3. Februar 2011

Sehr geehrter Herr Basran,

wir bestätigen hiermit die folgende Zimmerreservierung im Studentenwohnheim Ferdinandstraße:

Unterkunft: 1 Einzelzimmer mit Bad und Dusche
Fernseher mit Kabelanschluss auf dem Zimmer
Verpflegung: Gemeinschaftsküche (für kleine Mahlzeiten)
Mensa (Öffnungszeiten: 11.30 – 14.15 Uhr)
Daten: vom 31. März bis 9. April
Preis: 21,00 Euro pro Nacht (ohne Frühstück)

Das *Studentenwohnheim* liegt sehr zentral (Straßenbahnhaltestelle ca. 5 Minuten).
Freizeitmöglichkeiten: Sportzentrum (auf dem Campus)
Kino und Theater (Innenstadt)
Hallenbad und Fitness-Studio
Fahrradvermietung für Touren am Rhein

Mit freundlichen Grüßen

E. von Kummerfeld

> Formal letters begin:
> **Sehr geehrter Herr X**
> **Sehr geehrte Frau Z**
>
> Informal letters begin:
> **Lieber Hans**
> **Liebe Renate**

6 Am Fahrkartenschalter/At the ticket window

a *Vijay fliegt nach Düsseldorf und fährt dann mit dem Zug nach Bonn. Am Flughafen Düsseldorf gibt es einen Bahnhof und Vijay kauft eine Fahrkarte.*

Vijay:

Wann fährt der nächste Zug nach Bonn?
Muss ich umsteigen?
Wann kommt der Zug in Bonn an?
Was kostet eine Rückfahrkarte?
OK, ich nehme den Zug um 11.54.
Einmal Bonn, hin und zurück, bitte.

der Beamte:
Bitte?
Um 11.54.
Nein, er fährt direkt nach Bonn.
Um 12.46.
Mit dem Intercityzug, 32 Euro.

b „Sie müssen umsteigen …"

	Bitte schön?
Wann fährt der nächste Zug nach **a** _____?	Um **b** _____.
Muss ich umsteigen?	Ja, Sie müssen in Hamburg umsteigen.
Wann bin ich in Hamburg?	Um **c** _____.
Und wann fährt der Zug nach Kiel ab?	Um 14.35, von Gleis **d** _____.
Was kostet eine einfache Fahrt?	**e** _____.
Gut, zweimal einfach nach Kiel, bitte.	

c Wortsuche: die Dialoge **a** und **b**

i	Do I have to change?	**v**	Two singles to Kiel
ii	When does the train arrive?	**vi**	The next train
iii	How much is a return ticket?	**vii**	When does the train to Kiel depart?
iv	One return to Bonn	**viii**	From platform 3

d Rollenspiel: am Bahnhof.

i			**ii**	
Bremen?	8.14		Leipzig?	13.08
Umsteigen?	Nein		Umsteigen?	In Berlin
Ankommen?	9.17		Berlin ankommen?	13.46
Einfach?	27 Euro		Berlin abfahren?	13.55, Gleis 9
1 × einfach			Leipzig ankommen?	14.58
			Rückfahrkarte?	41 Euro
			2 × hin/zurück	

Auf Gleis neun – bitte einsteigen! Der Zug nach Bonn fährt ab …

Grammatik

<u>Verb families</u>: **umsteigen**, **einsteigen**: what do you think **aussteigen** means?

7 An der Rezeption

- Guten Morgen, ich heiße Vijay Basran. Ich komme aus England und ich mache den Sprachkurs hier.
- Herzlich willkommen! Wie kann ich Ihnen helfen?
- Ich habe ein Zimmer hier im Studentenheim *vom 31. März bis zum 9. April.* Wo bekomme ich den Schlüssel für das Zimmer?
- Ich habe den Schlüssel hier … Einen Moment, ja, *Zimmer Nummer 34, im dritten Stock.* Leider gibt es keinen Fahrstuhl, aber da ist *Fritz,* unser Pförtner. Geben Sie ihm den Koffer! Er zeigt Ihnen gern das Zimmer.
- Das ist schon in Ordnung, der Koffer ist nicht schwer.
- Ah, hier ist *Anna Schubert,* Ihre Teamleiterin. Sie organisiert *das Freizeitprogramm.* Sagen Sie ihr, wenn Sie Probleme haben.
- Freut mich, Sie kennen zu lernen.

a Listen carefully to the recording of Frau Hilfiger and Vijay Basran at the reception of the **Studentenwohnheim**. The transcript on the previous page is largely the same as the recording but there are some inaccurate details (in *italics*). What are they?

b Working with a partner, summarise the scene in English.

Grammatik

Dative pronouns

Four verbs in the above dialogue are followed by a pronoun in the dative.

geben – to give (to so.)   **Geben Sie ihm (dem Pförtner) den Koffer.**
Give him (the porter) the suitcase.

sagen – to say (to so.)   **Sagen Sie ihr, wenn Sie Probleme haben.**
Tell her if you have problems.

helfen – to give help (to so.)   **Wie kann ich Ihnen helfen?** How can I help you?
zeigen – to show (to so.)   **Er zeigt Ihnen gern das Zimmer.**
He'll be glad to show you the room.

The following dative pronouns occur in the dialogue above:
mir (to me)   **ihm/ihr** (to him/her)   **Ihnen** (to you – formal)

These pronouns are also used after prepositions taking the dative. Can you find the example in exercise 8?

8 Im Hotel

Vijay reserviert ein Hotelzimmer für seinen Freund James.

– Guten Tag, ich möchte ein Zimmer reservieren, bitte.
– Ja, … wann brauchen Sie das Zimmer?
– Vom 5. April bis zum 8. April.
– Also, drei Nächte. … Möchten Sie ein Einzelzimmer oder ein Doppelzimmer?
– Ein Doppelzimmer, bitte.
– Wir haben Zimmer mit Bad und Dusche und Zimmer mit Dusche.
– Was kosten die Zimmer?
– Mit Bad und Dusche, 72 Euro pro Nacht, einschließlich Frühstück. Mit Dusche, 59 Euro.
– Ich nehme ein Zimmer mit Bad und Dusche.
– Ein Doppelzimmer mit Bad und Dusche, Anreise am 5. April, Abreise am 8. April. … Wie heißen Sie, bitte?
– Das Zimmer ist für einen Freund von mir, Herrn White, und seine Freundin. Ich gebe Ihnen seine Adresse und seine Telefonnummer.
– Danke.

Grammatik

Ich gebe Ihnen seine Adresse I'll give <u>you</u> his address
This sentence has an *indirect* object (**Ihnen**) as well as a direct object (**seine Adresse**).
What I'm giving is the address, I'm giving it <u>to</u> you (dative in German).
– Which of the four sentences in the previous grammar box have both sorts of object?

Rollenspiel: Using the previous dialogue as a model, role-play a similar scene with a partner. The differences are:

You want a single room; with a shower; from 29 June to 2 July; i.e. four nights; the room is for you, so give your name when asked.

9 An der Straßenbahnhaltestelle

To get about most towns, you have to be able to use an automatic ticket machine. Can you follow the instructions? The questions will help you to focus on the key information.

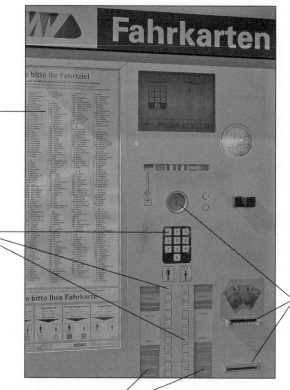

2 Zielwahl
Wenn Sie ein anderes Ziel erreichen wollen, suchen Sie es im alphabetischen Verzeichnis. Hier finden Sie die Zielnummer.

3 Fahrpreisinformation
– Drücken Sie eine Schnellwahltaste oder tippen Sie die Zielnummer.
– Wählen Sie die gewünschte Fahrkarte (Erwachsene, Kinder, Tageskarte).
Der Automat gibt Ihnen den Fahrpreis.

4 Zahlung
Sie können mit Münzen oder Geldscheinen zahlen. Restgeld erhalten Sie zurück.

1 Schnellwahl
Für Fahrtziele in der Innenstadt drücken Sie die entsprechende Taste.

a Read about the ticket machine and answer the questions in English:
 i What is the rapid choice option for? What do you have to do?
 ii What must you do if your destination is not included in the rapid choice menu?
 iii How do you get information on fares (two ways are mentioned)?
 iv What are the three sorts of ticket named?
 v What are we told about payment?

b Erklären Sie auf Deutsch, wie man eine Fahrkarte bekommt.

Extra!

10 Sprachkurs

Listen to two students talking about their advanced German summer course in Munich. Draw up a grid like the one below and fill it in in English, incorporating as much information as you can gather from the conversation.

	Personal details	Course information	Homework/ duties	Friends on course
Paloma				
Jean-Paul				

11 Hotel-Info

HEIDELBERG

Hotel Winter

– ab €89*
– Autobahn 1,5 km, Bahnhof 1,5 km, Flughafen 90 km
Preise inklusive Frühstück, Wellness-Bereich und Parkplatz

– Alle Zimmer mit Dusche und WC
– Alle Zimmer mit Kabelfernsehen, Telefon und Mini-Bar
– Parkplatz
– Ruhige Lage in einer Seitenstraße
– Seminarräume
– Terrasse und Biergarten
– Wellness-Bereich mit Fitnessgeräten, Solarium und Sauna
– Restaurant (gastronomisches Menü und regionale Spezialitäten)
– gemütliche Bar

Wir sind direkt am Neckarufer mit schöner Aussicht von der Terrasse. Innerhalb von wenigen Minuten erreichen Sie die weltberühmten Sehenswürdigkeiten Alt-Heidelbergs.

You and a friend are going by car to Heidelberg for a short break. Your friend favours staying in a student hostel, but you'd prefer to stay in this hotel. Draft an email in English in which you persuasively summarise what the hotel offers.

See how much you understand before referring to the vocabulary at the back of the book. Compare notes with a classmate.

Grammatik

~ Subordinate clauses ▶ G19.5

1 These clauses are introduced by subordinating conjunctions such as **wenn**, **weil** and **dass**. There must be a comma before the subordinating conjunction.

2 The verb in the clause goes to the end: **Du weißt, dass ich keine Zeit habe.**
This puts it after any infinitive which would be at the end anyway:

Er lernt Deutsch, weil er im Ausland arbeiten möchte.

3 Note the construction **um … zu** with an infinitive, expressing 'in order to':

Ich mache den Kurs, um mein Deutsch zu verbessern.

The infinitive goes to the end.

4 When a subordinate clause begins a sentence, it is treated as the first item in the sentence and so is followed by the verb of the main clause. A comma marks the end of the subordinate clause:

Wenn Sie ein anderes Ziel erreichen wollen,   **suchen Sie im Verzeichnis.**
       subordinate clause   main clause

~ seit

Ich lerne Deutsch seit September.   **Ich lerne Deutsch seit sechs Monaten.**
I've been learning German since September.   … for six months.

This preposition does the work of two English equivalents. Note that in German the present tense is used (because the situation is still going on).

Seit is followed by the dative: **Seit einem Jahr.**

~ Dative plural ▶ G4.3

Articles, possessives, adjectives and nouns all end in **-n**. Add the ending to the noun if its plural form does not already end in an **-n**. Exception: nouns with a plural ending in **-s**.

Sie können mit Münzen oder Geldscheinen zahlen.
Ich helfe dir mit den schweren Koffern.

~ Dative pronouns ▶ G4.3, G11, G12

mir   dir   ihm/ihr   uns   Ihnen   ihnen   euch

These pronouns are used for the indirect object in the sentence, and with certain prepositions and verbs (e.g. **gefallen**).

~ Ordinal numbers

der	erste	1st	siebte	7th	der	zwanzigste	20th
	zweite	2nd	achte	8th		einundzwanzigste	21st
	dritte	3rd	neunte	9th		…	
	vierte	4th	…			neunundneunzigste	99th
	fünfte	5th	neunzehnte	19th			

Dates: **der vierte April/am vierten April**

Grammatikübungen

1 Put the two sentences together, turning the underlined one into a subordinate clause. Use each of **dass**, **weil**, **wenn**. One of them has to be used twice. Be careful to get the word order right!

   a Sie kann leider nicht kommen. <u>Sie schreibt am vierzehnten einen Test.</u>

   b Ich weiß. <u>Er bekommt sehr gute Noten.</u>

   c Wir haben keine Zeit. <u>Wir arbeiten jeden Abend.</u>

   d <u>Das Wetter ist schlecht.</u> Ich komme schon am neunzehnten zurück.

   In the following, use **um ... zu** to put the English into German:

   e Sie fahren nach Deutschland *in order to do a German course.*

   f Ich habe einen Job *in order to earn money for the summer holidays.*

2 Translate the words in brackets into German: You'll need **seit**, and a noun in the dative.

   a (*For three years*) wohnt Dieter mit (*his friends*) Uwe und Hans zusammen.

   b (*Since November*) hilft er (*his parents*) im Büro.

3 Translate the following sentences into German. Take care to use the correct pronoun:

   a Klaus gives him a letter.

   b Markus goes with her to the cinema.

   c I can show you (formal) a good café.

   d Tell me if you (formal) have problems!

   e How are you (informal, singular)?

   f Ali shows them his new car.

4 a Write the dates in words:

   Example: der erste März

     i   1.3 (nach London fahren/ich)

     ii   26.6 (Geburtstag haben/sie *sing.*)

     iii 3.10 (zum Zahnarzt gehen/er)

     iv 15.5 (umziehen/wir)

     v   30.1 (einen Test schreiben/ich)

     vi 7.8 (zum Sprachkurs fahren/wir)

     vii 11.11 (anfangen/der Sprachkurs)

     viii 27.2 (essen gehen/wir)

   b Make sentences using the outlines given. Make sure you use the correct form of the verb and date. Also check your word order!

   Example: <u>Am</u> ersten März fahre ich nach London.

Vokabeln

See Appendix p. 190 for vocabulary for exercise 9.

Aufgabe 2

du weißt	you know
frei	free
verbringen	to spend (time)
Tage *pl*	days
zurückkommen *sep*	to come back
also	so, therefore
der Termin	appointment
der Zahnarzt	dentist
das Geld	money
die Sommerferien *pl*	summer holidays
verdienen	to earn
aufgeben* *sep*	to give up

Aufgabe 3

der Geburtstag	birthday

Aufgabe 4

seit	since, for (time) – see Grammatik
Monate *pl*	months
Spaß machen	to be fun
Noten *pl*	grades
verbessern	to improve
intensiv	intensive
der Sprachkurs	language course
stattfinden *sep*	to take place
zu Ostern	at Easter
dauern	to last
weil	because
das Studium	study
im Ausland	abroad

Aufgabe 5

bestätigen	to confirm
hiermit	herewith
folgend	following
die Zimmerreservierung	room booking
das Studentenwohnheim	hall of residence
die Unterkunft	accommodation
das Einzelzimmer	single room
der Kabelanschluss	cable connection
die Verpflegung	catering
die Gemeinschaftsküche	communal kitchen
pro Tag/Nacht	per day/night
ohne	without
liegen	to lie, be situated
die Straßenbahn	tram

ca. = circa = zirka	about
Freizeitmöglichkeiten *pl*	leisure opportunities
das Hallenbad	indoor swimming pool
das Fitness-Studio	keep-fit centre
die Fahrradvermietung	bicycle hire
Touren *pl*	tours
der Rhein	River Rhine

Aufgabe 6

fliegen	to fly
mit dem Zug	by train
der Flughafen	airport
die Fahrkarte	ticket (for travel)
Bitte?	How can I help you?
der (nächste) Zug	the (next) train
umsteigen *sep*	to change (trains/ buses)
ankommen *sep*	to arrive
kosten	to cost
die Rückfahrkarte	return ticket
mit dem Intercity(zug)	by Intercity
hin und zurück	return
abfahren* *sep*	to depart
Gleis x	Platform x
einfach	(here) single
einsteigen *sep*	to get on, board

Aufgabe 7

Herzlich willkommen!	Welcome!
der Schlüssel	key
der Fahrstuhl	lift
der Pförtner	porter
geben	to give
ihm	to him
der Koffer	suitcase
zeigen	to show
schwer	heavy
die Teamleiterin	team leader (f)
ihr	to her
(Es) freut mich, Sie kennen zu lernen	Pleased to meet you

Aufgabe 8

reservieren	to reserve, book
Nächte *pl*	nights
das Doppelzimmer	double room
einschließlich	including
die Anreise/Abreise	arrival/departure
die Adresse	address
die Telefonnummer	phone number

*Verb strong in present tense ▶**G14.2**

Partnerarbeit

1 Zuginformation

You are making arrangements for a trip in Germany. Your partner is a friend who you have asked to get some train information. He/She will give only information you specifically ask for.

You speak first.

- Tell your partner you want to go from Cologne to Darmstadt. Say you want to go between 9.00 and 10.00 in the morning. Ask if there is a train at that time.
- Find out if you have to change and where.
- When do(es) the train(s) get into Darmstadt?
- Check the details with your partner by summarising the information you have been given.
- Tell him/her which train you will get.

2 Wann fahren wir nach Spanien?

You discuss on the phone with your partner when you will be going to Spain together but there are a few problems …

Play your part in the conversation, using the prompts below. German is the only language you have in common.

You speak first:

Hi, (*name*), when can we go to Spain?

„ … "

July is fine. Have you got time after the 15th?

„ … "

On the 22nd? But my lectures start on the 1st of September.

„ … "

That is great. Do we take the train in Germany?

„ … "

How much does a return ticket cost?

„ … "

Oh! Can we fly from Düsseldorf?

„ … "

That is OK. Do we reserve a room in a hotel?

„ … "

Good idea. Is the hall of residence central?

„ … "

Thank you. I'll buy the train tickets to Düsseldorf.

Düsseldorf, Rheinturm

Partnerarbeit

B

1 Zuginformation

Your partner is a friend making arrangements for a trip in Germany and has asked you to get some information about trains.

He/She will speak first. Give only information you are asked for!

Köln	Umst.	an	ab	Darmstadt
9.29	Frankfurt	11.17	11.32	11.59
9.46	Mainz	11.31	12.09	12.32
10.22	Frankfurt	11.44	12.05	12.49

At the end of your conversation, your partner will give you back the information you have given him/her, so you can check he/she has understood correctly. He/She will also tell you which train he/she will get.

2 Wann fahren wir nach Spanien?

You are Partner A's friend. You discuss on the phone when you will be going to Spain together – but there are a few problems ... . Play your part in the conversation, using the prompts below. German is the only language you have in common.

Partner A speaks first.

„ ... "

Mmmhh, it is already June now... perhaps in July?

„ ... "

I'm sorry, no – the 15th is my birthday! ... And a week later?

„ ... "

Perhaps we can go on the 2nd of July?

„ ... "

No, that is too expensive.

„ ... "

Hmmm, just a moment ... about 180 euros.

„ ... "

Yes, that is no problem. But we have to go to Düsseldorf by train and change.

„ ... "

Perhaps in a student hall of residence. One can have single rooms or double rooms in Madrid.

„ ... "

Yes, only 10 minutes by bus to the city centre. I can reserve a room because I have the phone number.

„ ... "

'Bye!

Düsseldorf, Altes Rathaus

8 Gestern

In this unit you will learn to talk about events in the past. You will also learn how to describe states of mind and emotions, aches and pains.

1 Was hast du gestern gemacht?/What did you do yesterday?

a Listen to the recording and see if you can fill in the missing question and answer at the end of the conversation.

– Hallo, Horst ... Wie geht's?
– Danke gut, Sabine. Und dir? Was *hast* du denn gestern *gemacht*?
– Gestern ... ach ja, ich *habe* am Nachmittag bei Aldi für ein italienisches Essen *eingekauft*: Nudeln, Tomaten, Salat, Rotwein, Parmesan. Abends *habe* ich für Manfred und Vera *gekocht*, und dann *haben* wir zusammen Musik *gehört* und ein bisschen *getanzt*. Später – sehr spät, so gegen Mitternacht – *haben* wir noch Karten *gespielt* ...
– Ein toller Abend!
– _____ ?
– _____ .

b Fragen:
  i Wo hat Sabine eingekauft?
  ii Was hat sie gekauft?
  iii Was haben die Freunde nach dem Essen gemacht?
  iv Und was haben sie sehr spät gemacht?

Grammatik

The perfect tense
To talk about events in the past, you normally use the *perfect tense* in German.
Regular (weak) verbs form the perfect tense as follows:
the appropriate form of the verb **haben** plus the *past participle*.

ich	habe <u>gekocht</u>	wir	haben <u>gekocht</u>
du	hast <u>gekocht</u>	Sie	haben <u>gekocht</u>
er, sie, es	hat <u>gekocht</u>	sie	haben <u>gekocht</u>
		ihr	habt <u>gekocht</u>

NB: *Separable verbs*: **Sabine hat ein<u>gekauft</u>.**

Word order: Note the position of the the past participle:
Was hast du gestern <u>gemacht</u>?

2 Ein Tag in den Semesterferien

Listen to the recording and note the differences with the text below. The verbs (in *italics*) remain the same but the details are different. Write out the corrected text.

Um halb elf *hat* Verena gestern zwei Brötchen mit Marmelade *gegessen*, und dazu *hat* sie eine Tasse Kaffee mit Milch *getrunken*. Nach dem Frühstück *hat* sie einige E-Mails an ihre Freunde im Ausland *geschrieben*: an Markus in Australien, Inge in Israel und Rolf in Spanien. Sie *hat* lange Zeitung *gelesen* und dann nachmittags im Café Bauer ihre Mutter *getroffen*. Sie *haben* beide eine heiße Schokolade mit Sahne *getrunken* und viel geredet. Am Abend *hat* Verena ihre Freundin Susi *angerufen*, um sie ins Kino einzuladen. Leider hatte Susi keine Zeit, weil sie babysitten musste. Das war schade – der Film war spannend.

Grammatik

Strong verbs:
Note how the past participle is formed:

essen	**gegessen**	**lesen**	**gelesen**
trinken	**getrunken**	**treffen**	**getroffen**
schreiben	**geschrieben**	**anrufen**	**angerufen**

There is often a change of vowel in the past participle (see Grammar page 94).

NB: The verbs **haben**, **sein** and all *modal* verbs are usually used in the *simple past* or *imperfect tense* – **sie hatte**, … **war**, … **musste**, … **konnte**.

3 E-Mail an Andreas

```
Hallo Andreas
Heute habe ich endlich Zeit! Ich hatte in den letzten zwei Wochen schrecklich
viel zu tun, und deshalb konnte ich dir nicht schreiben.
Gestern war kein schöner Tag für mich. Ich bin zu spät aufgestanden und hatte
keine Zeit zum Frühstücken. Ich bin mit dem Bus zur Uni gefahren, denn es hat
geregnet. Mein Professor war krank - also keine Vorlesung! Ich bin den ganzen
Nachmittag in der Bibliothek geblieben und habe ein wichtiges Buch für meine
Dissertation gesucht, aber leider nicht gefunden. Zum Glück ist mein Freund
Julius gekommen, und wir sind ins „Café Chaos" gegangen. Das war interessant,
denn er hat mir von seiner neuen Arbeit erzählt. Um halb acht war ich wieder zu
Hause und habe den ganzen Abend ferngesehen … langweilig!
Ich muss jetzt gehen, denn ich treffe Marina um Viertel nach acht.
Harald
```

Grammatik

Some verbs form the perfect tense with the appropriate form of **sein** instead of **haben**.

a Read the text and find the past participles with **sein** (e.g: **ich bin aufgestanden**). There are four, in addition to the example given. What are the infinitives of those verbs (e.g. the infinitive of **aufgestanden** is **aufstehen**)?

b Harald did not think much of yesterday: summarise in English what happened.

c Without referring to the text, tell the story of Harald's day using the outline below. Use the **er**-form of the perfect tense. Remember to use **haben** or **sein** with the correct past participle (weak or strong) and remember the word order rules!

Harald ist …
spät aufstehen – Bus Uni fahren – regnen – Professor krank – Bibliothek bleiben – Buch suchen – nicht finden – Freund kommen – Café gehen – Abend fernsehen.

4 Was hat Carima gestern gemacht?

a Look at the pictures below and write a caption for each picture. Remember to use the perfect tense to talk about past events. Make sure you use the correct form of the verb. If in doubt, consult the grammar page 94.

b Compare your version with the recording.

5 Im Café

Zwei Konversationen in einem Café in Bielefeld

a Frau Huber und Frau Malzahn
   i   Warum hat Frau Huber letzte Woche nicht gearbeitet?
   ii Was hat sie in der Stadt gemacht?
   iii Wer war auch im Café?
   iv Was hat Herr Schulz gemacht?

b Uschi und Horst
   i   Warum ist Horst in Bielefeld?
   ii Wo hat er Monika das erste Mal gesehen?
   iii Was haben Horst und Monika dann gemacht?
   iv Wie lange ist Uschi schon mit ihrem Freund zusammen?

6 Hallo, Anna …

Write an email to your friend in Berlin telling her what you have been doing in the last couple of weeks. The verbs given below (in the infinitive) might give you some ideas.

> ausgehen   nach (London) fahren   ins Konzert gehen   viel arbeiten
> neuen Freund treffen   Aufsatz schreiben   ins Sportzentrum gehen …

7 Gestern Abend

Katrin ist böse auf Dieter.

- Hallo.
- *Schweigen*
- Was ist los?
- Dieter, wo warst du gestern Abend?
- Ich habe dir gesagt … ich war in der Bibliothek.
- Bis wann?
- Ich habe bis etwa 10 Uhr gearbeitet. Dann bin ich nach Hause gegangen. Ich war müde.
- Bist du direkt nach Hause gegangen?
- Fast … . Ich habe unterwegs ein Bier getrunken. … Mit Mario.
- Wo?
- In der Campus-Bar.
- Genau! Silvia hat dich dort gesehen. Du hast die ganze Zeit mit Antje gesprochen. Und du hast sie geküsst!
- Nein! Antje hat mich geküsst. Ich war total überrascht. Und wir waren nicht allein – Mario war da.
- Wirklich? Silvia hat ihn nicht gesehen …

Grammatik

Accusative pronouns: these are used for the *direct object* of a verb.

Sie hat <u>mich</u> geküsst ('She kissed <u>me</u>')   **Silvia hat <u>dich</u> gesehen** ('Silvia saw <u>you</u>')

Sie hat <u>ihn</u> nicht gesehen. ('She didn't see <u>him</u>')

Du hast <u>sie</u> geküsst ('You kissed <u>her</u>')

a Fragen:

    i   Wo war Dieter bis 10 Uhr?

    ii Warum ist er nach Hause gegangen?

    iii Er ist nicht direkt nach Hause gegangen – Wohin ist er gegangen?

    iv Was hat er gemacht? (Silvias Version!)

b Rollenspiel: Dieter und Silvia.

Silvia: Ich habe dich gesehen! Du hast …

Dieter antwortet: *Bibliothek arbeiten – 10 Uhr nach Hause – Bier trinken – Antje sprechen – mich küssen – überrascht*

8 **Was machst du jetzt?**/What are you going to do now?

Mario und Dieter

– Also … Man hat euch in der Bar gesehen?

– Noch schlimmer, Silvia hat uns gesehen! Sie hat Katrin alles erzählt.

– Was machst du jetzt?

– Ich sage die Wahrheit. Vielleicht ist sie nicht mehr so böse … Sie liebt mich!

– Hm …

Grammatik

Accusative pronouns:

Man hat <u>euch</u> gesehen ('you' plural, informal)   **Silvia hat <u>uns</u> gesehen** ('us')

a In the short passage above, find the German equivalents of:

    i even worse **ii** told **iii** the truth **iv** angry **v** loves

b Without reference to the text, role-play the scene with a partner, using these prompts:

Mario: – Bar gesehen?   Dieter: – Silvia! – Katrin erzählt

         – Jetzt?   – Wahrheit – böse – liebt!

c With a partner, script and role-play the resulting conversation between Dieter and Katrin. Act it out!

d Diskussion (10 Minuten Vorbereitungszeit): Was denken Sie über Silvias Reaktion? Warum hat sie Katrin alles erzählt?

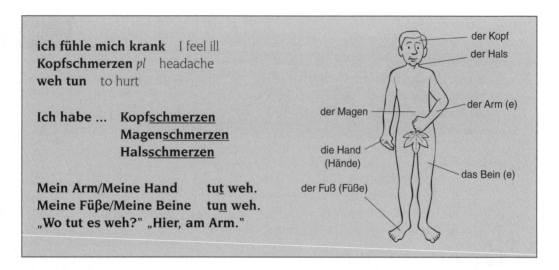

ich fühle mich krank   I feel ill
Kopfschmerzen *pl*   headache
weh tun   to hurt

Ich habe …   Kopf<u>schmerzen</u>
Magen<u>schmerzen</u>
Hals<u>schmerzen</u>

Mein Arm/Meine Hand   tu<u>t</u> weh.
Meine Füße/Meine Beine   tu<u>n</u> weh.
„Wo tut es weh?" „Hier, am Arm."

der Kopf
der Hals
der Arm (e)
der Magen
die Hand (Hände)
das Bein (e)
der Fuß (Füße)

9 **Wie geht's heute?**/How are things today?

a
1 krank	**a**	sad
2 optimistisch	**b**	in love
3 (un)glücklich	**c**	bored
4 hungrig	**d**	pleased
5 verliebt	**e**	(un)happy
6 gestresst	**f**	tired
7 ängstlich	**g**	optimistic
8 überrascht	**h**	disappointed
9 müde	**i**	ill
10 froh	**j**	anxious
11 enttäuscht	**k**	stressed
12 erkältet	**l**	hungry
13 traurig	**m**	suffering from a cold
14 gelangweilt	**n**	surprised

 b Complete each sentence with an appropriate adjective.

i Pauls Mannschaft, Bayern München, hat 2:0 gewonnen. Er ist …

ii Sabine hat heute Morgen gearbeitet. Am Nachmittag muss sie das Haus putzen und die Kinder von der Schule abholen. Sie ist …

iii Matthias hat den Arzt gesehen und muss drei Tage im Bett bleiben. Er ist …

iv Herr Christiansen will Cannelloni nach Italien exportieren. Er ist …

v Karin will Karl wieder sehen. Sie ist …

vi Ich habe im Sommer eine Prüfung. Ich bin …

  c And how do you feel at the moment? Tell your partner and explain why.

Extra!

10 Der Sprachkurs

Listen to Paloma and Jean-Paul (whom you have already met in Unit 7) talking about what they did during their time in Munich, where they attended different advanced German summer courses.

 Fragen:

a Wie lange ist Paloma in München geblieben?
b Wann hat der Unterricht angefangen?
c Was hat Paloma in ihrer Freizeit gemacht?
d Wer ist Paola?
e Hat Jean-Paul der Sprachkurs gefallen?
f Was sagt er über den Sprachkurs?
g Was hat er in seiner Freizeit gemacht?
h Wer ist Nathalie?

München

11 Mein Wochenende

Karin

Mein Wochenende? Das war schrecklich! Am Samstag habe ich zu lange geschlafen und ich bin erst um halb elf aufgestanden. Dann bin ich in die Stadt gegangen. Ich habe eine schicke Boutique gesucht, weil ich ein neues Kleid kaufen wollte. Ich habe zwölf Kleider anprobiert, aber ich habe nichts gefunden: zu klein, zu lang, zu teuer, zu langweilig … Dann war ich frustriert, es war kalt und es hat geregnet. Ich bin mit dem Bus nach Hause gefahren, aber das war auch schwierig. Der Fahrkartenautomat war kaputt, ich hatte kein Kleingeld und der Busfahrer konnte den Zehn-Euro-Schein nicht wechseln. Um halb sieben hat mein Freund angerufen und gesagt, dass er nicht mit mir ins Kino gehen kann – so eine Enttäuschung! Ich war traurig, habe eine Flasche Wein aufgemacht und den Fernseher angeschaltet … und am nächsten Morgen hatte ich schreckliche Kopfschmerzen!

Kurt

Mein Wochenende war ganz fantastisch. Ich bin um halb zehn aufgestanden, und meine Freundin hat Frühstück geholt – Croissants und Ei. Wir haben einen schönen Ausflug in die Berge gemacht und dann haben wir in einem kleinen Restaurant gegessen. Das Essen war köstlich und das Wetter gut. Am Nachmittag haben wir zu Hause ein bisschen im Garten gesessen und ein Glas Wein getrunken. Um acht Uhr sind wir zu einer Party gegangen, denn mein Freund Holger hatte Geburtstag. Er hat draußen im Garten gefeiert, weil es so warm war. Die Würstchen haben gut geschmeckt, die Musik war wunderbar und wir haben viel getanzt. Ich habe einige alte Freunde getroffen und viel Spaß gehabt. Um Mitternacht sind Nadine und ich nach Hause gegangen – das war ein toller Tag!

 a Summarise the two contrasting weekends in English.

b Write an account of your own weekend in German.

Grammatik

~ Perfect tense ▶ G16, G22

1 To talk about events that happened in the past, German-speakers tend to use the perfect tense. It has two elements:

an auxiliary verb (in the normal second position in the sentence)

and   a past participle (at the very end of the sentence)

2 The auxiliary is a present tense form of either:

haben ich habe, du hast, er/sie/es hat wir/Sie/sie haben, ihr habt	**sein** ich bin, du bist, er/sie/es ist wir/Sie/sie sind, ihr seid

or

3 The past participle follows one of two patterns, either:

weak **ge...t** **kaufen → gekauft** **einkaufen → eingekauft**	strong **ge...en** **kommen → gekommen** **ankommen → angekommen**

or

e.g.   **Wir <u>haben</u> ein neues Auto <u>gekauft</u>.**
Er <u>hat</u> ein Bier <u>getrunken</u>.
Ich <u>bin</u> in die Stadt <u>gegangen</u>.

4 While weak past participles are totally predictable, you have to learn the individual strong past participles, as many have a vowel change compared with the infinitive (**nehmen → genommen, trinken → getrunken**). The list of strong verbs in G22 also indicates which of them have **sein** as auxiliary.

5 All the verbs which are strong in the present tense (**du-** and **er/sie-** forms) follow the strong pattern for their past participle (e.g. **fahren** – present: **du fährst, er/sie fährt**; past participle: **gefahren**).

6 Some verbs which are not strong in the present tense follow the strong pattern for the past participle (e.g. **kommen** – present: **du kommst, er/sie kommt**; past participle: **gekommen**).

~ Accusative pronouns ▶ G11, G12

Accusative pronouns indicate the direct object in a sentence:
Sie hat <u>ihn</u> in der Campus-Bar gesehen. She saw <u>him</u> in the campus bar.
(She did the seeing, so she is the subject: she saw him, so he is the direct object.)

mich	**dich**	**ihn**	**sie**	**es**	**uns**	**Sie**	**sie**	**euch**
me	you (inf, sing)	him/it (m)	her/it (f)	it (n)	us	you (formal)	them	you (inf, pl)

Remember the accusative is also used after certain prepositions: always (e.g. **für, um, durch**) or sometimes (e.g. **in, auf, an**).

Grammatikübungen

1 Complete these perfect tense sentences with the past participle of the appropriate verb from the list and the correct form of the auxiliary.

    a Hans und Heide _____ in New York _____ .

    b Wir _____ gestern einen neuen Computer _____ .

    c Antje _____ mich _____ – ich war total überrascht!

    d „_____ du gut _____?" – „Ja, ich war sehr müde."

    e „_____ Sie den Brief _____?" – „Nein, noch nicht."

    f Ich _____ heute Vormittag nicht _____.

    g Wir _____ mit dem Bus _____.

    h „Wohin _____ ihr _____?" – „In die Stadt."

    i Peter _____ nicht zu unserer Party _____, er _____ zu Hause _____.

    j Anna _____ sehr früh _____ .

fahren	schlafen	küssen	schreiben	aufstehen (*sep*)
kaufen	frühstücken	gehen	kommen	bleiben wohnen

2 a Insert the correct accusative pronoun.

    i Julia hat _____ in der Stadt gesehen. (*her*)

    ii Er hat _____ geküsst. (*us*)

    iii Wir haben es für _____ gemacht. (*you, informal sing.*)

    iv Ich habe _____ gekauft. (*it, masc*)

    v Sie hat _____ in der Bar gesehen. (*you, informal plural*)

    vi „Wo sind die Brötchen?" – „Ich habe _____ alle gegessen!" (*them*)

b Put in the correct pronoun in the sentences below. Remember the difference between direct (accusative) and indirect (dative) objects, and bear in mind which form follows the prepositions.

    i Hast du (*ihn/ihm*) in der Vorlesung gesehen?

    ii Ich bin gestern mit (*sie/ihr*) ins Kino gegangen.

    iii Klaus hat (*ihn/ihm*) das Buch schon gegeben.

    iv Verena hat (*mich/mir*) gestern angerufen.

    v Diese Flasche Wein ist für (*dich/dir*).

    vi Er trifft (*sie/ihnen*) um halb neun vor dem Kino.

    vii Kannst du (*mich/mir*) helfen?

    viii Wir haben (*sie/ihnen*) getroffen.

Vokabeln

See Appendix on page 191 for more vocabulary from Extra! and Weitere Übungen.

Aufgabe 1

gestern	yesterday
Und dir?	And how are you?
gemacht	past participle of machen
das Essen	meal
eingekauft	pp of einkaufen
Tomaten *pl*	tomatoes
gekocht	pp of kochen
gehört	pp of hören
getanzt	pp of tanzen
gespielt	pp of spielen
Karten *pl*	cards

Aufgabe 2

Brötchen *pl*	rolls
die Marmelade	jam
gegessen	pp of essen*
getrunken	pp of trinken
geschrieben	pp of schreiben
Australien	Australia
lange	a long time
die Zeitung	newspaper
getroffen	pp of treffen*
heiß	hot
die Schokolade	chocolate
die Sahne	cream
geredet	pp of reden
reden	to talk
angerufen	pp of anrufen
babysitten	to babysit
spannend	exciting

Aufgabe 3

endlich	at last
in den letzten 2 Wochen	in the last 2 weeks
schrecklich	terribly
deshalb	therefore
aufgestanden	pp of aufstehen
zur Uni	to university
gefahren	pp of fahren*
geregnet	pp of regnen
krank	ill
den ganzen Nachmittag	all afternoon
geblieben	pp of bleiben
wichtig	important

gesucht	pp of suchen
gefunden	pp of finden
zum Glück	luckily
gekommen	pp of kommen
gegangen	pp of gehen
erzählt	pp of erzählen
erzählen	to tell
ferngesehen	pp of fernsehen*

Aufgabe 5

allen Kollegen	to all the colleagues

Aufgabe 6

der Aufsatz	essay

Aufgabe 7

böse (auf)	angry (with)
Schweigen	silence
Was ist los?	What's the matter?
bis wann?	until when?
müde	tired
unterwegs	on the way
gesprochen	pp of sprechen*
geküsst	pp of küssen
küssen	to kiss
überrascht	surprised

Aufgabe 8

noch schlimmer	even worse
alles	everything
die Wahrheit	truth
lieben	to love
denken	to think

Aufgabe 9

optimistisch	optimistic
(un)glücklich	(un)happy, (un)lucky
hungrig	hungry
verliebt	in love
gestresst	stressed
ängstlich	anxious, afraid
froh	glad, pleased
enttäuscht	disappointed
erkältet	suffering from a cold
traurig	sad
gelangweilt	bored
die Mannschaft	team
gewonnen	pp of gewinnen
gewinnen	to win
abholen *sep*	to collect (someone)
die Prüfung	exam

*Verb strong in present tense ▶**G14.2**
For parts of the body see panel on page 92.

Partnerarbeit

1 Was hat Karen gemacht?

Fill in the blanks in Karen's diary by asking questions about what she did then. Answer your partner's questions to help him/her fill the diary too.

Example: *Was hat Karen am Donnerstagnachmittag gemacht?*
           Sie hat/ist …

	Donnerstag	Freitag	Samstag
Vormittag	10 Uhr Vorlesung (Mathe)		Frühstück mit Sabine (10.30)
Nachmittag		nach Frankfurt fahren (Museum)	
Abend	Tischtennis spielen mit Markus (7.30)		mit Klaus ins Kino gehen (8 Uhr)

2 Und was hast du gemacht?

Now ask your partner what he/she did on certain days and complete the diary below, using the information you are given.

	Mittwoch	Samstag
Vormittag		
Nachmittag		
Abend		

Frankfurt am Main

3 Adjektive

a From this list of adjectives denoting physical condition, states of mind, feelings and emotions, your partner will mime five. You must work out which they are.

froh, erkältet, unglücklich, gestresst, hungrig, müde, fit, enttäuscht, optimistisch.

b Now it's your turn. Mime the following five adjectives:

ängstlich   krank   verliebt   gelangweilt   traurig

Partnerarbeit

1 Was hat Karen gemacht?

Fill in the blanks in Karen's diary by asking questions about what she did then. Answer your partner's questions to help him/her fill the diary too.

Example: *Was hat Karen am Donnerstagnachmittag gemacht?*
Sie hat/ist …

	Donnerstag	Freitag	Samstag
Vormittag		einkaufen (Aldi)	
Nachmittag	treffen im Café 1.30 – Eva		Ausflug nach Heidelberg/Eltern
Abend		arbeiten (Studentenbar)	

2 Und was hast du gemacht?

Now ask your partner what he/she did on certain days and complete the diary below, using the information you are given.

	Mittwoch	Samstag
Vormittag		
Nachmittag		
Abend		

Heidelberg

3 Adjektive

a Mime the following adjectives so that your partner can work out what they are:

müde froh gestresst erkältet hungrig

b Now your partner will mime five adjectives from the following list denoting physical condition, state of mind, feelings and emotions. You must work out which they are.

unglücklich, gelangweilt, optimistisch, krank, enttäuscht, verliebt, traurig, ängstlich, fit.

9 Lebensläufe

In this unit you will continue learning to use the perfect tense, this time in the context of your life, experience and education. You will also learn how to apply for a job. There is a particular focus on reading.

1 In welchem Jahr?/In which year?

a … ist Königin Victoria gestorben?
b … hat der Zweite Weltkrieg geendet?
c … sind die Amerikaner auf dem Mond gelandet?
d … ist die Berliner Mauer gefallen?
e … hat Spanien die Fußballweltmeisterschaft in Südafrika gewonnen?

1945 2010 1989
1901 1969

In the gaps below, **(i)** fill in the missing year from the five given above, and **(ii)** write out the current year:

neunzehnhundertfünfundvierzig   **zweitausendzehn**
neunzehnhunderteins   **neunzehnhundertneunundsechzig**

i _____   ii _____

2 Wer bin ich?

1 Ich bin im Jahre 1756 in Salzburg, Österreich geboren. Ich habe Opern, Symphonien, Violinkonzerte und Klavierkonzerte komponiert.

2 Ich bin 1918 in Südafrika geboren. Ich habe 26 Jahre im Gefängnis verbracht, aber später bin ich Präsident geworden.

3 Ich bin 1943 in New York geboren und bin Filmschauspieler. Ich habe zweimal einen Oscar erhalten: 1975 für meine Rolle als Don Corleone im Mafia-Film *Der Pate* II und 1981 für die Rolle vom Boxer Jake La Motta in *Wie ein wilder Stier*.

4 Ich bin im Jahre 1940 in Liverpool geboren. Ich war Sänger und Songschreiber und habe das Lied *Imagine* geschrieben.

a Identify the four people! – Das ist …

b Work out how to say the years of their birth on the basis of the examples in exercise 1.

c Then check your answers to **a** and **b** by listening to the recording.

d Write a similar description of a famous person, a woman this time. Your partner tries to work out who it is. Then he/she tries out a mini-biography on you.

Grammatik

Perfect tense

- Verbs with an infinitive ending in **-ieren** are weak but do not have the prefix **ge-** in their past participle: **komponieren** ('to compose') → **ich habe komponiert**.

- Verbs with the prefixes **ver-**, **be-**, **ent-** and **er-** (these are the commonest, there are others) also do without the **ge-** prefix in their past participle: **verbringen** ('to spend time'): **ich habe verbracht**. These are called *inseparable* prefixes.

- Mixed verbs: **verbringen** has features of both *strong* (it changes its vowel sound **i → a**) and *weak* (its past participle ends in **-t**) verbs. **Bringen** and all the verbs based on it follow this *mixed* pattern. Another mixed verb is **denken** ('to think') → **ich habe gedacht**.

3 Marias Leben/Maria's life

A
Sie haben es gar nicht verstanden. Mein Bruder und meine Schwester haben studiert und ich habe immer gute Noten bekommen, aber das Studium hat mich einfach nicht interessiert.

B
Ich habe mit 19 die Schule verlassen. Ich wollte nicht weiter studieren, ich wollte arbeiten, Geld verdienen, leben! Ich habe eine Stelle als Bankangestellte gefunden, habe ein bisschen Geld verdient und bin oft ausgegangen!

C
Ich bin im Jahre 1955 in Berlin geboren, aber meine Eltern sind bald danach umgezogen. Ich bin also in Hamburg aufgewachsen.

D
Wir haben drei Kinder. Ich habe 1985 meine Stelle bei der Bank aufgegeben, weil ich mehr Zeit mit den Kindern verbringen wollte. Ich arbeite nicht mehr – ich bin jetzt Großmutter und habe viel zu tun!

E
Meinen Mann habe ich im Sportverein kennen gelernt. Ich habe 1978 geheiratet und wir haben eine kleine Wohnung gefunden. Wir waren sehr glücklich, obwohl wir kein Geld hatten!

a The above extracts from an interview are not in the correct order. Re-arrange them, then check your version by listening to the recording. To guide you, here are the questions the interviewer asked:
  – Sind Sie Hamburgerin?
  – Haben Sie studiert?
  – Wie haben Ihre Eltern reagiert?
  – Wann haben Sie geheiratet?
  – Haben Sie Kinder?

b Wortsuche:

i	I found a job	**vi**	I got to know my husband
ii	I got married	**vii**	My parents moved house
iii	I grew up in Hamburg	**viii**	I was born
iv	I gave up my job	**ix**	I always got good grades
v	I left school		

c Fragen:

i	Ist Maria in Berlin aufgewachsen?	**iv**	Was hat sie im Jahre 1978 gemacht?
ii	Was haben ihre Eltern gemacht?	**v**	Warum hat sie die Stelle aufgegeben?
iii	Warum hat sie nicht studiert?	**vi**	Was ist sie jetzt von Beruf?

4 In Berlin geboren

Maria ist in Berlin geboren, aber …

umziehen – in Hamburg aufwachsen – gute Noten bekommen – Schule verlassen – Stelle finden – Mann kennen lernen – heiraten – drei Kinder: Stelle aufgeben

5 Der Lebenslauf von Brigitte Jacobs

Geburtsdatum: 8.11.1987
Geburtsort: Bad Schwartau   Staatsangehörigkeit: deutsch
Wohnort: Lübeck   Konfession: evangelisch
Familienstand: ledig

Schule	1994–1998 1998–2006	Grundschule Bad Schwartau Gymnasium Lübeck Abitur (Durchschnittsnote 2,8)

Hochschule   Universität Kiel
2006–2010   Studium: Theologie und Anglistik
      Studienabschluss: Magister

Berufserfahrung
April 2007–Sept. 2007   International Office, Methodist Church, London
April 2008–Sept. 2008   Pastorale Assistentin, St-Jürgen-Krankenhaus, Bremen
Ferienjobs   2007–9   Supermarkt Aldi, Kiel (Kasse), Barpersonal, Kellnerin usw.

Sprachkenntnisse: Englisch (fließend), Latein, Griechisch.

Using Brigitte's CV as a model, draft your own German **Lebenslauf**.

6 Beate sucht eine Stelle

„ **a** _____ August 1991 bis Juni 1999 habe ich das Ludwigsgymnasium in Tübingen besucht und mein **b** _____ mit der Durchschnittsnote 2,4 gemacht. Ich habe gleich **c** _____ dem Abitur mit dem Studium in Heidelberg **d** _____ – meine Studienfächer waren Anglistik und Computerlinguistik. Dieses Jahr im **e** _____ habe ich meine Magisterprüfung gemacht. Ich suche jetzt eine Stelle, und ich würde gern meine Sprachkenntnisse nutzen, denn ich **f** _____ fließend Englisch, ziemlich gut Französisch und ein **g** _____ Spanisch. In den Semesterferien habe ich in einer **h** _____ und in einem Übersetzungsbüro gearbeitet, das heißt, ich habe etwas Erfahrung in der Arbeitswelt gesammelt. Im Semester habe ich manchmal **i** _____ in einer Kneipe und in einem Restaurant **j** _____, weil das Studentenleben ziemlich teuer ist. Ich interessiere mich für Fremdsprachen, und natürlich auch für **k** _____. Ich möchte gern mit Menschen zusammenarbeiten, **l** _____ ich am liebsten in einem Team arbeite …"

spreche	Computer	April	angefangen	bisschen	von
Computerfirma	abends	Abitur	gearbeitet	nach	weil

Grammatik

ich würde gern … /ich möchte gern … 'I'd like to …'

To express plans, wishes or hopes, you can use one of these constructions:

ich/er, sie, es	würde/möchte	Sie/wir/sie	würden/möchten
du	würdest/möchtest	ihr	würdet/möchtet

Ich würde gern/möchte gern in einer Computerfirma <u>arbeiten</u>.

7 Hanna und Jens

a Machen Sie Notizen.

	Schule/Universität	Ferienjobs	Berufliche Pläne
Hanna			
Jens			

b Write a brief account for each person, using the information you have collected.
Beispiel: Hanna hat die Viktoriaschule besucht …

8 Und Sie?

a **Was haben Sie gemacht?** Work together with a partner and tell one another about your education and any work experience you have. Use the glossary and a dictionary if necessary.

b **Was würden Sie gern beruflich machen?** Now tell one another what you would like to do when you finish university. These can be realistic plans, but you can also use your imagination!

9 Referenz

On an employment agency evaluation form, applicants are rated on a set of characteristics, some of which are listed below.

a Can you work out what most of them mean? Check in the unit vocabulary list page 191.

motiviert	freundlich	gute Sprachkenntnisse
enthusiastisch	kommunikativ	Fähigkeit MS Office
selbständig	pünktlich	mobil
teamorientiert	zuverlässig	fleißig
flexibel	organisiert	

b Which of the above characteristics do you think would be required of someone thought suitable for the post advertised here? Explain why in German.

> **SPEZIALIST FÜR FLUGREISEN – EUROPAWEIT!**
> – Kundenberatung in unseren Läden in vier Ländern, am Telefon und im Internet.
> – Sind Sie motiviert und flexibel, besitzen Sie Teamgeist?
> – Wir bieten Ihnen ein interessantes Arbeitsfeld in unserem jungen Reservierungsteam.

c Which of the characteristics listed in **a** above do you possess?

10 Ich bewerbe mich um .../I am applying for ...

> # Übersetzer/in ins Englische
>
> *Wir* sind ein Übersetzungsbüro in Erlangen.
> *Wir* spezialisieren uns auf technische Übersetzungen.
> *Wir* suchen eine/n Übersetzer/in ins Englische.
> *Wir* bieten ein gutes Gehalt und eine gute Arbeitsatmosphäre.
>
> *Sie* haben ausgezeichnete Englisch- und Computerkenntnisse.
> *Sie* sind zuverlässig und pünktlich.
> *Sie* können selbständig arbeiten, aber *Sie* arbeiten auch gern im Team.
> *Sie* sind flexibel.
>
> *Bewerbungen an:* Frau Marion Hoffman, Übersetzungsbüro Urban, Kohlstr. 5, 91056 Erlangen oder hoffman@urbanueber.de

Grammatik

Reflexive verbs

sich interessieren, sich bewerben, sich spezialisieren, sich entscheiden
Ich interessiere _mich_ für Fremdsprachen I am interested in languages
Ich bewerbe _mich_ um diese Stelle I am applying for this job.
Er interessiert _sich_ für … He's interested in …
Sie bewirbt _sich_ um … She's applying for …

Sehr geehrte Frau Hoffmann,

ich habe Ihre Stellenanzeige mit Interesse gelesen und möchte mich um die Stelle als Übersetzerin bewerben. Ich habe das Studium der Anglistik und Computerlinguistik in Heidelberg mit der Magisterprüfung abgeschlossen. Ich spreche fließend Englisch und habe sehr gute Computerkenntnisse.

Ich habe fünf Monate in einem Übersetzungsbüro gearbeitet. Dort habe ich in einem Team von vier Kollegen gearbeitet. Ich musste flexibel sein, denn wir hatten viele wichtige Termine. Ich würde gern bei Ihnen arbeiten.

Mit freundlichen Grüßen,

Beate Winkler

---

a Read the job advertisement on the previous page. Once you are sure of the requirements of the job, match Beate's letter of application above and her interview (exercise 6) against them. Does she meet the requirements? Report back to the class.

b Then draft Uwe's similar letter applying for the job advertised on the right, using the CV details given below.

Uwe Heimann

geb.:	Feb. 1988
Mai 2007	Abitur (3,1)
	Liebigschule Dahlem
Sept. 2007	Krankenhausküche
Okt. 2009	Studienanfang FU
	(Informatik/Anglistik)

Französischkenntnisse: Abitur
Ferienjobs: Studentenbar/Pizzeria
Auto: ja
Arbeitszeit: nach 17 Uhr

Wir suchen …

Zuverlässiges Personal für unser Internationales Konferenzzentrum in Berlin.

Kellner/in für Cafeteria
Der/die Bewerber/in muss
- pünktlich und fleißig sein
- Englisch und Französisch sprechen
- teamorientiert und flexibel sein
- auch im Stress arbeiten können!
- Erfahrung im Restaurantmetier haben
- nachmittags/abends arbeiten können

Extra!

11 Und was würden Sie gern machen?

a You are listening to a radio programme from Germany. The presenter asks two young women who have just finished university about their education, situation now, and future plans. Draw up a grid and make a note of the relevant information – it doesn't matter if you do not understand everything.

	Ausbildung	Situation jetzt	Zukunftspläne
Alice			
Barbara			

b Using your notes, write a profile of the two women in German.

c **Was würden S***ie* **gern machen?** Write a short paragraph about your own plans for the future.

12 Kein typischer Student?

Herr Heydorn ist kein typischer Student. Er ist Rentner. Wann hat er sich entschieden, zur Universität zu gehen? „Das war vor vier Jahren", antwortet der Fünfundsechzigjährige. „Als meine jüngste Tochter ihr Studium begonnen hat, habe ich gedacht: Ich möchte so was machen! Ich habe mich informiert, bin zur Abendschule gegangen, habe das Abitur gemacht und … jetzt bin ich Student im ersten Semester." Warum wollte er studieren? „In meinem Alter studiert man, weil es Spaß macht", sagt er.

Fragen:
a In welchem Jahr hat Herr Heydorn sich entschieden, zur Universität zu gehen?
b Wie alt ist er jetzt? Wann ist er geboren?
c Was ist ein typischer Student?
d Warum wollte Herr Heydorn studieren?
e Und Sie? Warum studieren Sie? …
f Which are the two reflexive verbs in this passage? What tense are they in?

Grammatik

~ Perfect tense (continued) ▸G16.3, G23

1 Verbs with an infinitive ending in **-ieren** are weak but their past participle omits the prefix **ge-**:

Andreas hat nicht <u>studiert</u>. (← **studieren**)

2 Verbs with an inseparable prefix such as **be-**, **ver-**, **ent-**, **er-**, whether weak or strong, also omit the prefix **ge-** in their past participle:

Wir haben unseren Großvater <u>besucht</u> (← **besuchen** weak);
Meine Eltern haben es nicht <u>verstanden</u> (← **verstehen** strong).

3 Mixed verbs combine features of both weak verbs (a past participle ending in **-t**) and strong verbs (vowel change):

Mandela hat viele Jahre im Gefängnis <u>verbracht</u>. (← **verbringen**)

~ Reflexive verbs ▸G14.5

There are some reflexive verbs in the unit: these are formed with a reflexive pronoun:

sich interessieren

ich interessiere	<u>**mich**</u> für Bilder	**wir interessieren**	<u>**uns**</u> für Literatur
du interessierst	<u>**dich**</u>	**ihr interessiert**	<u>**euch**</u>
er/sie interessiert	<u>**sich**</u>	**Sie/sie interessieren**	<u>**sich**</u>

~ Expressing plans, wishes, hopes ▸G18

ich würde gern + infinitive / **ich möchte gern** + infinitive

ich/er, sie, es	**würde/möchte**	**wir/Sie/sie**	**würden/möchten**
du	**würdest/möchtest**	**ihr**	**würdet/möchtet**

Ich <u>würde gern</u> in einer Computerfirma <u>arbeiten</u>.
Remember the infinitive comes at the end!

~ Subordinating conjunctions ▸G19.5

1 You have met the subordinating conjunctions **wenn**, **weil** and **dass**. In this unit two more were introduced: **als** (which means 'when' referring to the <u>past</u>: note that **wenn** is used in statements in the present tense, **wann** in questions) and **obwohl** ('although').

2 Remember subordinating conjunctions send the verb to the end:

Wir waren glücklich, obwohl wir kein Geld <u>hatten</u>.
Er ist oft sehr müde, weil er abends <u>ausgeht</u>. (note position of separable prefix **aus**)

3 When the subordinate clause (the part of the sentence introduced by the subordinating conjunction) comes first, the main verb follows immediately, preceded by a comma which separates the two clauses:

Obwohl wir kein Geld hatten,   <u>waren</u> wir glücklich.
◄── subordinate clause ──►,   ◄── main clause ──►

Grammatikübungen

1 Complete the verb table. All these verbs can be found in this unit.

Infinitive	Past participle	Auxiliary	Meaning
sterben	_____	_____	_____
_____	geendet	_____	_____
_____	_____	_____	to fall
_____	gewonnen	_____	_____
komponieren	_____	_____	_____
_____	_____	haben	to spend (time)
_____	verstanden	_____	_____
_____	_____	_____	to interest
finden	_____	_____	_____
_____	verdient	_____	_____
_____	_____	_____	to move house
aufwachsen	_____	sein	_____
heiraten	_____	_____	_____

2 Reflexive verbs. Translate the sentences into German.
   a I'm applying for a job in London.
   b She's interested in sport.
   c They specialise in translations.
   d He has decided to find a job.

3 Using an appropriate form of the **würde gern** construction, express the following in German:

Example: … work in a translation bureau. (I) .

   Ich würde gern in einem Übersetzungsbüro arbeiten.

   a … work in a team. (*they*)
   b … attend the **Gymnasium** (grammar school). (*she*)
   c … use your knowledge of languages? (*you singular, informal*)
   d … find a job. (*we*)
   e … move house. (*he*)

4 Subordinating conjunctions
   a In the following two sentences, the two clauses are joined by **aber** ('but') – a *co-ordinating conjunction*. Join them with **obwohl** instead, remembering the word order rules.
      i Er hat viel Freizeit, aber er geht selten aus.
      ii Sie spricht fließend Italienisch, aber sie war noch nie in Italien.
   b Insert the appropriate word for 'when':
      i (*When*) bist du geboren?
      ii (*When*) ich letzte Woche in Berlin war, habe ich deinen Bruder gesehen.
      iii (*When*) ich im Ausland arbeite, nutze ich meine Sprachkenntnisse.

Vokabeln

See Appendix on p. 191 for more vocabulary from exercises 7, 9, 10 and 11

Aufgabe 1

die Königin	queen
gestorben	pp of sterben*
sterben*	to die
der Weltkrieg	world war
der Mond	moon
gelandet	pp of landen
landen	to land
die Berliner Mauer	Berlin Wall
gefallen	here = pp of fallen*
fallen*	to fall
die Weltmeisterschaft	World Cup
Südafrika	South Africa

Aufgabe 2

geboren	born
Opern *pl*	operas
Symphonien *pl*	symphonies
Violinkonzerte *pl*	violin concertos
Klavierkonzerte *pl*	piano concertos
komponiert	pp of komponieren
komponieren	to compose
das Gefängnis	prison
verbracht	pp of verbringen
der Präsident	president
geworden	pp of werden*
werden*	to become
der Filmschauspieler	film actor
erhalten*	to receive (also pp)
die Rolle	role
„Der Pate"	'The Godfather'
„Wie ein wilder Stier"	'Raging Bull'
der Sänger	singer
der Songschreiber	songwriter
das Lied	song

Aufgabe 3

gar nicht	not at all
verstanden	pp of verstehen
verstehen	to understand
studiert	pp of studieren
einfach	simply
interessieren	to interest
mit 19	at 19
verlassen*	to leave (also pp)
weiter	further

leben	to live
die Stelle	job, position
die Bankangestellte	bank employee (f)
bald danach	soon afterwards
umgezogen	pp of umziehen
umziehen *sep*	to move (house)
aufgewachsen	pp of aufwachsen*
aufwachsen* *sep*	to grow up
aufgegeben	pp of aufgeben*
mehr	more
der Sportverein	sports club
kennen gelernt	pp of kennen lernen
geheiratet	pp of heiraten
heiraten	to marry
obwohl	although
reagiert	pp of reagieren
reagieren	to react

Aufgabe 5

der Lebenslauf	CV
evangelisch	Protestant
die Grundschule	primary school
das Gymnasium	grammar school
das Abitur	A Levels (equivalent)
die Durchschnittsnote	average grade
Anglistik	English (academic subject)
Studienabschluss	degree, diploma
die Berufserfahrung	professional experience
die pastorale Assistentin	pastoral assistant
Ferienjobs *pl*	holiday jobs
das Barpersonal	bar staff
Sprachkenntnisse *pl*	knowledge of languages
fließend	fluent

Aufgabe 6

Studienfächer *pl*	subjects studied
Computerlinguistik	computer linguistics
nutzen	to use
Semesterferien *pl*	vacation(s)
die Firma	firm
das Übersetzungsbüro	translation agency
Erfahrung sammeln	to gain experience
die Arbeitswelt	world of work
das Studentenleben	student life
sich interessieren für	to be interested in
Fremdsprachen *pl*	foreign languages
Menschen *pl*	people
das Team	team

*Verb strong in present tense ▶G14.2

Partnerarbeit

A

1 Elkes Lebenslauf

You and your partner have different gaps in your copies of Elke Schwarzer's CV. Ask each other questions to complete the CV.

Geburtsdatum:	*21.12.89*
Geburtsort:	*Schwerin*
August 96 – Juni 00:	
September 00 – Mai 09:	*Bert-Brecht-Schule, Jena, Abitur mit Durchschnittsnote 1,8*
Juni 09 – September 09:	
Dezember 09 – Januar 10:	*Verkaufsassistentin bei Karstadt, Abteilung Damenmode.*
Februar 10 – Februar 11:	
Mai 11 – September 11:	*Kellnerin Café Rosenthal, Berlin Mitte.*
September 11 –	

2 Sommer in der Schweiz/Summer in Switzerland

You are looking for a holiday job this summer and your partner helps by giving you a mock initial interview with the agency you are using.

When you've completed the interview, swap roles.

Partnerarbeit

B

1 Elkes Lebenslauf

You and your partner have different gaps in your copies of Elke Schwarzer's CV.
Ask each other questions to complete the CV.

Geburtsdatum: Geburtsort:	
August 96 – Juni 00:	*Karl-Marx-Schule, Schwerin*
September 00 – Mai 09:	
Juni 09 –September 09:	*Büroangestellte, Arbeitsagentur Jena* *Computerkenntnisse: Word/Excel*
Dezember 09 – Januar 10:	
Februar 10 – Februar 11:	*Buchgeschäft Humboldt, Berlin* *Verkäuferin*
Mai 11 – September 11:	
September 11 –	*Studienbeginn Humboldt-Universität* *Studienfächer: Informatik und Graphik*

2 Sommer in der Schweiz/Summer in Switzerland

Your partner is looking for a holiday job in Switzerland this summer. She/He is about to
have an introductory interview with the agency and you have agreed to ask the questions
in a mock interview. You have obtained the following outline from the agency's website,
use it to formulate your questions.

```
FERIENJOBS IN DER SCHWEIZ

Vorstellungsgespräch - wir möchten Sie kennen lernen!

Name, wann und wo geboren, Familienstand (verheiratet/ledig),
Schule, Studium (Studienfächer), Qualifikationen, Sprachkenntnisse
(Deutsch, Französich, Italienisch), Berufserfahrung, Ferienjobs.
Was würden Sie gern tun? Warum?

Sind Sie: organisiert, zuverlässig, pünktlich?
Arbeiten Sie lieber im Team oder selbständig?
```

When you've completed the interview, swap roles.

10 Zukunftspläne

In this unit you will learn how to express wishes and hopes for the future, compare situations in the past and in the present and talk about your holiday plans.

 1 Im Ausland arbeiten/Working abroad

Markus Kühn hat Betriebswirtschaft und Politik studiert. Er arbeitet seit einem Jahr in einer akademischen Buchhandlung.

Read the following extract from an email Markus sent to his friend Gudrun, then translate it into English.

> Ich weiß nicht, ob ich lange in diesem Job bleibe. Die Arbeit ist ziemlich monoton und langweilig, und ich würde gern eine interessantere Stelle finden – ich brauche Abwechslung im Leben! Ich würde gern im Ausland arbeiten, vielleicht in Großbritannien oder Italien. Mein Englisch ist besser als mein Italienisch, aber ich möchte wirklich gern in einem warmen Land leben und arbeiten, denn das regnerische Wetter hier im Norden macht mich ganz melancholisch. Warst du schon mal in Italien? Ich habe letztes Jahr fast einen Monat in Verona verbracht. Das Klima, die Leute, das Essen – alles war fantastisch. Ich würde gern mehr Zeit dort verbringen, um das Leben dort besser kennen zu lernen.

Grammatik

Comparative form of the adjective

Die Stelle ist interessant	**eine interessante Stelle**
The job is interesting	an interesting job
Die Stelle ist interessanter	**eine interessantere Stelle**
The job is more interesting	a more interesting job

Irregular comparative: **gut – besser**.

 2 Meine Zukunftspläne/My future plans

Markus explains his plans for the future to his parents. Listen carefully to the recording and then complete the sentences below using the cues. Remember **weil** sends the verb to the end!

a Markus würde gern eine andere Stelle finden, weil ... (langweilig)
b Die Atmosphäre ist oft schlecht, weil ... (nett)
c Er möchte einen Intensivkurs in Italienisch machen, weil ... (sprechen/arbeiten)
d Das Leben in Italien ist angenehm, weil ... (freundlicher)
e Markus würde gern in einem anderen Land arbeiten, weil ... (Erfahrung)

3 Und Sie? Würden Sie gern im Ausland arbeiten?

Wo? Warum (nicht)?

4 Die ideale Partnerin

Markus ist ledig, aber er sucht eine Freundin. Er beschreibt seine ideale Partnerin.

a Listen to the recording and note down the key features of Markus' ideal partner (in German).

b Write a short description of this possible partner, and make sure you include the following key words and aspects:

Sinn für Humor – Sport – Kino – Politik – Musik – Freizeit – Ausland – Freunde

5 Er muss gern reisen/He must like travelling

Read this description of an ideal partner and check your understanding of it with a classmate. Would the woman who wrote this be interested in Markus? What evidence is there for your opinion? Explain in German.

> Mein idealer Partner...
> kann zwischen 1,58m und 1,78m groß sein
> muss sportlich sein
> muss flexibel und tolerant sein
> muss gern reisen
> darf mit seinen Freunden ausgehen
> darf nicht rauchen

Grammatik

Modal verb in addition to **müssen**, **können** and **wollen**:
dürfen 'be allowed to', 'may': **ich/er darf, Sie dürfen**

6 Ihre ideale Partnerin/Ihr idealer Partner

a Tell the others in the class about your ideal partner.

b Write a description of your perfect partner in German.

Für wen kauft er die Blumen?

7 Hoffnungen und Realität/Hopes and reality

Diese Woche, 20 Jahre nach der Weidervereinigung, besucht die Zeitschrift „Unser Leben" Marianne Hildebrandt in Jena. Marianne ist 1960 geboren, hat zwei Kinder – Jutta (28) und Klaus (26) – und ist seit 30 Jahren verheiratet. Sie hat ihr ganzes Leben in Jena gewohnt und möchte auch nicht umziehen. Nach der Wiedervereinigung ist sie natürlich mal nach Westdeutschland gefahren, um Verwandte zu besuchen. Ihr Bruder, die Schwester ihrer Mutter und der Bruder ihres Vaters wohnen alle im Westen. Aber sie ist auch gern wieder nach Jena zurückgekommen.

Natürlich hat die Wiedervereinigung viele Vorteile gebracht: mehr Freiheit zu reisen, mehr Auswahl beim Einkaufen, eine offenere Politik. Aber die Nachteile? Vor der Wiedervereinigung hatte Marianne einen relativ gut bezahlten Job als Bibliothekarin, dann war sie 11 Jahre lang arbeitslos. Jetzt hat sie einen Teilzeitjob in einem Supermarkt. Vorher hatten alle eine Stelle. Heute haben viele Jugendliche in Jena keine Arbeit und zu viel Zeit. Vorher war die Miete für die Wohnung billig, jetzt ist sie sehr viel teurer. Wir haben mit Marianne über ihre Hoffnungen und Zukunftspläne gesprochen.

UL *Frau Hildebrandt, vor der Wiedervereinigung war Ihr Leben ganz anders als jetzt. Welche Hoffnungen hatten Sie damals für die Zukunft?*

MH Ja, wissen Sie, ich war eigentlich ganz zufrieden. Meine Arbeit in der Bibliothek hat mir gut gefallen. Ich war unabhängig, weil ich auch Geld verdient habe. Das heißt, ich habe das Geld meines Mannes nicht gebraucht, wenn ich ein neues Kleid kaufen wollte. Ich habe gedacht, dass ich erst mit 65 aufhöre zu arbeiten. Als ich 1991 meine Stelle verloren habe, war das für mich ein Schock. Ich habe endlich im Jahre 2002 eine neue Stelle gefunden.

UL *Wie haben Ihre Kinder reagiert? Jutta und Klaus waren ja noch ziemlich klein?*

MH Damals war das OK, denn die Kinder haben sich gefreut, dass ich jeden Tag zu Hause war.

UL *Wie sehen Sie die Zukunft Ihrer Kinder jetzt?*

MH Sie haben immer noch schlechtere Chancen, einen Job zu finden. Sie wohnen im Moment beide zu Hause – Klaus studiert noch – und sie müssen keine Miete zahlen. Für mich war es damals leicht, eine Stelle zu bekommen. Nach der Hochzeit haben wir auch nicht lange gebraucht, eine schöne Wohnung zu finden. Das ist alles heute viel schwieriger.

Unser Leben, Oktober 2010

Fragen:

a Ist Marianne Hildebrandt ledig?

b Warum ist sie nach der Wiedervereinigung nach Westdeutschland gefahren?

c Welche Vorteile hat die Wiedervereinigung gebracht?

d Arbeitet Marianne?

e Wie ist die Situation jetzt in Jena?

f Warum hat Marianne gern gearbeitet?

g Wie sieht sie die Situation ihrer Kinder?

h Was ist ein anderes Wort für „die Schwester ihres Vaters"? (Suchen Sie im Wörterbuch.)

Grammatik

<u>Genitive: possessive/indefinite article pattern</u>

die Schwester ihres Vaters (her father's sister) = '... of her father'

der Bruder ihrer Mutter (her mother's brother) = '... of her mother'

Find the German equivalents of the following on page 113:

'My husband's money' (... 'of my husband') ...

'Your children's future' ('of your children') ...

8 Damals und jetzt

a You already know quite a lot about Marianne's situation before and after German reunification. Listen to the extract from an interview where Marianne talks in more detail about her hopes in 1990 and her current situation. Then complete the grid:

Damals	Jetzt
Wenig Kriminalität Alle hatten eine Stelle.	Teure Mieten

b With reference to the grid only, prepare a short talk in German on the contrast between life then and now. Give the talk to a group/the whole class.

c Write an account in German of Marianne's situation before and after reunification.

 ## 9 Und welche Zukunftspläne und Hoffnungen haben Sie/hast du?

Get together with a partner and talk about plans and hopes for the future. Then present these to the class.

Beispiel: *Michael möchte später in einer Großstadt wohnen. Er will ...*

10 Zwei Wochen in der Sonne

Read the message. In a similar way, describe briefly (to a partner/the class) what you will be doing in the next few weeks.

> Liebe Eva und Max
> Hallo! Wie geht's? Es ist die letzte Woche des Semesters.
> Morgen um 11 Uhr habe ich meine letzte Vorlesung. Dann gibt es
> die Prüfungen! Und danach muss ich einige Wochen arbeiten, aber
> am 16. August fahre ich in Urlaub – zwei Wochen in der Sonne!
> Was macht ihr in den Sommerferien? Möchtet ihr nach Spanien
> fahren? Vielleicht sehe ich euch am Tag der letzten Prüfung.
> Wir können zusammen ein Bier trinken! Schreibt bald!
> Tschüss
> Mehmet

Grammatik

Genitive: definite article pattern

Masculine and neuter nouns: **das Ende des Semesters** 'the end of the semester'

Feminine and plural nouns: **der Tag der Prüfung(en)** 'the day of the exam(s)'

11 Wir müssen uns entscheiden

Die Sommerpläne von Eva und Max

– Max, hast du die E-Mail von Mehmet gesehen?

– Nein, noch nicht.

– Er fährt im August **a** _____ Spanien und möchte wissen, was wir machen.

– Eine gute Frage: **b** _____ fahren wir eigentlich?

– Ich bin nicht sicher …

– Wir müssen uns entscheiden. Also … Deutschland oder **c** _____?

– Südeuropa ist zu warm …

– Also Deutschland. Fahren wir an die **d** _____ oder **e** _____ Land?

– An die **f** _____ – da kann man mehr machen.

– Nordsee oder Ostsee?

– Die Nordseeküste ist näher.

– OK – an die Arbeit! Wir finden bestimmt was im Internet.

Grammatik

Wohin?/Wo? With the prepositions **auf**, **an** and **in** the accusative is used when the sense is 'to', the dative is used when the sense is 'at'.

ins Ausland/im Ausland	abroad (to/at)
an die See/an der See	to the seaside/at the seaside
aufs Land/auf dem Land<u>e</u>	to the country(side)/in the country(side)

12 Was kann man an der Nordseeküste machen?

a Eva and Max have decided to spend their summer holiday in Ostfriesland, on the North Sea coast. They are interviewed for a radio travel programme.

Given the location, decide which of these activities they are likely to be looking forward to, then check on the recording to see if you were right!

tanzen

Ski fahren

lesen

einkaufen

fernsehen

schwimmen

wandern

Rad fahren

segeln

bergsteigen

in der Sonne liegen

Kunstgalerien besuchen

Die ostfriesische Küste

Freizeit: Bootvermietung
Fahrradvermietung
Wanderungen
Ausflüge

Unterkunft: Hotels
Pensionen
Apartments
Ferienwohnungen
Campingplätze

b Diskussion in Kleingruppen: 20 Minuten Vorbereitungszeit. Urlaub – an der See oder auf dem Lande?

13 Und du/Sie?

Find out what your partner is doing this summer, when he/she is going away and what he/she is planning to do.

Was machst du/machen Sie…?   *Wohin …?*
Wann gehst du/gehen Sie …?   *Was kann man dort machen?*

14 Meine Sommerpläne

Draft an email to a German friend describing what you are doing this summer.

Extra!

15 Hoffnungen und Realität

a You will hear four people talk on a radio programme about their hopes when they were younger, and how their lives developed in reality. Draw up a grid with the headings given below, then listen carefully and note down in English their hopes and current situations in key words.

	Hopes	Reality
Helga Stein		
Benjamin Blume		
Renate Otto		
Dietmar Lang		

b Using the information collected in your grid, write a short account in German of each person's life at present and their hopes.

16 Das Ende der DDR

> Zwischen 1949 und 1990 hat es zwei deutsche Staaten gegeben, die Bundesrepublik Deutschland im Westen und die Deutsche Demokratische Republik im Osten. Die kommunistische Regierung der DDR hat 1961 eine Mauer zwischen den Staaten gebaut, weil Tausende von Menschen die DDR verlassen haben, um ein neues Leben im Westen zu suchen.
>
> DDR-Bürger durften nicht in den Westen fahren, wie sie wollten. Man konnte Verwandte nur selten sehen. Im Jahre 1989 haben Hunderttausende demonstriert, besonders in Leipzig. Sie wollten mehr Freiheit, vor allem die Freiheit zu reisen. Am Ende hat die Regierung verstanden, dass sie das kommunistische System reformieren musste. Am 9. November 1989 hat sie die Reisefreiheit eingeführt. Am selben Abend sind die Ost-Berliner zur Mauer gegangen – sie wollten den Westen sofort sehen! Das war das Ende der Mauer.
>
> Es war auch das Ende des Staates DDR. Die Bürger haben in den freien Wahlen vom März 1990 für Parteien gewählt, die eine schnelle Vereinigung wollten. Die ökonomische Situation der DDR war katastrophal. Im Oktober sind aus dem Territorium der DDR und Berlins fünf neue Bundesländer der Bundesrepublik Deutschland geworden.

Try out your reading skills. Remember, you are not being asked to translate but to show that you have understood information. Resist the temptation to focus on what you don't know! Read the whole text, then compare your understanding with a partner's.

Grammatik

~ The genitive ▶ G4.4

masculine	**Er ist ein alter Freund meines Vaters.** (note **-s** on the noun!)
	He is an old friend of my father.
feminine	**Das ist das neue Auto seiner Mutter.**
	That is his mother's new car.
neuter	**Hast du ein Foto deines Babys?** (note **-s** on the noun!)
	Have you a photo of your baby?
plural	**Von hier kann man das Haus unserer Eltern sehen.**
	From here you can see our parents' house.

The pattern is the same for the definite article:

die Jacke des Lehrers (m); **der Parkplatz der Bibliothek** (f);
das Ende des Semesters (n); **die Ankunft der Züge** (pl).

~ Adjective endings and the comparative ▶ G8

1 German adjectives on their own after the verb 'to be' have no ending:

Sein Computer ist neu; die Schule ist modern; das Bier ist kalt; die Kinder sind müde.

2 They do take an ending after an article or possessive. For example, here is the indefinite article/possessive pattern in the nominative singular:

ein neuer Computer (m); **eine moderne Schule** (f); **ein kaltes Bier** (n).

3 In the accusative only the masculine is different: **einen neuen Computer**.

4 Similarly, the *comparative* form of an adjective ('older', 'more intelligent'), which always ends in **-er**, has no further ending in statements such as:

Der Wein ist billiger in Italien. The wine is cheaper in Italy.
Alles ist viel schwieriger. Everything is much more difficult.

5 After an article or possessive it adds the adjectival ending to the existing **-er**:

ein besserer Film (m) a better film/*accusative*: **einen besseren Film**
eine interessantere Stelle (f) a more interesting job
ein größeres Haus (n) a bigger house

6 Some adjectives add an umlaut in the comparative (**groß** → **größer**).

Note: **schlechtere Chancen** worse chances.

~ dürfen (to be allowed to, may) ▶ G14.4, G17

Dürfen has an irregular present tense along the same lines as the other modals, **müssen**, **können** and **wollen**.

Darf ich rauchen? May I smoke?

ich darf, du darfst, er/sie/es darf, wir/Sie/sie dürfen, ihr dürft.
Simple past: **ich durfte.**

Grammatikübungen

1 In the following exercise **von** and the dative is used to express the same idea as the genitive. Change into the genitive.

Example: Ein alter Freund von meinem Vater → Ein alter Freund meines Vaters.

   a Ein alter Freund von meiner Schwester. _____
   b Eine Freundin von seinem Bruder. _____
   c Der Anfang von dem Semester. _____
   d Die Handtasche von unserer Lehrerin. _____
   e Die Bücher von den Studenten. _____
   f Das Schlafzimmer von meinem Sohn. _____
   g Der Parkplatz von dem Sportzentrum. _____
   h Ein Foto von dem Baby. _____

2 Complete the following sentences with an appropriate comparative form from the list at the end of each paragraph. Make sure the adjectival ending, if any is needed, is correct.

Ich würde gern einen **a** _____ Job finden. In der Buchhandlung ist alles jetzt viel **b** _____. Der neue Boss ist **c** _____ und ich habe endlich einen **d** _____ Computer. Aber ich brauche mehr Geld: ich möchte ein **e** _____ Haus kaufen, weil wir ein neues Baby haben.

> **a** interessanteren/interessanter   **b** besser/besseren/besseres
> **c** netter/netterer/netteren   **d** schneller/schnelleren   **e** größeren/größeres/größer

Unsere Kinder haben **f** _____ Chancen, eine Stelle zu finden. Vor der Wiedervereinigung waren die Mieten **g** _____ und die Leute **h** _____. Ich hatte ein **i** _____ Leben als jetzt.

> **f** schlechter/schlechtere   **g** billigere/billiger   **h** glücklichere/glücklicher
> **i** angenehmeren/angenehmer/angenehmeres

3 Your friend Sean has been advised by his doctor to adopt a healthier lifestyle. Explain in an email to your German friend Klaus that Sean:

> may not eat chips, but has to eat fruit and vegetables and drink mineral water, isn't allowed to drink beer or wine, has to go for walks and must not smoke.

Bayern

Vokabeln

See Appendix on p. 191 for vocabulary from exercises 11–12 and caption p. 112.

Aufgabe 1

die Betriebswirtschaft	business management
die Politik	politics
die Abwechslung	variety
das Leben	life
Großbritannien	Great Britain
besser als	better than
regnerisch	rainy
das Wetter	weather
im Norden	in the North
melancholisch	melancholy
Warst du schon in …?	Have you ever been to …?
letztes Jahr	last year
das Klima	climate
die Leute *pl*	people

Aufgabe 2

die Atmosphäre	atmosphere
der Boss	boss
jeder	each (one)
billiger	cheaper
angenehm	pleasant
freundlicher	more friendly
kommunikativer	more communicative
das Straßencafé	pavement café
Städte *pl*	towns
die Kultur	culture
größer	bigger
mieten	to rent

Aufgabe 4

der Sinn für Humor	sense of humour
groß	(here =) tall
sportlich	sporty
der Federball	badminton
außerdem	besides
das Interesse an	interest in
Gespräche *pl*	conversations
modisch	fashionable
jeden Tag	every day
reisen	to travel
weggehen *sep*	to go away
öfters	often
unabhängig	independent

Aufgabe 7

Hoffnungen *pl*	hopes
die Zeitschrift	magazine
die Wiedervereinigung	reunification (of Germany, 1990)
Verwandte *pl*	relatives
alle	all, everybody
Vorteile *pl*	advantages
gebracht	pp of bringen
die Freiheit	freedom
die Auswahl	selection, choice
offener	more open
Nachteile *pl*	disadvantages
relativ	relatively
gut bezahlt	well paid
arbeitslos	unemployed
der Teilzeitjob	part-time job
vorher	previously
Jugendliche *pl*	young people
die Miete	rent
teurer	dearer
ganz anders	totally different
damals	at that time
die Zukunft	future
eigentlich	really, actually
zufrieden	content
gedacht	pp of denken
aufhören *sep*	to finish
verloren	pp of verlieren
verlieren	to lose
der Schock	shock
sich freuen	to be glad
schlechter	worse
leicht	easy
die Hochzeit	wedding
schwieriger	more difficult

Aufgabe 8

wenig	little, not much
die Kriminalität	criminality
Drogen *pl*	drugs

Aufgabe 10

die Sonne	sun
danach	after that
der Urlaub	holiday
in Urlaub fahren	to go on holiday

Aufgabe 11

wissen	to know (facts)
sicher	sure, certain
Südeuropa	Southern Europe

Partnerarbeit

1 Auf dem Auslandsamt/At the International Office

In this role-play, you are applying to spend a year of your studies working abroad and you go for an interview with the representative of a German firm which receives students on placement. The aim is to sustain a conversation about your reasons for wanting to work abroad and your plans for the future.

Take time to prepare for the interview. Do not refer to any notes during the role-play. The list below will give you some ideas.

Partner B starts the conversation off.

NB: Remember to use the correct verb forms!

- sich für die Kultur des Landes interessieren
- Sprachkenntnisse verbessern
- Erfahrungen in der Arbeitswelt sammeln
- ein anderes Land kennen lernen
- mit anderen Menschen zusammenarbeiten
- unabhängiger werden
- Abwechslung haben
- eine andere Lebensart/Küche kennen lernen
- bessere Chancen auf dem Arbeitsmarkt haben
- den Lebenslauf verbessern
- Flexibilität zeigen
- Geld verdienen
- ich möchte in … arbeiten, weil …

Mathildenhöhe Darmstadt

2 Im Ausland arbeiten – ja oder nein?

Discuss with your partner the advantages and disadvantages of living and working abroad. Take 10 minutes to prepare, summarising your points *for* working abroad in key words. Then discuss the question with your partner (who will argue against it), trying to respond to the arguments brought forward by him/her. You start the discussion.

Argumente dafür/ja

Ich glaube, dass …/Ich denke, dass …	I think that … (Beware word order!)
Meiner Meinung nach (*verb*) …	In my opinion …
Das ist nicht richtig, weil …	That is wrong because …
Du hast Recht, (aber …)	You are right (but…)
Das stimmt, (aber …)	You are right (but…)

Partnerarbeit

1 Auf dem Auslandsamt/At the International Office

In this role-play, you are interviewing someone who has applied to work abroad for a year during their time at university. You ask questions in order to find out why he/she wants to do this and what his/her plans for the future are. Take time to prepare for the conversation but do not use any notes during it: refer to the checklist below. Begin with these items, and ask two further appropriate questions of your own. The aim is to sustain conversation successfully.

You start the conversation. Remember to use **Sie**, not **du**.

- Warum möchten Sie im Ausland arbeiten (mehrere Gründe!)
- persönliche Motivation
- Welche Vorteile bringt das Jahr im Ausland?
- In welchem Land möchten Sie arbeiten? Warum?

Bayern

2 Im Ausland arbeiten – ja oder nein?

Discuss with your partner the advantages and disadvantages of living and working abroad. Take 10 minutes, summarising arguments *against* the notion in key-words. Then discuss the question with your partner (who will argue for it), trying to respond to the arguments brought forward by him/her. Partner A starts the discussion.

Argumente dagegen/nein

Ich glaube, dass …/Ich denke, dass …	I think that … (Beware word order!)
Meiner Meinung nach (*verb*) …	In my opinion …
Das ist nicht richtig, weil …	That is wrong because …
Du hast Recht, (aber …)	You are right (but…)
Das stimmt, aber …	You are right (but…)

Weitere Übungen
FURTHER PRACTICE

1 Studenten

  1 Länder/Countries

Give the missing countries or inhabitants.

a Deutschland   Deutscher/Deutsche   **f** _____   Österreicher(in)

b England   _____   **g** Schottland   _____

c Frankreich   _____   **h** Irland   _____

d _____   Spanier(in)   **i** _____   Belgier(in)

e Italien   _____

 2 Sommerkurs/Summer course

Below is a completed registration form for a German language summer school. How much of the information can you give in complete German sentences? Use the pronoun **sie** (she), e.g. *Sie heißt …*

SOMMERKURS „DEUTSCH LERNEN IN BONN AM RHEIN"	
Familienname *Jenkinson*	Vorname *Anne*
Wohnort *Oxford*	Land *England*
Beruf *Sekretärin*	

 3 Wer ist das?

Expand the following information into full sentences for each person. Do so first in sentences beginning **ich** 'I', as if you were the person concerned, then in sentences about each person, beginning **er** 'he' or **sie** 'she'. The sentences are on the recording for you to check your responses.

Name	aus …	Nationalität	Wohnort	Beruf
Lisa	Carlisle	Eng…	Sheffield	Studentin
Paul	Aberdeen	Schott…	Dortmund	Lehrer
Corinne	Lille	Franz…	München	Sekretärin
Wolfgang	Lüneburg	Deuts…	Hamburg	Busfahrer

4 Anja und David

Summarise in English the information the two people give about themselves during their conversation.

5 Brief von Alex/Letter from Alex

You receive the following message from a student. Give the contents in English.

```
Lieber (plus your name if m) or Liebe (plus your name if f)

Hallo! Mein Name ist Alex und ich komme aus Russland. Ich
studiere Geschichte und Politik. Ich bin auch Barmann im
Red Lion. Ich wohne in Redman Street. Ich lerne Deutsch. Die
Lehrerin ist Deutsche und heißt Frau Wolters. Kommst du aus
Deutschland oder lernst du Deutsch?

Alex
```

6 Brief an Alex/Letter to Alex

Reply to Alex. If you ask any questions, use the informal **du**.

L 7 Jutta und Peter

Fill in the gaps.

Das ist Peter Müller. Er **a** _____ aus Essen, er wohnt
b _____ Frankfurt am Main. Er **c** _____ als
Englischlehrer.

Jutta Schneider ist Peters **d** _____. Sie wohnt mit Peter in der
Taunusstraße und **e** _____ Psychologie an der Johann-Wolfgang-
Goethe-Universität in Frankfurt. Sie arbeitet **f** _____ Kellnerin in der
Studenten-Bar „Szene".

2 Bibliothek oder Diskothek?

1 Zahlen/Numbers

Say the numbers out loud, then check them on the recording

32   44   76   59   81   23   67   55

2 Wie viel Uhr ist es?

Write down (in figures) the times you hear.

a _____   b _____   c _____   d _____   e _____   f _____

3 Am Morgen

Listen to the account of a student's morning and give the information in English.

4 Wann hast du Zeit?/When are you free?

You are trying to arrange a meeting with a German friend. You receive the following email. What is he doing today? When does he seem to be free?

Heute habe ich am Morgen eine Vorlesung und ein Seminar. Ich gehe um 14 Uhr in das Sportzentrum und spiele Fußball. Trinkst du um 16 Uhr Kaffee? – Ich gehe in die Mensa. Die Englischstunde ist um 17 Uhr. Wann gehst du heute Abend nach Hause?

Ralf

5 Hallo, Ralf!

You ring Ralf. Speak after the prompts on the recording.

6 Ralfs Abend

Using the outline, describe Ralf's evening.

18.00	fernsehen
20.00	ausgehen/Stadt
20.30	Kneipe/Bier trinken
22.15	Diskothek/tanzen
1.00	nach Hause
1.45	ins Bett gehen

7 Schreiben/Writing

Make complete sentences. Remember to check word order. Use the correct form of the verb given here in the infinitive.

a ich	immer	zu Hause	bleiben.	
b du	oft	Musik	hören?	
c sie	manchmal	ein Buch	lesen	
d er	selten	fernsehen		
e Sie	nie	ausgehen?		

 8 Wortsuche/Wordsearch

Go through Unit 2 again and find as many nouns as you can which designate food and drink. Remember to give the definite article, too!

 9 Jutta und Peter

Fill in the gaps.

Peter Müller steht immer **a** _____ 6.30 Uhr auf. Zum
b _____ isst er Toast mit Butter und er **c** _____
eine Tasse Kaffee. Er hört Radio und um 7.30 Uhr **d** _____ er zur Arbeit.
Mittags isst er normalerweise ein **e** _____ und er trinkt eine Cola.
Um 15 Uhr geht Peter nach **f** _____. Er **g** _____
E-Mails und manchmal geht er in das Sportzentrum – er ist sehr fit! Peter
h _____ oft Basketball und Fußball. Abends **i** _____
er oft zu Hause und **j** _____ fern, zum Beispiel amerikanische Filme.

Jutta Schneider steht um 7.30 Uhr auf. Sie trinkt morgens Tee und isst ein Joghurt. Um 10
Uhr geht Jutta an die **k** _____ – die Vorlesung ist interessant. Um 12 Uhr
geht sie immer in die **l** _____ und isst Pizza oder Omelett. Nachmittags
m _____ Jutta Spanisch. Die Spanischstunde **n** _____
um 14 Uhr. Manchmal geht Jutta in die Stadt und kauft für das Abendessen ein: Wein,
Nudeln, Tomaten und Salat. Zu Hause **o** _____ sie Musik und
p _____ ein Buch. Abends arbeitet sie oft in der Studentenbar und sie
q _____ selten zu Hause. Sie geht in die **r** _____ und
tanzt. Um 0.30 Uhr geht Jutta ins Bett.

3 Familie

 1 Fragen und Antworten/Questions and answers

Here are the answers: what were the questions?

a Nein, ich bin ledig.

b Meine Freundin heißt Tina.

c Ja. Ich habe einen Sohn und eine Tochter.

d Ich bin Bibliothekar.

e Meine Mutter ist Architektin.

f Mein Großvater ist 81.

 2 Stimmt das?/Is that right?

Look at Stephanie's family album on page 25 and decide whether these statements are true (**richtig**) or false (**falsch**). Where necessary, correct the statement.

a Andreas hat keinen Sohn. richtig/falsch

b Christian ist Stephanies Großvater. richtig/falsch

c Jessica ist Carolines Schwester. richtig/falsch

d Stephanie hat zwei Schwestern. richtig/falsch

e Martina hat zwei Töchter. richtig/falsch

f Stephanie hat einen Bruder. richtig/falsch

g Caroline ist ledig. richtig/falsch

 3 Eine Familie

Listen to Dieter describing his family and sketch out a family tree.
Here are the names you will need: Ana/Carsten/Barbara/Silvia/Clara.

L 4 Mein oder dein?

Fill in the gaps with the correct form of the possessive from the list on the right.
Each word must be used once.

a Sie besuchen _____ Großeltern in Spanien.

b _____ Moped ist neu.

c _____ Tochter ist noch klein.

d Wir brauchen _____ Computer.

e Wie alt ist _____ Bruder?

| seine |
| dein |
| ihre |
| mein |
| unseren |

 5 Passt das?/Does that belong here?

a Which is the odd word out in each group?

b Give the gender of each noun. Check in the vocabulary at the end of the book where necessary.

i Fahrrad/Auto/Moped/Schwimmbad

ii Fernseher/E-Mail/Handy/Computer

iii Tochter/Bruder/Sohn/Vater

iv Radio/Film/CD-Spieler/Handy

6 Dialog im Schwimmbad

Complete this dialogue with the help of the English prompts, then listen to the conversation on the recording.

– Hallo, Claudia. Sag mal, wo ist denn deine Schwester?
– *My sister is at home. She is watching* TV.
– Und was macht dein Bruder?
– *My brother is working. He goes to the library in the mornings.* …
  I *have got his Beatles* CD. *Have you got your* CD *player?*
– Ja, den habe ich … Komm, wir hören die CD. Sie ist sehr gut.
– *What are you doing this afternoon?*
– Meine Eltern sind in Marburg und wir gehen ins Restaurant.
– I *never go to the restaurant. We always eat at home!*
– … Oh je, wie spät ist es denn?
– *It is almost one o'clock … why?*
– [in a panic] So spät! Aber wir gehen um 1.30 Uhr ins Restaurant …
– *Have you got your car?*
– Nein, ich habe mein Fahrrad!

7 Jutta und Peter

Fill in the gaps.

Juttas Familie ist groß – sie hat zwei Schwestern und einen **a** _____.
Ihr Bruder **b** _____ Jürgen und er ist verheiratet. Er hat
c _____ Kinder, aber er hat drei Katzen. Juttas große Schwester
Martina ist neunundzwanzig Jahre alt. Sie hat zwei **d** _____, Julia
und Klaus. Sie sind noch **e** _____ und gehen in den Kindergarten.
Martinas Mann ist Informatiker von **f** _____. Jutta ist
dreiundzwanzig Jahre alt und sie ist **g** _____, aber sie hat einen
Freund, Peter. Juttas „kleine" Schwester Ingrid ist zwanzig Jahre alt und sie studiert
Theaterwissenschaft, das ist sehr interessant. Jutta geht oft abends ins Theater. Theater
und Musik sind ihre **h** _____.

Peters Familie ist klein und er hat keine **i** _____. Manchmal besucht
er seine **j** _____. Sie wohnen in Offenbach und sie sind Rentner.
Peter hat ein Auto, aber Jutta hat ein **k** _____ – das ist sehr gesund!
Peter schreibt oft E-Mails und er braucht **l** _____ Computer. Seine
Hobbys sind Sport, Filme und Computerspiele. Normalerweise **m** _____
er abends zu Hause und manchmal sieht er mit Michael einen Film. Michael ist sein
Freund und er **n** _____ auch in Frankfurt. Michael und Peter
o _____ oft Pizza und trinken ein Bier. Abends
p _____ Jutta und Peter manchmal in ein Restaurant – „Bella Italia".
Das Restaurant ist sehr gut und Spaghetti Napoli fantastisch!

4 Am Wochenende

L 🎧 1 Was machst du gern am Wochenende?

Decide which verb form goes in which space, then check your decision by listening to the recording.

Silvia   Ich **a** _____ spät _____ Ich **b** _____ gern zu Hause
und **c** _____ oder **d** _____ Musik …

Anna   Und du **e** _____ .

Silvia   Ja, ich **f** _____ gern.

Anna   Ich **g** _____ nicht gern zu Hause. Samstags **h** _____ ich in die
Stadt – ich **i** _____ gern _____ . Manchmal **j** _____
ich mit Markus _____ . Er **k** _____ gern Auto.

gehe	lese	fährt	kochst	kaufe … ein
höre	gehe … aus	koche	stehe … auf	bleibe × 2

✏️ 2 Das mache ich gern

Write to Katrin outlining your likes and preferences: you like going to the cinema, reading and shopping. You like walking but prefer cycling. What you like doing most of all at the weekend is cooking. You like smoking – but you do not like drinking wine or beer.
Ask her if she likes cooking.

L 3 Wann denn?

Fill in the gaps with the words below.

Wann **a** _____ Heinz mit Anja **b** _____ ? Am Montag und am
Dienstag **c** _____ er für sein Examen **d** _____ .
e _____ spielt sie Badminton. Am Donnerstag hat er **f** _____
Zeit: Seine Spanischstunde ist um 6 Uhr und dann **g** _____ er mit Martin
und Paul in die Kneipe **h** _____ . Am Freitag **i** _____ Anja
mit Sandra **j** _____ Theater und am Wochenende besucht sie ihre
k _____ in München.

geht	Mittwochs	kann	ins	arbeiten	will
Eltern	ausgehen	keine	muss	gehen	

🎧 4 Willst du mitkommen?

Listen to the short conversation between Anna and Christian and summarise what happens in English. Then check the answer at the end of the book.

5 Im Restaurant

Reconstruct the dialogue by putting what the diner and waiter say into the correct order. Then check by listening to the recording.

a Und was möchten Sie trinken?

b Ja, ich nehme den Tomatensalat, bitte.

c Guten Abend.

d Danke, das ist alles.

e Was bekommen Sie?

f Guten Abend, haben Sie einen Tisch für eine Person?

g Ja, hier am Fenster.

h Ich möchte das Steak, bitte

i Möchten Sie auch einen Salat?

j Danke.

k Sonst noch etwas?

l Ein Bier, bitte.

L 6 Jutta und Peter

Fill in the gaps.

Heute **a** _____ gehen Jutta und Peter ins Restaurant „Bella Italia". Jutta geht besonders **b** _____ italienisch essen, und auch Peter isst gern Pizza und Spaghetti. Um **c** _____ nach acht treffen sie Michael – Peters Freund – und um halb neun sind sie im Restaurant. Sie nehmen den **d** _____ am Fenster und der Kellner bringt die **e** _____. Jutta **f** _____ immer Spaghetti Napoli, aber Peter isst **g** _____ Pizza. Michael möchte Huhn mit Sahnesauce und einen Salat. Die drei Freunde wollen auch etwas **h** _____, und der Kellner bringt die Weinkarte. „Wir nehmen **i** _____ Rotwein Nummer 14", sagt Peter.

Das Essen ist **j** _____ und der Wein ist auch sehr gut. Um zwanzig vor zehn gehen Jutta, Peter und Michael. „Wir haben noch **k** _____ – was wollen wir machen?", sagt Jutta. Michael möchte gern in die Studentenbar „Szene" gehen, aber Jutta **l** _____ lieber tanzen! Der Kompromiss: Sie gehen in die Diskothek und um 11 Uhr in die Bar. Dort können sie noch ein Glas **m** _____ trinken und Freunde treffen. Um halb eins gehen sie nach **n** _____, denn morgen ist Donnerstag und Peter muss um halb sieben **o** _____ – das ist sehr früh! Michael muss auch früh arbeiten. Er ist Techniker von Beruf und arbeitet bei Siemens. Jutta **p** _____ bis neun Uhr schlafen. Ihre Vorlesung **q** _____ um 10 Uhr.

5 Zu Hause

 1 Wer wohnt da?/Who lives there?

Read carefully the descriptions of three different sets of people. Decide which set of people lives in the room illustrated. Give the reasons for your decision in German, and add a brief description of the room.

a Klaus und Marianne Schubert sind verheiratet und haben ein Kind. Ihre Tochter Annelie ist drei Jahre alt und geht in den Kindergarten. Klaus ist Ingenieur und muss jeden Tag eine halbe Stunde zur Arbeit fahren. Die Familie hat zwei Autos, denn Marianne muss Annelie jeden Tag in den Kindergarten bringen und dann zu ihrer Arbeit fahren. Sie arbeitet von 9 Uhr bis 12 Uhr in einem Eiscafé.

b Herr und Frau Werner sind Rentner. Sie haben zwei Töchter und drei Enkelkinder, aber jetzt wohnen sie natürlich allein – fast allein, denn sie haben einen Hund. Der Hund heißt Fido und geht gern spazieren. Herr und Frau Werner fahren manchmal Rad, und sie lesen gern und telefonieren oft. Sie haben kein Auto, denn sie wohnen im Stadtzentrum.

c Ulrike, Thomas und Jürgen sind Studenten in Leipzig. Ulrike studiert Architektur, und Thomas und Jürgen studieren Computerwissenschaften. Alle drei schlafen morgens gern lange und gehen abends oft aus. Sie kochen viel, denn Restaurants sind teuer. Sie waschen aber nicht gern ab und putzen auch nicht oft. Sie wohnen zentral und fahren normalerweise mit dem Fahrrad zur Universität. Sie brauchen kein Auto, aber Thomas hat ein altes Moped.

 2 Ute Schneiders Wohnung

Listen to Ute talking about her flat in Bremen. Describe in German (**a**) the living room and (**b**) the kitchen. You will probably need to listen to the recording more than once.

3 Einladung

Listen to the telephone conversation between Christine and Axel and answer the questions.

a Wann will Christine grillen, und warum?

b Wo grillt sie?

c Was bringt Axel mit?

d Was braucht Christine noch?

e Wo muss Axel am Freitag einkaufen?

f Was macht Christine zum Essen?

g Wer kommt zum Barbecue?

h Warum muss Axel gehen?

4 Wo?

Read the sentences below carefully: the locations are mixed up – put each in the correct sentence so they all make better sense.

a Wir wohnen *im Restaurant*.

b Ich arbeite *in der Bismarckstraße*.

c Man kocht *auf einem Stuhl*.

d Sie essen *am Schreibtisch*.

e Er sitzt *in der Garage*.

f Das Auto ist *in der Diskothek*.

g Petra steht *in der Küche*.

h Ich tanze gern *unter der Dusche*.

PRINZ-CHRISTIANS-WEG
13 – 25

5 Jutta und Peter

Fill in the gaps.

Jutta arbeitet nachmittags oft in der Universitätsbibliothek. Heute geht sie auch in die Bibliothek, aber um vier Uhr will sie in die **a** _____ gehen. Sie muss eine gute Flasche **b** _____ kaufen, denn heute Abend gehen Jutta und Peter zu Michael. Michael hat eine neue **c** _____, im Prinz-Christians-Weg 25. Michael kocht ein gutes **d** _____, und seine Freunde bringen Wein und Bier mit. Um acht Uhr **e** _____ die Party – Musik gibt es auch. Michael hat ein sehr **f** _____ Wohnzimmer und man kann tanzen. Aber jetzt gibt es Essen! Michael kocht gern französisch, und heute **g** _____ es Quiche und Salat, mit Rotwein von Jutta. Das Esszimmer ist **h** _____ und gemütlich – es gibt sechs alte Stühle von Michaels **i** _____, einen Tisch und eine altmodische **j** _____.

Die Freunde sind jetzt **k** _____ Wohnzimmer und tanzen. Jutta tanzt sehr **l** _____, aber Peter will nach Hause gehen. Er muss früh **m** _____ und arbeiten. „Was machen **n** _____?", fragt Jutta. „Ich will jetzt ins Bett!", sagt Peter. „Stop – ihr müsst hier bleiben … ", sagt Michael. In Michaels Wohnung stehen Bierflaschen **o** _____ dem Fernseher, es gibt Gläser **p** _____ dem Stuhl und Tassen **q** _____ dem Computer. „Ich **r** _____ nicht allein aufräumen!", sagt Michael.

6 In der Stadt

 1 Wo ist das Krankenhaus?

Summarise in English the directions given.

 2 Gibt es eine Bank in der Nähe?

Listen to the prompts and speak in the gaps.

 3 Das Geburtstagsgeschenk/The birthday present

a Answer the questions, without looking at the script:

   i Where are Marco and Fatma meeting?

   ii Where is the bookshop?

   iii What will Marco find there?

   iv Where is the flower shop?

b Now read the script to confirm your answers to **a**, and find the German equivalent of 'bouquet'.

Marco:	Es ist Fatmas Geburtstag heute, ich treffe sie in einer Stunde und ich habe kein Geschenk für sie!
Heike:	Wo triffst du sie?
Marco:	Vor dem Bahnhof.
Heike:	Einfach! … Am Bahnhof gibt's eine Buchhandlung. Fatma liest gern Krimis – du findest ganz bestimmt etwas für sie. … Und neben der Buchhandlung ist ein Blumengeschäft. Kauf einen schönen Blumenstrauß!
Marco:	Genial!

 4 Die Jacke kann ich nicht kaufen

Without referring to the script, listen to the recording and answer the true/false questions. Then check your answers by reading the script. Alter them where necessary!

Julia und Hans sind im Kaufhaus.

Richtig/falsch:

a Hans nimmt die Jacke.

b Die Jacke gefällt Julia nicht.

c Die Jacke ist zu groß.

d Die Jacke ist nicht zu teuer.

e Karin kauft die Jacke.

H: Nimm diese blaue Jacke!
J: Ich weiß nicht …
H: Gefällt sie dir nicht?
J: Nein … sie gefällt mir sehr.
H: Ist das nicht deine Größe?
J: Nein … die Größe ist richtig.
H: Ist sie zu teuer?
J: Nein … sie kostet nur 81,50 Euro.
H: Also … warum kaufst du sie nicht?
J: Die Jacke kann ich nicht kaufen – Karin hat so eine!

5 Einkaufsbummel/Shopping trip

Ulrike and Klaus are going shopping. Listen to the dialogue and answer the following questions in English.

a What does Ulrike need?
b Why does Klaus object? (4 reasons)
c What would he rather buy with the money?
d What size is the garment?
e Where will Ulrike and Klaus meet?

L 6 Jutta und Peter

Fill in the gaps.

Heute ist Samstag, und wie jeden Samstag wollen Jutta und Peter in die
a _____ gehen und einkaufen. Jetzt ist es schon 11
b _____ , und sie sind mit dem Frühstück fertig. „Fahren wir mit dem
c _____ oder laufen wir in die Stadt?", fragt Peter. „Wir laufen, denn
samstags ist das Parkhaus immer voll. Wir können aber auch mit dem
d _____ fahren." „Das ist zu teuer – das kostet 4,50 Euro. … Wir
laufen." Jutta und Peter wohnen in der **e** _____ von der Innenstadt,
und nach 20 Minuten sind sie im Zentrum. „Was brauchen wir?", fragt Jutta. „Wir müssen
Essen fürs Wochenende kaufen, und ich will heute **f** _____ einen
guten Film sehen … also erst in die Videothek, und dann zum **g** _____."
Jutta will auch in ein Blumengeschäft **h** _____ – morgen ist
Muttertag, und sie braucht ein Geschenk für ihre Mutter. Aber sie hat kein Geld   also
müssen die beiden zur Bank gehen. Die Bank ist um die **i** _____ ,
und neben **j** _____ Bank ist die Videothek. Jutta kauft den Strauß
für ihre Mutter, und dann **k** _____ sie Peter vor dem Café. „Und was
ist mit deiner Mutter?" fragt Jutta. „Meine Mutter … ich weiß nicht, ich habe keine Idee."
„Männer!"

7 Fahren

1 Paola

a On the train to Bonn Vijay gets to know Paola. What do you think he asks her to get the following answers?

   i Ich komme aus Rom.

   ii Ich lerne seit einem Jahr Deutsch.

   iii Weil ich im Ausland arbeiten will.

b Without looking at the text below, listen to the recording as the conversation continues. Answer the questions, then check your understanding against the text.

   i Wann kommt der Zug in Bonn an?

   ii Was macht Paola in Bonn?

   iii Warum?

   iv Was macht Vijay?

   P: … Ja, ich auch. Ich kann schon Französisch und jetzt …

   „Meine Damen und Herren, in wenigen Minuten erreichen wir Bonn Hauptbahnhof."

   P: Oh! Ich steige hier aus!

   V: Ich auch! Was machst du in Bonn?

   P: Ich mache einen Sprachkurs. Ich will mein Deutsch verbessern.

   V: Ich auch! Ich helfe dir mit den Koffern, wenn du willst.

   P: Oh ja, danke.

2 Der nächste Zug

Listen to the recording and take part in the dialogue, using the prompts given.

[L] 3 In den Sommerferien

Fill in the gaps in the letter.

a _____ 10. August fahre ich **b** _____ Bremen, um einen Sommerkurs zu **c** _____ . Ich lerne **d** _____ zwei Jahren Deutsch und will es **e** _____ . Der Kurs **f** _____ drei Wochen und man **g** _____ junge Leute aus der ganzen Welt kennen. Ich **h** _____ um 10.40 in Bremen an. Vom Flughafen fahre ich **i** _____ der Straßenbahn in die Stadtmitte. Ich **j** _____ dann mit dem Bus zur **k** _____ .

machen	mit	Universität	am	dauert	seit
fahre	nach	verbessern	lernt	komme	

4 Ich darf nicht zu spät kommen!/I mustn't be late!

a Listen to the dialogue between Axel and Michael, and then answer the questions.

   i Warum kann Axel nicht mit ins Sportzentrum kommen?
   ii Was will Klaus am Samstag machen?
   iii Wie müssen sie nach Köln fahren?
   iv Warum will Axel nicht nach Köln fahren?
   v Was will er am Freitag machen?
   vi Was will Klaus in der Stadt kaufen?

b And you? Write down what you must/can/want to do on particular days of the week.

 5 Ich kann nicht so viel trinken …/I can't drink that much …

Listen to Gabi and Karl-Heinz and decide if the statements are true (**richtig**) or false (**falsch**).

a Gabi will mit ins Schwimmbad kommen.   r/f
b Sie geht mit Karl-Heinz essen.   r/f
c Karl-Heinz will mit Gabi in die Kneipe gehen.   r/f
d Gabi trinkt gern Wein.   r/f
e Sie hat morgen Abend keine Zeit.   r/f

 6 Jutta und Peter

Fill in the gaps.

Heute ist der Freitag vor Ostern, und Jutta und Peter müssen zwei Wochen nicht **a** _____ , sie haben frei. Sie wollen für 10 Tage **b** _____ Cuxhaven fahren, denn sie haben eine Freundin dort und **c** _____ bei Sabine wohnen. Die Stadt ist sehr **d** _____ – direkt am Wasser! Jutta und Peter schwimmen gern, aber **e** _____ April ist das Wasser noch sehr kalt. Man **f** _____ in den Restaurants gut und billig Fisch essen, und man kann lange am Wasser **g** _____. Die Koffer sind fertig und sehr schwer – Jutta und Peter wollen nicht mit dem **h** _____ fahren, sie nehmen ein Taxi zum Bahnhof. Dort **i** _____ sie eine Fahrkarte kaufen. Jutta geht zum **j** _____ und sagt: „Zwei **k** _____ nach Cuxhaven, bitte." Aber das ist sehr kompliziert. Mit Bahncard ist der Fahrschein billiger, aber Jutta und Peter haben keine Bahncard. Sie **l** _____ kein TwenTicket kaufen, **m** _____ Peter 26 Jahre alt ist – man muss jünger als 25 sein. „Und ein Guten Abend-Ticket?" – „Nein", antwortet Jutta, „wir wollen vor 19 Uhr fahren." „Wollen Sie den Super-Sparpreis?" Aber dann kann **n** _____ nicht freitags oder sonntags fahren! „Und das Wochenendticket?" Dann können wir nur am **o** _____ fahren. „Vielleicht bleiben wir zu **p** _____!", sagt Peter.

8 Gestern

 1 Ich habe gelacht/I laughed

Read the following.

Ich bin gestern Abend spät ins Bett gegangen und habe gut geschlafen. Zu gut, denn ich bin heute Morgen spät aufgestanden. Ich habe nichts gegessen, nur ganz schnell ein Glas Wasser getrunken. Ich bin pünktlich um 7.30 an der Bushaltestelle angekommen, um ins Büro zu fahren. Erst dann habe ich gesehen, dass ich ganz allein war. „Oh Gott ... es ist Samstag. Ich arbeite heute nicht!", habe ich laut gesagt. Dann habe ich gelacht.

Cover the text and write an account of what happened in the **er-**form of the perfect tense, using the following prompts:

spät ins Bett gehen – gut schlafen – aufstehen – essen – trinken
7.30 Haltestelle ankommen – sehen – allein – „Samstag!" – sagen – lachen

 2 Mein Wochenende

„Wie war dein Wochenende?"

„Katastrophal! Man hat meine Kreditkarte gestohlen. Unsere Fußballmannschaft hat schlecht gespielt. Ich habe die Bücher für meinen Aufsatz nicht gefunden. … Und es hat stundenlang geregnet. Nächstes Wochenende bleibe ich im Bett!"

Give (in English) the negative features of this person's weekend. What conclusion does he draw?

 3 Warum (nicht)?

You haven't been able to join your friend(s)/fulfil obligations because of other pressing engagements. Match up the two halves of each sentence to give a credible excuse.

1 Ich habe am Freitag nicht Tennis gespielt,
2 Ich bin gestern nicht in die Vorlesung gegangen,
3 Ich habe Peter nicht angerufen,
4 Ich bin gestern nicht nach Hause gekommen,
5 Ich bin am Samstag nicht zu deinen Eltern gefahren,
6 Ich konnte nicht essen,

a ... weil meine Schwester mein Handy hat.
b ... weil ich samstags arbeite.
c ... weil der Professor so langweilig ist!
d ... weil ich die ganze Nacht in der Bibliothek war.
e ... weil ich Magenschmerzen hatte.
f ... weil ich nicht fit genug bin.

①
②
③

4 Gestern

The following sentences are in the present tense. Put them into the perfect. Make sure you know which verbs are strong and which weak, and which verbs take the auxiliary **sein**. Listen to the recording to check your version.

a Ich kaufe bei Aldi ein und koche für meine Freunde. Nach dem Essen hören wir Musik und später spielen wir Karten.

b Sie isst Brot mit Marmelade und trinkt eine Tasse Tee. Sie schreibt E-Mails an ihre Freunde. Dann liest sie die Zeitung.

c Ich stehe um sieben Uhr auf und fahre mit dem Bus zur Uni. Ich bleibe den ganzen Nachmittag in der Bibliothek. Ich suche ein Buch für meine Dissertation, aber finde es nicht.

L 5 Jutta und Peter

a Fill in the gaps.

Gestern war ein wichtiger Tag für Jutta und Peter: sie **a** _____ zu einem Rolling Stones Konzert nach Köln gefahren. Sie sind spät

b _____, so gegen halb elf, und haben dann gemütlich

c _____. Um drei Uhr mussten sie am

d _____ sein, weil samstags der schnelle ICE schon um 15.17 Uhr von Frankfurt nach Köln fährt. Peter war sehr aufgeregt, weil er ein großer Fan ist und die Stones noch nie live **e** _____ hat. Der Zug war pünktlich, die Fahrt angenehm, und um 17.32 Uhr sind Jutta und Peter in Köln

f _____. Sie **g** _____ noch viel Zeit – zwei Stunden! „Was wollen wir **h** _____?", hat Jutta gefragt. Peter hatte eine Idee: „Wir **i** _____ vielleicht in der Stadt in eine Kneipe gehen ..." Jutta war nicht enthusiastisch – sie wollte lieber den Dom sehen und am Rhein spazieren gehen. „Ich möchte nicht trinken oder rauchen. ... Ich will die Stadt

j _____." Jetzt war Peter enttäuscht: „Ein Kompromiss – ich gehe in die Kneipe, du **k** _____ zum Dom, und wir **l** _____ uns um zwanzig **m** _____ acht an der Konzerthalle." „OK", hat Jutta gesagt. Zwei Stunden später war Jutta am Eingang. Um acht Uhr war Peter immer noch nicht da! Um Viertel nach acht **n** _____ Peter endlich gekommen – viel zu spät! Das Konzert hat schon **o** _____, und Peter war sehr frustriert. „Meine Uhr ist kaputt – was machen wir denn jetzt?"

b Think of an ending to Jutta and Peter's story – what did they do when they realised that they could not see the concert? Write a short paragraph in German to conclude the story.

9 Lebensläufe

1 Wann?

Write out the following years in words, then check them on the recording.

a 1947 **b** 1921 **c** 2003 **d** 1912 **e** 1815 **f** 1993 **g** 1874 **h** 2005

2 Verben

The following sentences are in the present tense; put them into the perfect tense.

a Meine Eltern verstehen mich nicht.
b Seine Brüder studieren in Frankfurt.
c Er wird nach dem Studium Lehrer.
d Erhalten Sie gute Noten?
e Wir verlassen mit 16 die Schule.

3 Die Stelle gefällt mir nicht

a Ask the questions in this conversation, following the prompts on the recording.

b Listen to the conversation again and summarise in English what the interviewee tells you in reply.

4 Jobs!

Read the three job ads and decide for which of them the two people described are best suited.

a
> **Studenten!**
>
> Wir suchen selbständige Interviewer in der Marktforschung.
>
> Gute Bezahlung. Flexible Arbeitszeiten.
>
> Sie sind: Pünktlich, zuverlässig und mobil.

b
> **Fitness-Center** sucht Teamleiter/in für organisatorische und administrative Aufgaben.

c
> **SERVICE/BAR**
>
> Golfanlage „Schloss Jesinghausen"
> Wir suchen ab sofort Teil- oder Vollzeitkräfte.
>
> Nette, freundliche Persönlichkeit und soziale Kompetenz erforderlich.

Simon arbeitet am liebsten in einem Team. Er ist tolerant, populär und hat viel Humor. Er studiert Englisch und Sport.

Anja ist organisiert, fleißig und kommunikativ. Sie hat ein Auto. Sie studiert Soziologie.

5 Auf dem Arbeitsamt

a Listen to the conversation at the job centre and answer the following questions in English.

  i When did Herr Helwig do his **Abitur**, and what was his grade?
  ii For how long did he work as an ambulance driver?
  iii Why did he do nothing for a while?
  iv Where did he apply eventually?
  v What was his job?
  vi What are his qualities/abilities for the job market?
  vii What did he do on Lanzarote?

b Listen to the recording again. Can you finish it by formulating a suitable reply for Herr Helwig? What do you think he might want to do now?

6 Sie möchte gern ...

Finish the sentences by choosing a suitable reason from the list below.

Example: Ulrike möchte in der Bibliothek arbeiten, weil sie gern liest.

a Markus möchte im Krankenhaus arbeiten, weil …
b Carima möchte im Museum arbeiten, weil …
c Mehmet möchte im Sportzentrum arbeiten, weil …
d Helga möchte in einer Kneipe arbeiten, weil …
e Andreas möchte im Theater arbeiten, weil …

NB: The verbs must be put into an appropriate form as they are given in the infinitive below. Make sure your word order is right. And beware … there is one surplus reason in the list!

> gern sehr spät ins Bett gehen   sich für Literatur interessieren   sportlich sein
> gern anderen Menschen helfen   gut Englisch sprechen   sich für Bilder interessieren

7 Jutta und Peter

Fill in the gaps.

Jutta muss einen Ferienjob finden, weil sie kein **a** _____ mehr hat. Jutta und Peter **b** _____ gern im September nach Italien fahren, und Hotels sind teuer. Heute ist Samstag und Jutta **c** _____ beim Frühstück die Zeitung: „Peter, hier ist eine **d** _____ im Schwimmbad …" „Aber du **e** _____ doch überhaupt nicht gut schwimmen – das ist keine gute Idee." Jutta sieht eine andere Anzeige. „Im Krankenhaus suchen sie eine Küchenhilfe …" „Aber du kochst nicht gern, und du **f** _____ nicht gern ab." Jutta antwortet nicht. „Im Konferenzzentrum **g** _____ man Personal für die Cafeteria. ‚Muss abends arbeiten **h** _____'." „Nein!", sagt Peter „Nicht in den Ferien! Ich will **i** _____ abends sehen." Jetzt ist Jutta wirklich böse auf Peter. „OK, dann **j** _____ wir den ganzen Sommer zu Hause – ohne Geld keine Toskana!"

10 Zukunftspläne

1 Markus und die Zukunft/Markus and the future

L

a Choose the right words to fill the gaps. Note that there are three more words than you need in the list at the end!

Markus findet seine Arbeit in **a** _____ Buchhandlung
b _____ . Er **c** _____ gern im
d _____ arbeiten. Das **e** _____ in einem
südeuropäischen **f** _____ ist **g** _____ und
die Kultur ist **h** _____ . Markus **i** _____
einen **j** _____ machen, um **k** _____ zu
lernen. Er geht **l** _____ Ausland, um neue **m** _____
zu sammeln. Wenn er **n** _____ , **o** _____ er
hoffentlich mehr Geld!

Land	zurückkommt	nach	langweilig	ins	der	würde	Italienisch
will	Erfahrungen	Ausland	Leben	interessanter	verdient	Jobs	
angenehmer	Sprachkurs	Italien					

b Then translate the passage into English.

2 Die Badehose/The swimming trunks

Complete the text below with an appropriate form of a modal verb. Then check your answers by listening to the recording.

Oskar **a** _____ heute Nachmittag ins Kino gehen, aber das ist leider nicht möglich. Er **b** _____ seine Eltern besuchen, denn sein Vater hat heute Geburtstag. Leider hat Oskar noch kein Geschenk für ihn ... Panik! Er hat ihm schon oft Bücher gegeben, denn er arbeitet in einer Buchhandlung. Sein Vater **c** _____ keinen Alkohol trinken, also **d** _____ er ihm keine Flasche Wein kaufen. Da sein Vater keine Hobbys hat, ist es wirklich schwierig, ein schönes Geschenk für ihn zu finden. Aber Oskar hat eine Idee – sein Vater **e** _____ einmal in der Woche schwimmen gehen, denn er ist nicht fit genug. Also eine Badehose!

3 Urlaub in Norddeutschland/Holidays in Northern Germany

> ### Zwischen Nordsee und Ostsee – eine magische Landschaft
>
> Fahrradtouren durch Holstein …
>
> Malerische alte Dörfer, traditionelle Bauernhöfe, schöne Wälder und Seen, ruhige Strände, kleine Häfen … das ist Holstein.
>
> Informieren Sie sich auch über unsere Touren …   zu Fuß
> auf dem Wasser
> zu Pferde
>
> ### Zwischen Nordsee und Ostsee – eine magische Landschaft

a Dictionary work: try to find the singular of the seven plural nouns in the advertisement. What is noteworthy about the noun **See** (plural **Seen**)?

b How many different ways of forming the plural are represented here?

c Which of the adjectives do you think means 'picturesque'?

d On the basis of this information, describe what you can do and see in Holstein:

In Holstein kann man … (Remember the word order rule: infinitive to end!)

es gibt …

L 4 Jutta und Peter

Fill in the gaps.

Zum Glück hat Jutta am Anfang der Semesterferien einen guten **a** _____ gefunden, und so **b** _____ Jutta und Peter doch in die Toskana in Italien fahren. Sie sind sehr glücklich . „Wir müssen das Hotel bald buchen, um ein

c _____ Zimmer zu bekommen", sagt Peter. „Du hast Recht … Wir gehen morgen in die Stadt. Aber es gibt eine andere wichtige Frage: fahren wir

d _____ dem Auto, oder mit **e** _____ Zug?", fragt Jutta. „Wir können fliegen! Fliegen ist viel schneller, aber vielleicht **f** _____ als mit dem Auto. Wir können nach Florenz fliegen und dann ein Auto mieten – ich glaube, das ist der beste Plan." Jutta ist nicht zufrieden … „Aber mit dem

g _____, können wir **h** _____, wohin und wann wir wollen. Das finde ich viel besser. Außerdem muss man einen Flug früh buchen, und wir wissen noch nicht, an welchem Tag wir reisen wollen. Und wie kommen wir

i _____. Flughafen? Mein Vater kann uns nicht fahren,

j _____ meine Eltern sind auch in Urlaub. Und …" Jutta redet und redet.

Peter versteht das nicht. „Jutta, was ist denn **k** _____ Problem?" Nach einer langen Pause **l** _____ Jutta: „Ich habe Angst vor dem Fliegen." Peter lacht. „Jetzt kenne ich dich schon so lange, und ich habe nicht gewusst, dass du nicht **m** _____ fliegst! OK, dann fahren wir mit dem Auto …"

GUIDE TO GRAMMATICAL TERMS

Language learners often feel unsure about grammatical terms. The following list gives some simple definitions. Examples are underlined, and terms used which are defined elsewhere in the list are given in bold. Examples are drawn from English: reference is made to German only when something distinctive about that language needs to be noted. This Guide is concerned only with the meanings of grammatical terms: there is a German Grammar Summary beginning on page 147.

Accusative   In German, **case** used for the **direct object** and after certain **prepositions**.

Adjective   A word used to describe a **noun** ('an <u>interesting</u> woman', 'the curry is <u>hot</u>'). See also **demonstrative adjective**, **possessive adjective**.

Adverb   A word which describes the action of a **verb** ('she sings <u>beautifully</u>', 'he cooks <u>well</u>') or modifies (= gives further information about) an **adjective** ('it's a <u>really</u> expensive car') or another adverb ('she sings <u>really</u> well').

Article   <u>The</u> (called the definite article), <u>a</u> or <u>an</u> (the indefinite article).

Auxiliary verb   A **verb** combining with another verb to form a compound tense. ('She has gone' = perfect tense formed by combining the auxiliary verb 'to have' with the past participle of 'to go'.)

Case   In German, a category defined by function within the sentence. See **accusative**, **dative**, **genitive**, **nominative**.

Clause   Subdivision of a sentence. Every clause has a verb. See also **main clause**, **subordinate clause**.

Coordinating conjunction   A **conjunction** which joins two **clauses** of equal importance. ('The man is tall <u>and</u> his name is John.')

Comparative   Form of an **adjective** ('that room is <u>bigger</u> than this one'; 'they've bought a <u>more expensive</u> car') or **adverb** ('it happens <u>more often</u> than you think') expressing a greater or lesser degree.

Conjunction   A word which joins parts of a sentence ('he was tired <u>and</u> he wanted to go home'; 'they arrived early <u>because</u> they wanted a good seat'). See **coordinating conjunction**, **subordinating conjunction**.

Dative   In German, **case** used for the **indirect object** and after certain **prepositions**.

Demonstrative adjective   'Points out' **nouns** (<u>this</u> chair/<u>these</u> chairs; <u>that</u> house/<u>those</u> houses).

Direct object   The word which directly undergoes the action of the verb. In the sentence 'she sent her mother <u>a present</u>', what she sent was a present, so that is the direct object. She didn't send her mother! See also **indirect object**.

Gender   In German, all **nouns** have a grammatical **gender**, masculine, feminine or neuter.

Genitive   In German, **case** expressing ownership, belonging.

Imperative   **Verb** form used in giving commands and instructions ('<u>Turn</u> left now!').

Indirect object   A secondary **object**. In the sentence 'she sent <u>her mother</u> a present', the **direct object**, the thing which is sent, is the present. It was sent *to* her mother, the indirect object.

Infinitive   The basic form of a **verb** ('to sing', 'to write').

Irregular verb   **Verb** that does not follow a standard pattern.

Main clause   The principal statement in a sentence. To make sense, a **subordinate clause** depends upon the information in the main clause. 'Peter stayed at home (because the weather was so bad.')

Mixed verb   In German, a **verb** that combines features of both **strong** and **weak** verbs.

Modal verb   E.g. 'can', 'must'. Often combines with another **verb**: 'he can go tomorrow'.

Nominative   In German, **case** used for the **subject**.

Noun   Word denoting a person ('student'), thing ('book') or abstract idea ('happiness').

Object   see **direct object**, **indirect object**

Past participle   Part of the **verb** which combines with an **auxiliary verb** to form the perfect tense ('they have arrived', 'I have seen').

Plural   More than one: the plural of 'man' is 'men'.

Possessive adjective   e.g. 'my house', 'your friend', 'his car' etc.

Preposition   e.g. 'on the table', 'under the chair', 'to the station', 'for the teacher' etc.

Pronoun   Word taking the place of a **noun**. 'Paul saw the waitress' becomes 'he saw her'.

Reflexive verb   In German, **verb** formed with an extra **pronoun** (called a 'reflexive **pronoun**'): e.g. sich setzen (to sit down), 'ich setze mich'.

Regular verb   **Verb** that follows a standard pattern.

Separable verb   In German, **verb** that has a detachable prefix: e.g. aufstehen → 'Ich stehe um 7 Uhr auf'.

Singular   One rather than many: the singular of 'bananas' is 'banana'.

Strong verb   **Verb** which has an internal vowel change, e.g. in the English past tense (swim → swam).

Subject   Who or what carries out the action of the **verb**. 'A student sent me this email.'; 'We are travelling next week.', 'The letter arrived yesterday.'

Subordinate clause   Part of a sentence introduced by a **subordinating conjunction**. To make sense it depends on the information in the **main clause**. '(Peter stayed at home) because the weather was so bad.'

Subordinating conjunction   **Conjunction** that introduces a **subordinate clause**: e.g. because, when, that.

Tense   Form taken by a **verb** to show when the action takes place, e.g. present tense: 'they live in New York'; past: 'they lived in New York'; future: 'they will live in New York' etc.

Weak verb   In German, a regular verb without any internal vowel change. See also **verb**, **strong verb**.

Verb   Word indicating an action ('they ate their dinner') or state ('the book lay on the table'). Different **tenses** are used to show when something happened. See also **irregular verb**, **mixed verb**, **modal verb**, **reflexive verb**, **regular verb**, **separable verb**, **strong verb**, **tense**, **weak verb**.

THE SOUNDS OF GERMAN

 Das Alphabet

a b c d e f g h i j k l m n o p q r s t u v w x y z

ä   ö   ü   ß

Ich buchstabiere meinen Namen ... / I'll spell my name ...

 German spelling ...

... is highly regular and predictable. Once you have learnt how the sounds are represented, you will be able to write down a word you hear but have not seen in print. Use these examples for some pronunciation practice, too!

ä	Universität	ö	Köln
ach	Bach	s	Apfelsaft
au	Audi	sch	Schweiz
äu	Löwenbräu	sp (initial)	Sport
d (final)	Abend	st (initial)	Stuttgart
e (final)	Porsche	u (long)	Hut
ee	Kaffee	ü	München
ei	Wein	v	Volkswagen
eu	Deutschland	w	Wasser
ich	Zürich	z	Mozart
ie	Bier	ss	dass
j	ja	ß	Spaß

 Using numbers

Geld:	€15,90	€0,75		
Gewicht:	74 kg	3,5 kg	500 g	1 Pfund
	Ich wiege ... ('I weigh ...')			
Länge:	55 km	700 m	1,80m	30 cm
	Ich bin ... groß ('I am ... tall')			
Telefon:	00 49	2 28	67 43 10	
	Deutschland	*Vorwahlnummer*		
Temperatur:	23 °C			

For numbers 1–99 see unit 2; for 100+ see page 99.

GRAMMAR SUMMARY

This is a short summary of basic German grammar. If you are not familiar with grammatical terms, you will probably find the 'Guide to Grammatical Terms' on pages 144–5 very useful as an introduction to this section.

1 Nouns – gender

To use a German noun properly, you must know its gender: masculine, feminine or neuter. Words denoting males (**Mann**, **Vater**, **Lehrer**) are masculine and those denoting females are feminine (**Frau**, **Mutter**, **Lehrerin**; the exception: **Mädchen** 'girl' is neuter), but objects (**der Tisch** 'table' is masculine), and ideas (**die Hoffnung** 'hope' is feminine) have a grammatical gender too and can be any of the three genders. Learn a noun with its *definite article* and you will automatically learn its gender.

Feminine forms of nouns denoting a job often add **-in** to the masculine form: **Lehrer/Lehrerin**.

Compound nouns have the gender of the last element: **die Abendzeitung** 'evening paper' is feminine because **Zeitung** is feminine, as are all nouns ending in **-ung**.

2 Nouns – plurals

In English, the overwhelming majority of nouns form their plural by adding '-s' but there are other ways which survive from an earlier stage of the language: change of vowel (man → men); no change (sheep → sheep); addition of '-en' (ox → oxen).

German has the same four ways of forming the plural of nouns but also has several others:

Add **-s**	**das Auto → Autos**
Vowel change (add Umlaut)	**der Bruder → Brüder**
No change	**der Amerikaner → Amerikaner**
Add **-en**	**das Bett → Betten**
Add **-n**	**die Schwester → Schwestern**
Add **-e**	**der Tag → Tage**
Vowel change (Umlaut) plus **-e**	**die Nacht → Nächte**
Add **-er**	**das Kind → Kinder**
Vowel change (Umlaut) plus **-er**	**das Land → Länder**

As you get to know the language better, you will see there are some patterns to this (e.g. feminine nouns ending in **-e** add an **-n** in the plural). The best advice is to learn the plural of each noun. The overall glossary beginning on page 160 gives the plurals of nouns in brackets.

3 Nouns – capitals

German nouns always begin with a capital letter.

4 The case system: articles, possessives and *dieser, welcher, jeder*

Nouns usually have accompanying words which give information on their function in the sentence. Here, we shall be looking at the *definite* and *indefinite* articles (**der** and **ein** etc.) and the *possessives* (**mein**, **dein**, **sein** etc.) as well as **dieser**, **welcher** and **jeder**, which follow the definite article pattern. Later sections deal with *adjectives* and *prepositions*.

As you have worked your way through the units of this book, you have seen a system of categories unfold. These categories, nominative, accusative, dative and genitive, are characterised by specific patterns, and using German grammar correctly is largely a matter of becoming familiar with the patterns. The categories are referred to as *cases*.

4.1 Nominative

This is the form used when the noun is the *subject*. It is also used after the verb **sein** 'to be':

	masc	fem	neut	pl
Definite article	**der**	**die**	**das**	**die**
dieser 'this', **welcher?** 'which?' **jeder** 'each'	**dieser**	**diese**	**dieses**	**diese** etc.
Indefinite article and **kein**	**(k)ein**	**(k)eine**	**(k)ein**	**keine**
Possessives	**mein**	**meine**	**mein**	**meine** etc.
(all possessives follow this pattern: see section 9 below)				

Dieser Rock ist zu teuer.　　　　　**Wo ist mein Buch?**
Eine Limonade kostet €2,00.　　　　**Das** Haus liegt in der Goethestraße.

4.2 Accusative

- This is the form used when the noun is the *direct object*.
- It is also used after certain *prepositions* (see section 11 below) and the construction **es gibt**.

Only the masculine changes: the feminine, neuter and plural forms are all the same as the basic, nominative form:

Definite article	**den**
dieser/welcher/jeder	**diesen** etc.
Indefinite article and **kein**	**(k)einen**
Possessives	**meinen** etc.

Wann hast du diesen Computer gekauft?　　**Ich suche einen Job.**
Er arbeitet für seinen Bruder.　　　　　　**Es gibt einen Park in der Nähe.**

4.3 Dative

- This form is used when the noun is the *indirect object*.
- It has to be used after the verbs **helfen** and **gefallen**.
- It is also used after certain *prepositions* (see section 11).

	masc. + neut.	fem.	pl.
Definite article	**dem**	**der**	**den**
dieser/welcher/jeder	**diesem**	**dieser**	**diesen** etc.
Indefinite article and **kein**	**(k)einem**	**(k)einer**	**keinen**
Possessives	**meinem**	**meiner**	**meinen** etc.

* In the dative plural, nouns not already ending in an **-n** add one (except those with a plural ending in **-s**).

Zu ihrem Geburtstag gebe ich <u>meiner</u> Schwester Blumen.
Klaus hilft <u>seinem</u> Großvater in <u>dem</u> Garten.
Wir bekommen oft Briefe von <u>unseren</u> Freunde<u>n</u> in Mexiko.

4.4 Genitive

This form is used to express belonging and ownership.

	masc. + neut.	fem. + pl.
Definite article	**de<u>s</u>**	**der**
dieser/welcher/jeder	**dies<u>es</u>**	**dies<u>er</u>** etc.
Indefinite article and **kein**	**(k)ein<u>es</u>**	**(k)ein<u>er</u>**
Possessives	**mein<u>es</u>**	**mein<u>er</u>** etc.

* Masculine and neuter nouns add **-(e)s**.

Er ist ein Freund <u>meines</u> Vater<u>s</u>.　　　**Das ist das Auto <u>der</u> Lehrerin.**
Am Ende <u>der</u> Ferien fahre ich nach Hause.

5 The case system: adjectives before the noun

When used before a noun and following a definite or indefinite article, **dieser**, **welcher**, **jeder** or a possessive, an adjective has an ending. The system is quite simple:

5.1 The adjective has the ending **-en** in:

– the masculine accusative singular (after **den/einen** etc.)
– the dative singular (any gender) (after **dem/einem** and **der/einer** etc.)
– the genitive singular (any gender) (after **des/eines** and **der/einer** etc.)
– the plural (all cases) (after **die/der/den** and **keine/keiner/keinen** etc.)

Ich trage gern diesen blau<u>en</u> Rock. (masculine accusative)
Es ist das Haus eines alt<u>en</u> Freundes. (masculine genitive)
Die neu<u>en</u> Stühle sind im Wohnzimmer. (plural nominative)

5.2 Otherwise, the adjective has the following endings:

(a)　**-e** after the *definite* article and **dieser**, **welcher**, **jeder**:
　　　– masc. nominative (after **der/dieser**)
　　　– fem. nominative + accusative (after **die/diese**)
　　　– neut. nominative + accusative: (after **das/dieses**)

(b)　**-er**, **-e**, or **-es** as follows after the *indefinite* article and **kein/mein** etc:
　　　– masc. nominative (**ein/kein/mein** etc.)　　　　　　**-er**
　　　– fem. nominative + accusative (after **eine/keine/meine** etc.)　**-e**
　　　– neut. nominative + accusative (after **ein/kein/mein** etc.)　　**-es**

a	b
Der italienisch<u>e</u> Anzug ist zu teuer.	**Ein neu<u>er</u> Computer kostet mehr!**
Diese weiß<u>e</u> Bluse gefällt mir nicht.	**Deine blau<u>e</u> Bluse ist schön.**
Heinz hat das alt<u>e</u> Fahrrad da, aber …	**Lucy hat ein klein<u>es</u> Auto gekauft.**

Grammar summary

5.3 At-a-glance summary of articles/adjectival endings

	masc.	fem.	neut.	pl.
nom.	der -E	die -E	das -E	die -EN
	ein -ER	eine -E	ein -ES	keine -EN
acc.	den -EN	die -E	das -E	die -EN
	einen -EN	eine -E	ein -ES	keine -EN
dat.	dem -EN	der -EN	dem -EN	den -EN
	einem -EN	einer -EN	einem -EN	keinen -EN
gen.	des -EN	der -EN	des -EN	der -EN
	eines -EN	einer -EN	eines -EN	keiner -EN

6 Adjective after the noun: no ending

Das Haus ist sehr modern.   **Die Arbeit ist langweilig.**

7 Adjective + plural noun

When there is no article, the nominative and accusative plural adjectival ending is **-e**.
Ihr habt tolle Sessel.

8 Comparison of adjectives

The comparative form of the adjective ends in **-er**: **interessant → interessanter**.
Some adjectives change their internal vowel (Umlaut): **groß → größer**, **lang → länger**.
The most common irregular comparative is: **gut → besser**

The resulting forms then follow the normal pattern for adjectives (see sections 5, 6 and 7):
Das war ein besserer Film.   **Ich habe einen schnelleren Computer gekauft.**
masculine nominative   masculine accusative

Ist dein Job jetzt interessanter?
no ending

9 Possessives

These follow the pattern of the indefinite article **ein** (see section 4 above).

my	**mein**	our	**unser**
your (informal)	**dein/euer** (sing./pl.)	your (formal)	**Ihr**
his/its (m/n)	**sein**	their	**ihr**
her/its (f)	**ihr**		

10 Amount, number

viel/viele	much/many	**viel Geld/viele Studenten**
wenig/wenige	little (not much)/ few (not many)	**wenig Geld/wenige Studenten**
weniger	less	**Andrew bekommt weniger Geld als Kevin.**
mehr	more	**Kevin bekommt mehr Geld als Andrew.**
einige	some	**Gundula hat einige Freunde eingeladen.**
mehrere	several	**Mehrere Studenten warten im Korridor.**

11 Prepositions

11.1 Always followed by the accusative:

für ('for'), **um** ('around', 'at' – time), **durch** ('through'), **gegen** ('towards', 'against', 'about' – time), **bis** ('until'), **ohne** ('without'), **entlang** ('along'), normally after the noun.

Er arbeitet für seinen Bruder.   Sie gehen durch den Park.   Wir fahren ohne ihn.

11.2 Always followed by the dative:

aus ('out of'), **bei** ('at someone's house', 'for a firm (working)'), **gegenüber** ('opposite'), **mit** ('with'), **nach** ('after'), **seit** '(since'), **von** ('from', 'of'), **zu** ('to').

Er kommt um drei Uhr aus dem Bahnhof.   Er wohnt gegenüber einer Bäckerei.

11.3 Followed by accusative or dative:

an ('at'), **auf** ('on'), **in** ('in'), **über** ('over', 'about'), **unter** ('under') are the prepositions most commonly found in both cases.

The following are followed by the accusative when the rule below requires it, but are much more likely to be found in contexts which require a dative:

hinter ('behind'), **neben** ('next to'), **vor** ('in front of', 'before'), **zwischen** ('between').

Rule: These prepositions are followed by a dative form when they are giving a location but by an accusative form when they express a change of place:

Example: **Sie tanzt in <u>der</u> Diskothek** is in the *dative* because this sentence tells us where she is dancing (location), i.e. in the disco. The *accusative* **Sie tanzt in <u>die</u> Diskothek** would be talking about a change of place and telling us that she dances into the disco!

Sein Buch liegt auf <u>dem</u> Tisch. Here **liegen auf** + *dative* tells us where the book is – on the table.

Er legt das Buch auf <u>den</u> Tisch. Legen auf + *accusative* describes a change of place – he puts the book on(to) the table.

The verbs **liegen** 'to lie' and **legen** 'to lay, put down' underline the difference in context between using one of these prepositions with the dative and using it with the accusative.

Er steht unter <u>der</u> Dusche. 'He is standing under the shower.'– **Unter** + *dative* gives location.
Er geht unter <u>die</u> Dusche. 'He is going under the shower.' – **Unter** + *accusative* describes a change of place.

11.4 Meaning of prepositions

English and German often use prepositions differently, so beware when translating them!

For example, the German preposition **auf** is translated differently in each of the following:

Die Katze sitzt auf meinem Schreibtisch. The cat is sitting <u>on</u> my desk.
Wir wohnen auf dem Lande. We live <u>in</u> the country.
Sie fahren auf das Land. They are going <u>to</u> the country.
Ich warte auf den Bus. I am waiting <u>for</u> the bus.
Sie ist böse auf mich. She is angry <u>with</u> me.

12 Pronouns

nominative		accusative		dative	
ich	I	**mich**	me	**mir**	(to) me
du	you – familiar sing.	**dich**	you	**dir**	(to) you
er	he, it	**ihn**	him/it	**ihm**	(to) him/it
sie	she, it	**sie**	her/it	**ihr**	(to) her/it
es	it	**es**	it	**ihm**	(to) it
wir	we	**uns**	us	**uns**	(to) us
Sie	you – formal sing & pl.	**Sie**	you	**Ihnen**	(to) you
sie	they	**sie**	they	**ihnen**	(to) them
ihr	you – familiar pl.	**euch**	you	**euch**	(to) you

Ich liebe dich. Er hat ihr ein Geschenk gegeben. **Arbeitest du mit ihnen?**
nom   acc   nom   dat   *nom   dat*
I love you.   He gave her a present. ('to her')   Do you work with them?

Gefällt dir dieser Rock? – Nein, er ist zu kurz.
Do you like this skirt? – No, it is too short.
Er = 'it' here because it refers to **Rock**, a masculine noun.

13 Verbs – the infinitive

This is the basic form of the verb and the one given in dictionaries and word-lists.
The infinitive of all verbs ends in **-n**. With very few exceptions the ending is **-en**: e.g. **wohnen** 'to live', **ausgehen** 'to go out', **sich waschen** 'to get washed'.

Infinitives can be turned into neuter nouns:

essen → **das Essen** eating, food, meal
schwimmen → **das Schwimmen** swimming

14 Verbs – present tense

German has no continuous present ('She is eating a pizza'). The present tense outlined here covers both that and the English simple present ('She eats pizza every day').

As in English, the German present tense can also refer to the future:

Wir fahren nächste Woche nach Spanien. We are travelling to Spain next week.

14.1 Regular verb pattern (also called weak pattern)

ich wohn<u>e</u>	wir wohnen
du wohn<u>st</u>	Sie wohnen
er/sie/es wohn<u>t</u>	sie wohnen
ihr wohn<u>t</u>	

The three forms on the right are identical with the *infinitive*. The other four forms add the endings **-e**, **-st** and **-t** to the *stem* of the infinitive: **wohn-**. Most verbs follow this pattern. If the stem ends in **-t** or **-d**, or in a consonant combination such as **-gn**, an **-e** is put in before the normal endings of the **du-** and **er/sie/es**-forms to make pronunciation possible: e.g. **er arbeit<u>et</u>**.

Note also that verbs with a stem ending in **-s**, **-ß** or **-z** don't add an extra **-s** in the **du**-form: **du heißt**, **du sitzt**.

14.2 Strong verb pattern

ich schlafe	wir schlafen
du schl<u>ä</u>fst	Sie schlafen
er/sie/es schl<u>ä</u>ft	sie schlafen
ihr schlaft	

The endings are the same as in the regular pattern but there is an internal vowel change (here it is from **a** to **ä**) in two forms: the **du**-form and the **er/sie/es**-form. Other common strong verbs in the present tense include: **fahren**, **essen**, **nehmen**, **lesen**. There is a list in section 22.

14.3 Separable verbs

In verbs such as **aufstehen**, the prefix separates off and comes at the end of the clause: **Anna steht um 7 Uhr auf.** Other examples include: **ausgehen**, **umsteigen**, **einkaufen**, **anrufen**. Some separable verbs are weak, some are strong. They follow the appropriate pattern as outlined earlier. There is a list in section 24.

14.4 Modal verbs

ich kann	wir können
du kannst	Sie können
er/sie/es kann	sie können
ihr könnt	

Modals all have a distinctive form without an ending for the **ich**-form and **er/sie/es**-form, which also provides the basis of the **du**-form. The other forms are regular. Modals are typically used with the infinitive of another verb, which comes at the end of the clause.

Ich <u>kann</u> nächsten Montag um 4 Uhr <u>kommen</u>. I can come next Monday at 4 o'clock.

Other modals: **müssen** 'must, to have to' – **ich muss**; **wollen** 'to want to' – **ich will**; **dürfen** 'may, to be allowed to' – **ich darf**.

14.5 Reflexive verbs

e.g. **sich setzen** 'to sit down'.

ich setze <u>mich</u>	wir setzen <u>uns</u>	**Imperative:**
du setzt <u>dich</u>	Sie setzen <u>sich</u>	**Setz dich!/Setzt euch!/Setzen Sie sich!**
er/sie/es setzt <u>sich</u>	sie setzen <u>sich</u>	
ihr setzt <u>euch</u>		

These have a *reflexive pronoun* in each form. Some are weak and some strong.

Er setzt sich an seinen Schreibtisch. He sits down at his desk.
(Do not confuse this verb with **sitzen** 'to be sitting': **Er sitzt an seinem Schreibtisch.**)

Other reflexives include: **sich freuen auf** 'to look forward to'; **sich waschen** 'to get washed'; **sich bewerben um** 'to apply for'; **sich entscheiden** 'to decide'.

14.6 Two irregular verbs: **sein** and **haben**

sein 'to be'		**haben** 'to have'	
ich bin	wir sind	ich habe	wir haben
du bist	Sie sind	du hast	Sie haben
er/sie/es ist	sie sind	er/sie/es hat	sie haben
ihr seid		ihr habt	

15 The imperative

This is the form used to give instructions. It is based on the three 'you'-forms of the present tense.

– Familiar singular: **du**-form of the verb minus its **-st** ending.
  Geh geradeaus. Go straight on. **Ruf morgen an.** Phone tomorrow. **Warte!** Wait!

– Familiar plural: **ihr**-form of the verb without the pronoun.
  Geht geradeaus.

– Formal singular and plural: **Sie**-form of the verb, with the pronoun second.
  Gehen Sie geradeaus.

Irregular: **sein**   **sei/seid/seien Sie**

16 The perfect tense

Like the perfect tense in English ('Have you ever been to America?'), the German perfect tense is a *compound* tense: it is made up of two elements, an *auxiliary* verb (**haben** or **sein**) combined with the *past participle* of the verb you are using.

Unlike its English equivalent, it is the tense most often used for talking about the past:
Ich habe um ein Uhr gegessen is used where English would have 'I ate at one o'clock'.
It is also used when English requires a perfect tense: **Wir haben schon gegessen.** 'We have already eaten.'

16.1 Weak verbs

auxiliary	present tense of **haben** **ich habe …** etc.	past participle (at end of clause) **ge____t** e.g. **gekocht ← kochen** separable verb: **eingekauft ← einkaufen**

Er hat eine wunderbare Paella gekocht.   **Ich habe den ganzen Abend getanzt.**
Am Nachmittag haben wir eingekauft.

A few weak verbs have **sein** as their auxiliary: **Sie sind gelandet. (← landen)**

16.2 Strong verbs

auxiliary:	present tense of **haben** **ich habe …** etc.	past participle (at end of clause) **ge____en** e.g. **gegessen ← essen**
or	present tense of **sein** **ich bin …** etc.	e.g. **gefahren ← fahren** separable verb: **ferngesehen ← fernsehen**

Wir haben Paella gegessen.   **Hast du das Buch schon gelesen?**
Er ist nach Rom gefahren.   **Sie hat bis 11 Uhr ferngesehen.**

* With the perfect tense, the simplest approach is to learn the strong verbs as a category: those that have a past participle ending in **-en**. Some verbs (e.g. **gehen → gegangen**) are strong in the perfect tense but do not have a vowel change in the present tense **du-** and **er/sie**-forms. Equally, not all strong verbs have a vowel change in the perfect (e.g. **sehen → gesehen**). See the list in section 22.

16.3 Special past participle patterns

– Verbs with an infinitive ending in **-ieren** have a weak past participle without the prefix **ge-**: **er hat in Amerika studiert (← studieren)**.

– Verbs with an inseparable prefix (e.g. **be-, er-, ent-, ver-**) also have a past participle without the **ge-**: **ich habe meine Eltern besucht (← besuchen)**.

– As in the present tense, verbs with a stem ending in **-t**, **-d**, or consonant combinations such as **-gn** add **-et** rather than **-t**: **es hat geregn<u>et</u>**.

17 Simple past tense

haben to have
ich hatte I had etc.	**wir hatten**
du hattest	**Sie hatten**
er/sie/es hatte	**sie hatten**
ihr hattet	

sein 'to be' is irregular:
ich war I was etc.	**wir waren**
du warst	**Sie waren**
er/sie/es war	**sie waren**
ihr wart	

Modals follow the same pattern:
wollen → ich wollte	I wanted to
müssen → ich musste	I had to
können → ich konnte	I was able to
dürfen → ich durfte	I was allowed to

When talking about the past using **sein**, **haben** or a modal verb, the simple past tense, or imperfect, is preferred to the perfect.

Wir wollten heute ins Restaurant gehen, aber wir konnten nicht, weil Petra babysitten musste.

18 'Would like to'

There are two verb forms we can use: **möchte (gern)/würde gern** + infinitive

ich möchte; du möchtest; er/sie/es möchte; wir/Sie/sie möchten; ihr möchtet
ich würde, du würdest, er/sie/es würde, wir/Sie/sie würden, ihr würdet

Ich würde gern im Ausland arbeiten.

19 Verbs and word order

19.1 The verb is the second item in a sentence but not necessarily the second word.

Peter <u>studiert</u> in Manchester.
1   2

Die drei deutschen Studenten <u>sind</u> jetzt in Manchester.
◄——————— 1 ———————► 2

The subject is one word in the first sentence and four words in the second, but it is still a single item, so the verb comes next. The verb is still the second item if the sentence does not begin with the subject:

Jetzt <u>sind</u> die drei deutschen Studenten in Manchester.

Note that here the subject follows the verb. This is unlike English where, if something other than the verb begins the sentence, the subject still comes in its normal place, before the verb:

Now the three German students are in Manchester.

19.2 Questions are formed by inverting the subject and the verb:

Geht er oft ins Kino? Hast du Michael gesehen? Wann können Sie uns besuchen?

Note that in the first examples the inversion of subject and verb means that the verb is in first place in the sentence. When the question begins with one of the question-forms in **w-** (**warum** 'why', **was** 'what', **wann** 'when', **wie** 'how', **wer** 'who', **wo** 'where') the verb comes second.

19.3 An infinitive comes at the end of the clause.

The two constructions you have met where this comes into play are: (i) **um ... zu** 'in order to' followed by an infinitive and (ii) modal verbs with an infinitive, where the modal verb takes second position in the clause.

(i) Sie macht einen Intensivkurs, um ihr Deutsch zu <u>verbessern</u>.
(ii) Ich will im Ausland <u>arbeiten</u>.

19.4 Like infinitives, past participles come at the end of the clause.

The auxiliary verb comes in second place:

Ich <u>habe</u> am Nachmittag Basketball <u>gespielt</u>.

19.5 In a subordinate clause, the verb comes at the end:

Wir bleiben zu Hause,   weil wir im Moment viel Arbeit haben.
◄—— Main clause ——►   ◄————Subordinate clause ————►

When the subordinate clause begins the sentence, the verb in the main clause follows immediately because the subordinate clause is then the first item and the main verb must be the second item:

Weil wir viel Arbeit haben,   bleiben wir zu Hause.
◄— Subordinate clause —►   2

19.6 TMP: Time, Manner, Place

Time expressions precede place expressions:

Der Zug kommt um drei Uhr in Heidelberg an.

English usually has them the other way round: 'The train arrives in Heidelberg at three o'clock.' Expressions of manner ('how') come between time and place expressions:

Ich fahre im Sommer mit meinem Bruder nach Spanien.
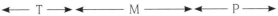
◄——— T ——►◄——— M ———►◄— P ——►

20 Adverbs

20.1 In German, the adverb normally has the same form as the adjective without an ending:

Er schreibt gut. He writes well.

20.2 Adverbs come immediately after the verb, unlike in English:

Er schreibt <u>oft</u> an seine Mutter. He often writes to his mother.

20.3 Gern, lieber, am liebsten

The useful adverb **gern** means that the subject of the preceding verb likes doing whatever that verb denotes:

Er <u>spielt gern</u> Karten. He <u>likes playing</u> cards.
<u>Gehst</u> du <u>gern</u> ins Kino? Do you <u>like going</u> to the cinema?
Ja, aber ich <u>gehe lieber</u> in die Diskothek. Yes, but I <u>like going</u> to the disco <u>more</u>.
Ich <u>bleibe am liebsten</u> zu Hause. I <u>like staying</u> at home <u>most of all</u>.

21 Negation

Nouns: think of **kein** as the negative form of **ein** (it also follows the same pattern, see section 4 above): **Ich habe einen Computer**, negative: **Ich habe <u>keinen</u> Computer** 'I don't have a computer'. Unlike **ein**, it can be used in the plural: **Er hat <u>keine</u> Freunde** 'He hasn't any friends'.

Verbs are negated by the negative adverb **nicht**: **Er geht <u>nicht</u> in die Bibliothek.**

22 Common strong verbs

infinitive	meaning	er/sie-form present	past participle
beginnen (I)	to begin	X	begonnen
bleiben	to stay, remain	X	geblieben*
essen	to eat	isst	gegessen
fahren	to go (in vehicle)	fährt	gefahren*
fallen	to fall	fällt	gefallen*
anfangen	to begin	fängt ... an	angefangen
finden	to find	X	gefunden
fliegen	to fly	X	geflogen*
geben	to give	gibt	gegeben
gehen	to go	X	gegangen*
gewinnen (I)	to win	X	gewonnen
helfen	to help	hilft	geholfen
kommen	to come	X	gekommen*
einladen	to invite	lädt ... ein	eingeladen
laufen	to run, walk	läuft	gelaufen*
lesen	to read	liest	gelesen
nehmen	to take	nimmt	genommen
rufen	to call, shout	X	gerufen
schlafen	to sleep	schläft	geschlafen
schreiben	to write	X	geschrieben
sehen	to see	sieht	gesehen
sitzen	to sit	X	gesessen
sprechen	to speak	spricht	gesprochen
stehen	to stand	X	gestanden
sterben	to die	stirbt	gestorben*
steigen	to climb, rise	X	gestiegen*
tragen	to wear, carry	trägt	getragen
treffen	to meet	trifft	getroffen
trinken	to drink	X	getrunken
tun	to do	X	getan
vergessen (I)	to forget	vergisst	vergessen
verlieren (I)	to lose	X	verloren
wachsen	to grow	wächst	gewachsen*
waschen	to wash	wäscht	gewaschen
werden	to become	wird	geworden*
ziehen	to pull	X	gezogen

(I) Inseparable (section 25)

X Not strong in present tense

* Forms perfect tense with **sein** as auxiliary

23 Mixed and irregular verbs

infinitive	meaning	er/sie-form present	past participle
bringen	to bring	X	**gebracht**
denken	to think	X	**gedacht**
haben	to have	**hat**	**gehabt**
sein	to be	**ist**	**gewesen***

* Forms perfect tense with **sein** as auxiliary.

In this book, **sein**, **haben** and the modals are encountered in the simple past, not the perfect.

24 Some separable verbs

24.1 Strong (for vowel changes see list in section 22, e.g. for **abfahren** see **fahren**)

abfahren* to depart
ankommen* to arrive
anfangen to begin
anrufen to phone
aufgeben to give up
aufstehen* to get up
aufwachsen* to grow up
ausgehen* to go out
aussteigen* to get off (bus etc.)

einladen to invite
einsteigen* to get on (bus etc.)
fernsehen to watch TV
mitkommen* to come/go along
umsteigen* to change (trains etc.)
umziehen* to move (house)
vorbeigehen* to go past
weggehen* to go away
zurückkommen* to come back

* Forms perfect tense with **sein** as auxiliary

24.2 Weak
abholen to collect
anprobieren to try on
aufhören to stop

aufmachen to open
einführen to introduce
einkaufen to shop

25 Some inseparable verbs

Prefix: **be-, er-, ge-, ver-, zer-**

25.1 Strong (see list in section 22): **beginnen, gewinnen, vergessen, verlieren**

25.2 Mixed: **verbringen** to spend (time) (see **bringen**, section 23)

25.3 Weak: **besuchen** (to visit), **erreichen** (to achieve), **erzählen** (to tell), **verdienen** (to deserve), **versuchen** (to try), **zerstören** (to destroy)

VOCABULARY

Plurals of nouns (see Grammar summary, section 2) are given in brackets after the noun.

pl after a noun means it is already in the plural.

/in at the end of a noun means that the feminine form has **-in** added to it: (**Amerikaner/ Amerikanerin**).

* after a verb means the verb is strong in the present tense; *sep* means the verb is separable; *refl* means it is reflexive

pp = past participle

ab	from (time)
der Abend (e)	evening
am Abend	in the evening
das Abendessen (-)	dinner, evening meal
zum Abendessen	for dinner
abends	in the evening (regularly)
die Abendschule (n)	evening classes
aber	but
abfahren* *sep*	to depart (train, bus)
abgeschlossen	pp of **abschließen**
abholen *sep*	to collect (someone)
das Abitur	A-Levels (equivalent)
die Abreise (n)	departure (person from hotel)
abschließen *sep*	to complete
abwaschen* *sep*	to wash up
die Abwechslung (en)	variety
die Adresse (n)	address
(das) Aerobic	aerobics
der Alkohol (e)	alcohol
alle	everybody, all
allein	alone
alles	everything
als	as; when (past)
also	so, therefore
alt	old
das Alter	age
altmodisch	old-fashioned
am = an dem	at the, by the
der/die Amerikaner/in (-/nen)	American (m/f)
die Ampel (n)	(set of) traffic lights
an	at, by, to, on
anders	different(ly)
anfangen* *sep*	to begin, start
angenehm	pleasant
angerufen	pp of **anrufen**
angeschaltet	pp of **anschalten**
die Anglistik	English (academic subject)
die Angst (vor)	fear (of)
Angst haben	to be afraid
ängstlich	anxious, afraid
ankommen *sep*	to arrive
die Ankunft (Ankünfte)	arrival (train)
anprobieren *sep*	to try on
die Anreise (n)	arrival (person in hotel)
anrufen *sep*	to phone
anschalten *sep*	to switch on
antworten	to answer
die Anzeige (n)	advert
der Anzug (Anzüge)	suit
der Apfelsaft	apple juice
die Apotheke (n)	pharmacy
die Arbeit	work
zur Arbeit	to work
arbeiten	to work
das Arbeitsfeld (er)	area of work
arbeitslos	unemployed
die Arbeitswelt (en)	world of work
der/die Architekt/in (e/nen)	architect (m/f)
die Architektur	architecture
der Arm (e)	arm
der/die Assistent/in (en/nen)	assistant
die Atmosphäre (n)	atmosphere
auch	also, as well
auf	on
die Aufgabe (n)	exercise
aufgeben* *sep*	to give up
aufgegeben	pp of **aufgeben**
aufgemacht	pp of **aufmachen**
aufgeregt	excited
aufgestanden	pp of **aufstehen**
aufgewachsen	pp of **aufwachsen**
aufhören *sep*	to finish
aufmachen *sep*	to open
aufräumen *sep*	to tidy up
aufstehen *sep*	to get up
aufwachsen* *sep*	to grow up
aus	out of; from (place)
der Ausflug (Ausflüge)	trip
ausgehen *sep*	to go out
ausgezeichnet	excellent
das Ausland	foreign countries
im Ausland	abroad
außerdem	besides
die Aussicht (en)	view
aussteigen *sep*	to get off (transport)
Australien	Australia
die Auswahl	selection, choice
das Auto (s)	car
Auto fahren*	to drive a car
die Autobahn (en)	motorway

der Automat (en)	vending machine
der/die Automechaniker/in (-/nen)	motor mechanic (m/f)
babysitten	to babysit
backen	to bake
der Bäcker (-)	baker
die Bäckerei (en)	baker's/bakery
die Badehose (n)	swimming trunks
die Badewanne (n)	bath(tub)
das Badezimmer (-)	bathroom
die Bahncard	railcard
der Bahnhof (Bahnhöfe)	railway station
bald (danach)	soon (afterwards)
der Balkon (s)	balcony
die Bank (en)	bank
der/die Bankangestellte	bank employee (m/f)
der Barmann	barman
das Barpersonal	bar staff
der Basketball	basketball
bauen	to build
der Bauernhof (Bauernhöfe)	farm
Bayern	Bavaria
der Beamte (n)	(here) ticket clerk
beantworten	to answer
beginnen	to begin
bei	at (someone's house or shop); for (a company)
beide	both
beige	beige
das Bein (e)	leg
bekommen	to get
Belgien	Belgium
der/die Belgier/in (-/nen)	Belgian (m/f)
bequem	comfortable
der Berg (e)	mountain
bergsteigen	to go mountain-climbing
die Berliner Mauer	Berlin Wall
der Beruf (e)	profession
die Berufserfahrung	professional experience
besitzen	to possess
besonders	especially
besser (als)	better (than)
bestätigen	to confirm
die Bestätigung (en)	confirmation
bestimmt	definitely
besuchen	to visit
die Betriebswirtschaft	business management
das Bett (en)	bed
im Bett	in bed
ins Bett gehen	to go to bed
sich bewerben um* *refl*	to apply for
der/die Bewerber/in (-/nen)	applicant (m/f)
die Bewerbung (en)	application
bewirbt	**er/sie**-form of **bewerben**
die Bibliothek (en)	library

der/die Bibliothekar/in (e/nen)	librarian (m/f)
das Bier (e)	beer
die Bierflasche (n)	beer bottle
der Biergarten (Biergärten)	beer garden
bieten	to offer
billig(er)	cheap(er)
bin	**ich-**form of **sein**
die Biologie	biology
bis	until
bis wann?	until when?
bis zu	as far as
bisschen	bit
bist du?	are you?
bitte	please
Bitte?	How can I help you?
blau	blue
bleiben	to stay, remain
die Blume (n)	flower
das Blumengeschäft (e)	flower shop
der Blumenstrauß (-sträuße)	bouquet
die Bluse (n)	blouse
böse	angry
der Boss (e)	boss
das Brandenburger Tor	Brandenburg Gate, Berlin
brauchen	to need
braun	brown
die BRD	Federal Republic of Germany
der Brief (e)	letter
der Briefkasten (-kästen)	mail box
die Brieftasche (n)	wallet
bringen	to bring; to take
das Brötchen (-)	bread roll
der Bruder (Brüder)	brother
das Buch (Bücher)	book
buchen	to book
das Bücherregal (e)	bookshelves
der Buchladen (-läden)	bookshop
Bundesländer *pl*	federal states
die Bundesrepublik	Federal Republic
bunt	colourful
der Bürger (-)	citizen
das Büro(s)	office
der Bürodrehstuhl (-stühle)	office chair
der Bus (se)	bus
der/die Busfahrer/in (-/nen)	bus driver (m/f)
die Butter	butter
ca. = circa = zirka	about
der Campingplatz (-plätze)	campsite
der CD-Spieler (-)	CD-player
die/das Cola (s)	cola

Vocabulary

der Computer (-)	computer
die Computerlinguistik	computer linguistics
das Computerspiel (e)	computer game
die Computerwissenschaften *pl*	
	computer science
damals	at that time
danach	after that
der/die Däne/Dänin	
(n/nen)	Dane (m/f)
Dänemark	Denmark
dann	then
das geht	that's OK
das ist alles	that's all
das stimmt	that's right
das war schade	that was a pity
dass	that (conjunction)
dauern	to last
die DDR	GDR, Communist East
	Germany 1949–1990
dein	your (*informal sing*)
demonstrieren	to demonstrate
denken	to think
denn	because
deshalb	therefore
Deutsch	German (language)
(die/der) Deutsche(r)	German (f/m)
Deutschland	Germany
die Deutschstunde (n)	German class
Dienstag	Tuesday
direkt	directly
die Diskothek (en)	discotheque, club
der Dom (e)	cathedral
Donnerstag	Thursday
das Doppelzimmer (-)	double room
das Dorf (Dörfer)	village
dort	there
dort drüben	over there
draußen	outside
dritt... (der dritte etc.)	third
die Droge (n)	drug
die Drogerie (n)	chemist's, drug store
drücken	to press
du	you (*informal sing*)
dunkel	dark
durch	through
die Durchschnittsnote	
(n)	average grade
die Dusche (n)	shower
die Ecke (n)	corner
an der Ecke	on the corner
um die Ecke	round the corner
eher als	rather than
das Ei (er)	egg
eigentlich	really
einfach	simple/simply; single (ticket)

einführen *sep*	to introduce
eingekauft	pp of **einkaufen**
einige	some
einkaufen *sep*	to go shopping
einladen* *sep*	to invite
die Einladung (en)	invitation
einmal	once (when ordering a meal = 'one')
die Einrichtung (en)	equipment
einschließlich	including
einsteigen *sep*	to get on, board
der Eintritt	entrance, admission
das Einzelzimmer (-)	single room
der Einzug (-züge)	moving in
das Eiscafé (s)	ice-cream parlour
der Elektroherd (e)	electric cooker
Eltern *pl*	parents
die E-Mail (s)	email
das Ende (n)	end
endlich	finally
der/die Engländer/in	
(-/nen)	Englishman/woman
Englisch	English (language)
Enkelkinder *pl*	grandchildren
enthusiastisch	enthusiastic
sich entscheiden *refl*	to decide
entschuldigen Sie …	excuse me (*formal*)
entsprechend	appropriate
enttäuscht	disappointed
die Enttäuschung (en)	disappointment
er	he; it (*masc*)
die Erfahrung (en)	experience
Erfahrung sammeln	to gain experience
erhält	**er/sie**-form of **erhalten**
erhalten*	to receive (also pp)
erkältet	suffering from a cold
erreichen	to get to
erst... (der erste etc.)	first
erst	only, not until
der/die Erwachsene	adult
erzählen	to tell
erzählt	pp of **erzählen** (also **er/sie**-form)
es	it (*neut*)
essen*	to eat
das Essen (-)	food, meal, eating
der Esstisch (e)	dining table
das Esszimmer (-)	dining room
etwa	about, roughly
etwas	something
euer/eure etc.	your (*pl, informal*)
Europa	Europe
der/die Europäer/in	
(-/nen)	European (m/f)
europaweit	throughout Europe
das Examen (-)	exam
exklusiv	exclusive

die Fähigkeit (en)	ability, capability
fahren*	to go, drive
die Fahrkarte (n)	ticket
der Fahrpreis (e)	fare
das Fahrrad (Fahrräder)	bicycle
die Fahrradvermietung	bicycle hire
der Fahrschein (e)	ticket
der Fahrstuhl (-stühle)	lift
fährt	er/sie-form of **fahren**
das Fahrtziel (e)	destination
fallen*	to fall
fällt	er/sie-form of **fallen**
die Familie (n)	family
der Fan (s)	fan
fängt … an	er/sie-form of **anfangen**
fantastisch	fantastic
die Farbe (n)	colour
fast	almost
der Federball	badminton
feiern	to celebrate; party
das Fenster (-)	window
der Ferienjob (s)	holiday job
ferngesehen	pp of **fernsehen**
fernsehen* *sep*	to watch TV
der Fernseher (-)	TV set
fertig	finished
der Film (e)	film
der Filmschauspieler (-)	film actor
finden	to find
die Firma (Firmen)	firm
der Fisch (e)	fish
Fitnessgeräte *pl*	fitness equipment
das Fitness-Studio	keep-fit centre
das Fitnesstraining	fitness training
das Fleisch	meat
fleißig	hard-working
flexibel	flexible
fliegen	to fly
fließend	fluent(ly)
Florenz	Florence
der Flughafen (-häfen)	airport
Flugreisen *pl*	air travel
folgend	following
Frankreich	France
der/die Franzose/ Französin (n/nen)	Frenchman/woman
französisch	French
Frau	Mrs, Ms
die Frau (en)	woman; wife
frei	free
die Freiheit	freedom
Freitag	Friday
Freizeitmöglichkeiten *pl*	leisure opportunities
die Fremdsprache (n)	foreign language
sich freuen *refl*	to be glad
sich freuen auf *refl* (+ accusative)	to look forward to

freut mich, Sie kennen zu lernen	pleased to meet you
der Freund (e)	(boy)friend
die Freundin (nen)	(girl)friend
freundlich	friendly
froh	glad, pleased
das Frühstück (e)	breakfast
zum Frühstück	for breakfast
frühstücken	to have/eat breakfast
frustriert	frustrated
der/die Fünfundsechzigjährige	65-year-old (m/f)
für	for
furchtbar	terrible
der Fuß (Füße)	foot
der Fußball	football
der Fußboden (-böden)	floor
ganz	complete(ly)
gar nicht	not at all
die Garage (n)	garage
der Garten (Gärten)	garden
der Gasherd (e)	gas cooker
gastronomisch	gastronomic
gebaut	pp of **bauen**
geben*	to give
geblieben	pp of **bleiben**
geboren	born
gebracht	pp of **bringen**
der Geburtstag (e)	birthday
gedacht	pp of **denken**
gefahren	pp of **fahren***
gefallen	pp of **fallen***
gefallen*	lit. 'to please' (but see unit 6 grammar page 70)
gefällt	er/sie-form of **gefallen**
das Gefängnis (se)	prison
gefunden	pp of **finden**
gegangen	pp of **gehen**
gegen	about (time); against
gegenüber	opposite
gegessen	pp of **essen***
das Gehalt (Gehälter)	salary
geheiratet	pp of **heiraten**
gehen	to go
geholt	pp of **holen**
gehört	pp of **hören**
der Geist (er)	spirit
gekocht	pp of **kochen**
gekommen	pp of **kommen**
gelandet	pp of **landen**
gelangweilt	bored
gelb	yellow
das Geld	money
der Geldschein (e)	banknote
gelernt	pp of **lernen**
gemacht	pp of **machen**
der Gemeinschaftsbereich (e)	communal area

Vocabulary

die Gemeinschaftsküche (n)	communal kitchen
das Gemüse (-)	vegetable(s)
die Gemüsesuppe (n)	vegetable soup
gemütlich	cosy
genau	exactly
gerade	just now
geradeaus	straight on
geredet	pp of **reden**
geregnet	pp of **regnen**
gern	(see Grammar Summary page 157)
die Gesamtmiete	full rent
die Geschichte (n)	history; story
geschmeckt	pp of **schmecken**
geschrieben	pp of **schreiben**
Geschwister *pl*	brothers and sisters, siblings
gesessen	pp of **sitzen**
gespielt	pp of **spielen**
das Gespräch (e)	conversation
gesprochen	pp of **sprechen***
gestohlen	pp of **stehlen***
gestorben	pp of **sterben***
gestresst	stressed
gesucht	pp of **suchen**
gesund	healthy
getanzt	pp of **tanzen**
getrunken	pp of **trinken**
gewinnen	to win
gewonnen	pp of **gewinnen**
geworden	pp of **werden***
gewünscht	desired
gibt	**er/sie**-form of **geben**
die Gitarre (n)	guitar
die Gitarrenstunde (n)	guitar lesson
das Glas (Gläser)	glass
glauben	to think, believe
gleich	immediately
Gleis x	Platform x
das Glück	luck, happiness
zum Glück	fortunately
glücklich	happy, lucky
der/die Grieche/Griechin (n/nen)	Greek (m/f)
Griechenland	Greece
grillen	to barbecue
groß	big; tall
Großbritannien	Great Britain
die Größe (n)	size
Großeltern *pl*	grandparents
größer	bigger
der Großvater (-väter)	grandfather
grün	green
gut	good, well
gut bezahlt	well paid
gut, danke	fine, thanks
guten Abend	good evening

guten Morgen	good morning
guten Tag	hello
das Gymnasium (Gymnasien)	grammar school
haben	to have
der Hafen (Häfen)	harbour, port
halb	half (to the next hour)
halb…	half
halblinks	fork left
das Hallenbad (-bäder)	indoor swimming pool
hallo	hello (*informal*)
Halsschmerzen *pl*	sore throat
die Haltestelle (n)	stop (bus, tram)
die Handtasche (n)	handbag
das Handy (s)	mobile phone, cellphone
Hannover	Hanover
hat	**er/sie**-form of **haben**
hatte	had
die Hauptstadt (-städte)	capital city
das Haus (Häuser)	house
nach Hause	(to) home
zu Hause	at home
der Hausmeister (-)	caretaker
die Haustür (en)	front door
heiraten	to marry
heiß	hot
heißen	to be called
helfen*	to help
hell	bright
das Hemd (en)	shirt
der Herd (e)	cooker
die Herrenabteilung (en)	men's department
hervorgehen aus *sep*	to emerge from
Herzlich willkommen!	Welcome!
heute	today
heute Nachmittag	this afternoon
hier	here
hiermit	herewith
die Hilfe	help
hilft	**er/sie**-form of **helfen**
hin und zurück	return
hinter	behind
Hobby (s)	hobby
die Hochzeit (en)	wedding
hoffentlich	hopefully
in Höhe von	to the amount of
holen	to fetch; go and get
Holstein	region of N. Germany to the north of Hamburg
hören	to hear
die Hose (n)	(pair of) trousers
hübsch	pretty
das Huhn (Hühner)	chicken
der Hund (e)	dog
hungrig	hungry
ich	I

ich bin's	it's me
die Idee (n)	idea
ihm	him, it (*dative*)
ihr	her/their; you (*pl, familiar*); to her
Ihr	your (*formal*)
im = in dem	in the
immer	always
die Informatik	computer science
sich informieren *refl*	to inform oneself
der/die Ingenieur/in (e/nen)	engineer (m/f)
inklusive	including
die Innenstadt (-städte)	town/city centre
innerhalb von	within
ins = in das	into
intensiv	intensive
interessant	interesting
das Interesse (n) (an + dative)	interest (in)
interessieren	to interest
sich interessieren für *refl*	to be interested in
der/die Ire/Irin (n/nen)	Irishman/woman
Irland	Ireland
isst	**er/sie**-form of **essen**
ist	is
Italien	Italy
Italiener/in (-/nen)	Italian (m/f)
italienisch	Italian
die italienische Küche	Italian cuisine
Italienisch	Italian language
ja	yes
die Jacke (n)	jacket
das Jackett (s)	(elegant) jacket
das Jahr (e)	year
jeden Tag	every day
jeder	each (one)
jetzt	now
der or das Joghurt	yoghurt
der/die Journalist/in (en/nen)	journalist (m/f)
Jugendliche *pl*	young people
jung	young
jüngst	youngest
das Kabelfernsehen	cable TV
der Kaffee	coffee
die Kantine (n)	canteen
kann	can – **ich-**, **er/sie**-form of **können**
kaputt	broken
Karten *pl*	cards
das Käsebrot (e)	cheese sandwich
katastrophal	catastrophic
die Katze (n)	cat
kaufen	to buy
das Kaufhaus (-häuser)	department store

die Kaution (en)	deposit
der/die Kellner/in (-/nen)	waiter/waitress
kennen	to know (be familiar with)
kennen lernen	to get to know
das Kind (er)	child
kinderfreundlich	welcoming to children
der Kindergarten (-gärten)	kindergarten
das Kino (s)	cinema
die Kirche (n)	church
das Kissen (-)	cushion
kitschig	kitschy
das Klavierkonzert (e)	piano concerto
das Kleid (er)	dress; *pl* (also) clothes
der Kleiderschrank (-schränke)	wardrobe
klein	small
das Kleingeld	small change
das Klima	climate
die Kneipe (n)	pub
kochen	to cook
der Koffer (-)	suitcase
der Kollege (n)	colleague
Köln	Cologne
kommen (aus)	to come (from)
kommunikativ	communicative
kommunistisch	communist
kompakt	compact
kompliziert	complicated
komponieren	to compose
komponiert	pp of **komponieren**
die Königin (nen)	queen
konnte	was able to, could – simple past of **können** (**ich**, **er/sie**-forms)
das Konzert (-e)	concert
der Kopf (Köpfe)	head
Kopfschmerzen *pl*	headache
kosten	to cost
köstlich	delicious
krank	ill
das Krankenhaus (-häuser)	hospital
die Krawatte (n)	tie
die Kreditkarte (n)	credit card
der Kreisverkehr	roundabout
die Kreuzung (en)	junction, crossroads
der Krimi (s)	detective story
die Kriminalität	criminality
die Küche (n)	kitchen; cuisine
der Kuchen (-)	cake
die Küchenhilfe (n)	kitchen assistant
der Kugelschreiber (-)	ballpoint pen
der Kühlschrank (-schränke)	refrigerator
die Kultur	culture
die Kundenberatung	advising customers
die Kunstgalerie (n)	art gallery

Vocabulary

kurz	short
küssen	to kiss
die Küste (n)	coast
der Laden (Läden)	shop, branch
lädt … ein	**er/sie**-form of **einladen**
die Lage (n)	situation
die Lampe (n)	lamp
das Land (Länder)	country
landen	to land
lang	long
lange	a long time
langweilig	boring
laufen*	to go on foot
läuft	**er/sie**-form of **laufen**
laut	(a)loud
leben	to live
das Leben (-)	life
der Lebenslauf (-läufe)	CV
ledig	single, unmarried
legen	to lay, put down
der/die Lehrer/in (-/nen)	teacher (m/f)
leicht	easy
das Leid	sorrow
es tut mir leid	I'm sorry
leider	unfortunately
lernen	to learn
die Lesefähigkeit	reading ability
lesen*	to read
letzt	last
letztes Jahr	last year
Leute *pl*	people
lieben	to love
das Lied (er)	song
liegen	to lie
liest	**er/sie**-form of **lesen**
die Linie (n)	bus/tram route
links	left
links von	to the left of
die Literatur	literature
machen	to do; make
der Magen (Mägen)	stomach
Magenschmerzen *pl*	stomach ache
die Mahlzeit (en)	meal
manchmal	sometimes
der Mann (Männer)	man; husband
die Mannschaft (en)	team
der Mantel (Mäntel)	coat
die Markthalle (n)	market hall
die Marmelade (n)	jam
Mathematik	mathematics
mehr	more
mein	my
melancholisch	melancholy
die Mensa	student canteen
der Mensch (en)	person, human being; *plural* – people

das Menü (s)	set menu
das Metier (s)	profession
die Mietdauer	period of tenancy
die Miete (n)	rent
mieten	to rent
die Mietzahlung (en)	payment of rent
die Mikrowelle (n)	microwave
die Milch	milk
das Mineralwasser	mineral water
mit	with
mit 19	at 19
mit dem Bus	by bus
mit dem InterCity	by Intercity
mitkommen *sep*	to come along/come too
das Mittagessen (-)	lunch
zum Mittagessen	for lunch
der Mittagstisch	lunchtime menu
Mittwoch	Wednesday
mobil	mobile
möchte(n) *irreg*	would like (to)
modern	modern
modisch	fashionable
der Moment (e)	moment
im Moment	at the moment
der Monat (e)	month
der Mond	moon
Montag	Monday
montags	on Mondays (regularly)
das Moped (s)	moped
morgen	tomorrow
der Morgen (-)	morning
am Morgen	in the morning
morgens	in the morning (regularly)
motiviert	motivated
müde	tired
München	Munich
die Münze (n)	coin
das Museum (Museen)	museum
die Musik	music
Musik hören	to listen to music
musste	had to – simple past of **müssen** (**ich**, **er/sie**-forms)
die Mutter (Mütter)	mother
nach	after; to (a place)
der Nachmittag (e)	afternoon
am Nachmittag	in the afternoon
nachmittags	in the afternoon (regularly)
nächst	next; nearest
nächste Woche	next week
nächstes Jahr	next year
die Nacht (Nächte)	night
der Nachteil (e)	disadvantage
der Nachttisch (e)	bedside table
nahe	near
in der Nähe	nearby

nähen	to sew
näher	nearer
nahmen teil	took part – simple past of **teilnehmen** (*pl.* forms)
der Name (n)	name
natürlich	of course
neben	next to
das Neckarufer	bank of the River Neckar
nehmen*	to take
nein	no
nett	nice
neu	new
nicht	not
nicht weit von	not far from
nichts	nothing
nie	never
nimmt	**er/sie**-form of **nehmen**
noch	still
Norddeutschland	N. Germany
der Norden	the North
die Nordsee	North Sea
normalerweise	normally
die Note (n)	grade
Nudeln *pl*	pasta, noodles
die Nummer (-n)	number
nutzen	to use
der Oberschrank (-schränke)	wall cupboard
das Obst	fruit
obwohl	although
oder	or
oder?	isn't it?
offener	more open
Öffnungszeiten *pl*	opening hours
oft	often
öfters	often
ohne	without
ökonomisch	economic
das Omelett (e or s)	omelette
die Oper (n)	opera
optimistisch	optimistic
der Orangensaft	orange juice
die Ordnung	order
in Ordnung	OK, all right
organisiert	organised
der Osten	East
Ostern	Easter
zu Ostern	at Easter
Österreich	Austria
der/die Österreicher/in (-/nen)	Austrian (m/f)
Ostfriesland	island and coastal region on the North Sea coast
die Ostsee	Baltic Sea
das Papier (e)	paper
der Park (s)	park

das Parkhaus (-häuser)	multi-storey car park
der Parkplatz (-plätze)	car park
die Partei (en)	political party
die Party (s)	party
Partys feiern	have parties
die Pension (en)	boarding house
das Personal	personnel, staff
Personen *pl*	persons
das Pferd (e)	horse
zu Pferde	on horseback
der Pförtner (-)	porter
die Pizza (s or Pizzen)	pizza
der Plan (Pläne)	plan, map (town)
der Platz (Plätze)	place, seat; square
die Politik	politics
der/die Polizist/in (en/nen)	policeman/woman
Pommes frites *pl*	chips, French fries
die Post	post office
praktisch	practical
der Präsident (en)	president
prima!	great!
pro Tag/Nacht	per day/night
die Prüfung (en)	exam
die Psychologie	psychology
der Pullover (-)	pullover
pünktlich	punctual, on time
putzen	to clean
Rad fahren*	to cycle
das Radio (s)	radio
im Radio	on the radio
das Rathaus	town hall
rauchen	to smoke
reagieren	to react
reagiert	pp of **reagieren**
Recht haben	to be right
rechts	right
rechts von	to the right of
reden	to talk
reformieren	to reform
die Regierung (en)	government
regnen	to rain
regnerisch	rainy
der Reichstag	German parliament building, Berlin
... rein	into ...
die Reise (n)	journey
das Reisebüro (s)	travel agency
reisen	to travel
relativ	relatively
der/die Rentner/in (-/nen)	pensioner
reparieren	to repair
reservieren	to reserve, book
das Restgeld	change
der Rhein	River Rhine
richtig	right, correct

Vocabulary

der Rock (Röcke)	skirt
die Rolle (n)	role
rot	red
der Rotwein (e)	red wine
die Rückfahrkarte	return ticket
ruhig	quiet
Russland	Russia
sagen	to say
die Sahne	cream
die Sahnesauce	cream sauce
der Salat (e)	salad
Samstag	Saturday
der Sänger (-)	singer
die Sauna	sauna
schade	(that's a) pity
Schau mal	Look!
schick	elegant, chic
das Schinkenbrot (e)	ham sandwich
schlafen*	to sleep
schläft	**er/sie**-form of **schlafen**
das Schlafzimmer (-)	bedroom
schlank	slim
schlecht	bad(ly)
schlechter	worse
der Schlüssel (-)	key
schmecken	to taste (good)
schnell	fast
die Schnellwahl	rapid choice
der Schock (s)	shock
die Schokolade	chocolate
das Schokoladeneis	chocolate ice cream
der Schokoladenkuchen (-)	
	chocolate cake
schon	already
schön	beautiful
der/die Schotte/	
Schottin (n/nen)	Scot (m/f)
Schottland	Scotland
der Schrank (Schränke)	cupboard
schrecklich	terrible/terribly
schreiben (an)	to write (to)
der Schreibtisch (e)	desk
der Schuh (e)	shoe
die Schule (n)	school
schwarz	black
Schwedisch	Swedish (language)
die Schweiz	Switzerland
schwer	heavy
die Schwester (n)	sister
schwierig	difficult
das Schwimmbad	swimming pool
schwimmen	to swim
das Schwimmen	swimming
der See (n)	lake
die See (n)	sea
segeln	to sail
sehen*	to see

die Sehenswürdigkeit (en)	sight worth seeing
sehr	very
sein (*possessive*)	his; its
sein (*verb*)	to be
seit	since
die Seite (n)	side; page
auf der rechten Seite	on the right-hand side
die Seitenstraße (n)	side street
die Sekretärin (nen)	secretary (f)
selbständig	independent
selten	seldom, rarely
Semesterferien *pl*	university vacation
das Seminar (e)	seminar
der Seminarraum (-räume)	seminar room
der Sessel (-)	armchair
sich setzen *refl*	to sit down
sicher	sure, certain
sie	she, it (*fem*), they
Sie	you (*formal*)
sieht	**er/sie**-form of **sehen**
der Sinn für Humor	sense of humour
sitzen	to sit
Ski fahren	to ski
so	so
so was	something like that
die Socke (n)	sock
das Sofa (s)	couch
sofort	at once, immediately
der Sohn (Söhne)	son
das Solarium	solarium
der Sommer	summer
Sommerferien *pl*	summer holidays
der Songschreiber (-)	songwriter
Sonnabend	Saturday (N. Germany)
die Sonne	sun
Sonntag	Sunday
sonst noch etwas?	anything else?
Spanien	Spain
der/die Spanier/in (-/nen)	Spaniard (m/f)
Spanisch	Spanish (language)
spannend	exciting
der Sparpreis (e)	low price
Spaß haben	to have fun
Spaß machen	to be fun
spät	late
später	later
spazieren gehen	to go for a walk
die Speisekarte (n)	menu
der Sperrmüll	bulky refuse (often picked up by bargain-hunters)
sich spezialisieren auf (+ accusative) *refl*	to specialise in
spielen	to play
der Sport	sport
sportlich	sporty
der Sportverein (e)	sports club

das Sportzentrum (-zentren)	sports centre
die Sprache (n)	language
Sprachkenntnisse *pl*	knowledge of languages
der Sprachkurs (e)	language course
sprechen*	to speak
spricht	**er/sie**-form of **sprechen**
der Staat (en)	state
die Stadt (Städte)	town
die Stadtmitte	town centre
das Stadtzentrum (-tren)	town centre
der Stammbaum (-bäume)	family tree
die Station (en)	station (on underground)
stattfinden *sep*	to take place
das Steak (s)	steak
stehen	to stand
stehlen*	to steal
die Stelle (n)	job
die Stellenanzeige (n)	job advert
sterben*	to die
stirbt	**er/sie**-form of **sterben**
der Stock (-)	floor (of building)
im ersten Stock	on the first floor
der Strand (Strände)	beach
die Straße (n)	street
die Straßenbahn (en)	tram
das Straßencafé (s)	pavement café
der Strauß (Sträuße)	bouquet
das Studentenleben	student life
das Studentenwohnheim (e)	hall of residence
der Studienabschluss	degree, diploma
das Studienfach (-fächer)	subject
studieren	to study
studiert	pp of **studieren** (also **er/sie**-form)
das Studium (Studien)	study/studies
der Stuhl (Stühle)	chair
die Stunde (n)	hour; lesson
stundenlang	for hours
suchen	to look for
Südafrika	South Africa
Südeuropa	Southern Europe
der Supermarkt (-märkte)	supermarket
die Symphonie (n)	symphony
das System (e)	system
der Tag (e)	day
die Tageskarte (n)	day ticket
täglich	daily
die Tankstelle (n)	petrol station
tanzen	to dance
die Tanznacht (-nächte)	dance night
die Tasse (n)	cup
die Taste (n)	button, key
tausend	a thousand

das Taxi (s)	taxi
das Team (s)	team
der/die Teamleiter/in (-)/(nen)	team leader
teamorientiert	team-orientated
technisch	technical
der Tee	tea
teilnehmen* an (+ *dative*) *sep*	to take part in
das Telefon (e)	telephone
telefonieren	to phone
die Telefonnummer (-n)	phone number
das Teller (-)	plate
der Termin (e)	appointment, deadline
die Terrasse (n)	terrace
das Territorium (-orien)	territory
der Test (s)	test
einen Test schreiben	to do/take a test
teuer	dear, expensive
teurer	dearer
das Theater (-)	theatre
die Theaterwissenschaft	theatre studies
tippen	to type
der Tisch (e)	table
der Tischtennis	table tennis
der Toast	toast
die Tochter (Töchter)	daugher
die Toilette (n)	toilet
toll	great
die Tomate (n)	tomato
die Tomatensuppe	tomato soup
die Toskana	Tuscany
die Tour (en)	tour
tragen*	to wear; carry
trägt	**er/sie**-form of **tragen**
traurig	sad
treffen*	to meet
sich treffen* *refl*	to meet up
trifft	**er/sie**-form of **treffen**
trinken	to drink
das T-Shirt (s)	T-shirt
tun	to do
die Tür (en)	door
tut mir leid	I'm sorry
das TwenTicket	young person's ticket
typisch	typical
die U-Bahn	underground
über	about, over, across
überrascht	surprised
die Überraschung (en)	surprise
der/die Übersetzer/in (-/nen)	translator
das Übersetzungsbüro (s)	translation agency
die Uhr (en)	clock, watch
zwei Uhr	two o'clock
um	at (time); around (place)
um wie viel Uhr?	what time?

Vocabulary

um … zu	in order to
umgezogen	pp of **umziehen**
umsteigen *sep*	to change (trains/buses)
umziehen *sep*	to move (house)
unabhängig	independent
und	and
Und dir?	And how are you?
unglücklich	unhappy, unlucky
die Universität (en)	university
unser	our
unter	under
die Unterkunft	accommodation
der Unterricht	lesson(s), class(es)
im Unterricht	in class
die Untersuchung (en)	investigation
unterwegs	on the way
der Urlaub (e)	holiday
in Urlaub fahren	to go on holiday
das Vanilleeis	vanilla ice-cream
der Vater (Väter)	father
verbessern	to improve
die Verbindung (en)	connection
verbracht	pp of **verbringen**
verbringen	to spend (time)
verdienen	to earn
verheiratet	married
verlassen*	to leave (also pp)
verlässt	**er/sie**-form of **verlassen**
verliebt	in love
verlieren	to lose
verloren	pp of **verlieren**
die Vermietung	hire
die Verpflegung	catering
verstanden	pp of **verstehen**
verstehen	to understand
Verwandte *pl*	relatives
das Verzeichnis (se)	index
die Videothek (en)	video shop/library
viel	a lot
viel zu machen	a lot to do
viele	many
vielen Dank	many thanks
vielleicht	perhaps
das Viertel (-)	quarter
Viertel nach/vor	quarter past/to
das Violinkonzert (e)	violin concerto
voll	full
von	from; of
vor	before, in front of; (before time expression) ago
vorbeigehen *sep*	to go past
am Krankenhaus vorbei	past the hospital
vorher	previously
die Vorlesung (en)	lecture
der Vorteil (e)	advantage

wächst auf	**er/sie**-form of **aufwachsen**
Wahlen *pl*	elections
wählen	to choose
die Wahrheit	truth
der Wald (Wälder)	forest
der/die Waliser/in (-/nen)	Welshman/woman
wandern	to go on a hike, walk
Wanderungen *pl*	hikes, walks
wann	when (in questions)
war	was
warm	hot
Warst du schon in … ?	have you ever been to …?
warum	why
was	what
Was ist los?	What's the matter?
die Waschmaschine (n)	washing machine
wäscht … ab	**er/sie**-form of **abwaschen**
das Wasser	water
wechseln	to change money
weggehen *sep*	to go away
weh tun	to hurt
weil	because
der Wein (e)	wine
die Weinkarte (n)	wine-list
weiß	white
weiß	**ich-, er/sie**-form of **wissen**
der Weißwein (e)	white wine
weiter	further
welche(r/s)	which
der Wellness-Bereich (e)	health and fitness area
weltberühmt	world-famous
die Weltmeisterschaft (en)	World Championship
wen	whom
wenig	little, not much
wenn	if, when
wer	who
werden*	to become
der Westen	West
das Wetter	weather
wichtig	important
wie	how
wie alt	how old
Wie geht's?	How are you?
Wie heißt du?	What's your name?
Wie kann ich Ihnen helfen?	How can I help you?
wie komme ich zu …	how do I get to …
wie lange	how long (time)
wieder	again
die Wiedervereinigung	reunification (of Germany, 1990)
Wien	Vienna
wird	**er/sie**-form of **werden**

wirklich	really
wirst	**du**-form of **werden**
wissen*	to know
wo(her)	where (from)
die Woche (n)	week
das Wochenende (-)	weekend
wohin?	where to?
wohnen	to live
der Wohnort	place of residence
die Wohnung (en)	flat
das Wohnzimmer (-)	living room
wollte	wanted (to) – simple past of **wollen** (**ich**, **er/sie**-forms)
das Wörterbuch (-bücher)	dictionary
wunderbar	wonderful
die Wurst (Würste)	sausage
das Würstchen (-)	(small) sausage
die Zahl (en)	number
zahlen	to pay
die Zahlung (en)	payment

der Zahnarzt (-ärzte)	dentist
Zahnschmerzen *pl*	toothache
zeigen	to show
die Zeit (en)	time
die Zeitschrift (en)	magazine
die Zeitung (en)	newspaper
das Zentrum (Zentren)	centre
ziemlich	quite
das Zimmer (-)	room
die Zimmerreservierung	room booking
zu	to; too (+ adjective)
zufrieden	content
der Zug (Züge)	train
die Zukunft	future
zurückerhalten* *sep*	to get back
zurückkommen *sep*	to come back
zusammen	together
der Zusammenhang (-hänge)	connection, context
zusammenleben mit *sep*	to live with
zuverlässig	reliable
zwischen	between

171

ANSWERS

UNIT 1

5 **a** Deutschland **b** Österreich **c** England
d Griechenland **e** Frankreich **f** Schottland
g Belgien **h** Irland **i** Spanien **j** Dänemark
k Wales **l** Italien

6 **a** Spanien **b** Deutschland **c** Frankreich
d Österreich **e** Griechenland

8 **a** Wie heißt du? **b** Wie heißen Sie?
c Woher kommst du? **d** Woher kommen
Sie? **e** Wo wohnst du? **f** Wo wohnen Sie?
g Bist du Engländer(in)? **h** Sind Sie
Engländer(in)? **i** Bist du Student(in)?
j Sind Sie Student(in)?

9 **a** **i** Sind Sie Engländer? **ii** Wo wohnen Sie?
iii Kommen Sie aus Frankfurt?
b **i** Wo wohnen Sie? **ii** Sind Sie
Engländerin? **iii** Sind Sie Studentin?

11 **a** **i** Das ist Marianne Möller. **ii** Nein, sie ist
Lehrerin. **iii** Sie wohnt in Manchester.
iv Sie kommt aus Hamburg. **v** Nein, sie
ist Deutsche.
b **i** Er heißt Tom Paschke. **ii** Nein, er ist
Lehrer. **iii** Nein, er wohnt in London.
iv Nein, er kommt aus Berlin. **v** Ja, er ist
Deutscher.
c **i** Nein, er heißt Marc Berlande. **ii** Nein,
er ist Student. **iii** Er wohnt in Glasgow.
iv Er kommt aus Marseille. **v** Nein, er ist
Franzose.
d **i** Das ist Sue Edwards. **ii** Sie kommt aus
Birmingham. **iii** Sie wohnt in Leipzig.
iv Nein, sie lernt Deutsch. **v** Nein, sie ist
Engländerin.

12 **a** **i** bin, heiße, komme **ii** heiße, bin, lerne
iii heiße, komme, bin, lerne **iv** heiße,
komme, bin, wohne
b **i** Sie ist Deutsche. Sie heißt Silke und
kommt aus Stuttgart. Sie studiert Sport
und Englisch. **ii** Sie heißt Eva. Sie ist

Spanierin, aber sie studiert in England.
Sie studiert Literatur und lernt Englisch
– und Deutsch! **iii** Er heißt Michael. Er
kommt aus Cork in Irland. Er ist Student
in Birmingham. Er studiert Biologie. Er
lernt auch Deutsch. **iv** Er heißt Yannis
und er kommt aus Griechenland. Er ist
Student hier in England. Er wohnt in
Brighton und studiert Psychologie.

15 **a** **i** Er kommt aus Leipzig. **ii** Nein, er
studiert in Marburg. **iii** Cristina ist
Martins Freundin. **iv** Nein, sie ist
Italienerin. **v** Sie ist Sekretärin. **vi** Sie
arbeitet in Frankfurt.
b **i** Ja, sie arbeitet als Kellnerin. **ii** Nein, sie
ist Französin. **iii** Lyon ist in Frankreich.
iv Sie wohnt in London.
c **i** Er heißt Bernd Voigt. **ii** Bremen ist in
Deutschland. **iii** Nein, er ist Deutscher.
iv Er ist Journalist.

Extra!

18 **Annie** studiert Literatur. Sie kommt aus
Frankreich, aber sie wohnt in Düsseldorf.
Sie arbeitet als Kellnerin.
Jürgen kommt aus Österreich. Er wohnt in
London und er ist Journalist von Beruf.
(Jürgens Freundin ist Engländerin.)
Padma ist Engländerin und sie kommt aus
Birmingham. Sie studiert Psychologie in
Leeds.

19 **a** *Your summary should be similar to the
following*: Ursula Eggebrecht is from
America, but she is studying psychology
at Bremen University. She is studying in
Europe because her father is German
and her mother Dutch, and she feels
European as well as American. She has
also got a job as a car mechanic.

b i Sie wohnt in Bremen. **ii** Sie kommt aus New York. **iii** Sie studiert Psychologie. **iv** Nein, sie studiert in Deutschland. **v** Ja, sie ist Automechanikerin / sie repariert Autos.

Grammatikübungen

1 **a** Studentin/Deutsche **b** Student/ Deutscher **c** Spanierin/Lehrerin **d** Italiener/Journalist

2 **a** Er **b** Sie **c** ich **d** ich **e** er **f** du **g** Ich

3 **a** heißt **b** wohnt (arbeitet) **c** kommt **d** kommen **e** komme **f** Ist **g** bin **h** sind

4 **a** Wie heißt sie? **b** Wo wohnst du? / Wo wohnen Sie? **c** Bist du Student? / Sind Sie Student? **d** Wo arbeitet er? **e** Woher kommst du? / Woher kommen Sie? **f** Bist du / Sind Sie Franzose/ Spanier/Italiener...? **g** Was ist er von Beruf? **h** Was lernt sie?

5 **a** Wer **b** Wo **c** Wie **d** Woher **e** Was **f** Was

UNIT 2

1 **b** 5, 9, 12, 14, 17
  c 13, 8, 6, 11, 16, 2, 1, 15

3 **a** **73** dreiundsiebzig
     54 vierundfünfzig
     66 sechsundsechzig
     47 siebenundvierzig
     95 fünfundneunzig
     81 einundachtzig
     38 achtunddreißig
  b **30** dreißig **40** vierzig **50** fünfzig
     60 sechzig **70** siebzig **80** achtzig
     90 neunzig
  c **i** 34 **ii** 54 **iii** 56 **iv** 87 **v** 98

5 **a** **i** 7.45 Uhr **ii** 8.05 Uhr **iii** 8.30 Uhr **iv** 9 Uhr **v** 10.15 Uhr **vi** 11 Uhr
  b **i** Nein, er steht um 7.45 Uhr auf. **ii** Er frühstückt um 8.05 Uhr. **iii** Er geht um 8.30 Uhr an die Universität. **iv** Die Vorlesung beginnt um 9 Uhr. **v** Nein, er trinkt um 10.15 Uhr Kaffee. **vi** Er geht um 11 Uhr in die Bibliothek.

9 *Note possible variations in word order!* Er geht um 13.30 Uhr in die Bibliothek. **oder:** Um 13.30 Uhr geht er in die Bibliothek. Er geht um 14.30 Uhr in die Stadt. Um 16 Uhr hat er eine Deutschstunde. Er spielt um 17.10 Uhr Fußball. / Er geht um 17.10 Uhr in das Sportzentrum. Um 18.45 Uhr geht er nach Hause.

10 1c **2**e **3**f **4**a **5**g **6**h **7**d **8**b

11 **Bernd:** Ich gehe oft aus. Manchmal trinke ich ein Bier, manchmal spiele ich Fußball.
   Petra goes out rarely, but she often watches TV or listens to music. She sometimes reads.
   Ralf never stays at home. He goes to the pub or the disco.
   Jasmin always stays at home. She writes emails, but rarely watches TV. She goes to bed at 11 pm.
   Bernd goes out a lot. He sometimes goes for a beer, and sometimes he plays football.

14 **a** Sie trinkt (morgens) eine Tasse Kaffee. / Morgens trinkt sie eine Tasse Kaffee. **b** Sie geht immer in die Mensa. **c** Sie isst um 13 Uhr (zum Mittagessen) ein Käsebrot. **d** Nein, sie trinkt zum Mittagessen eine Cola. **e** Sie isst Nudeln mit Fisch oder Salat. **f** Sie trinkt ein Glas Orangensaft.

Extra!

16 **a** Nein, Vera trinkt mit Susanne Kaffee.

b Nein, Veras Vorlesung beginnt um 16 Uhr. **c** Am Abend geht sie ins Kino und in die Bar. **d** Sie geht um 20.30 Uhr ins Kino. **e** Walter steht um 7 Uhr auf. **f** Er frühstückt, geht schwimmen und in die Vorlesung. **g** Um 12 Uhr geht er in die Bibliothek. **h** Nein, er bleibt zu Hause. / Nein, er liest ein Buch.

17 **Some important points:**
Annette is studying psychology. She goes out in the evenings to the theatre or pub. She has lectures during the day and fish or pasta for dinner.
Klaus is studying sports and literature. He usually stays in in the evenings. In the morning he goes to the library and he often eats pizza. (*This is an informal conversation.*)
Herr Wolf comes from Magdeburg and is a teacher. He now lives in Heidelberg and he is in town to do some shopping. He often goes for a coffee and he watches TV in the evenings. He is also learning French.
Frau Petri comes from Heidelberg. She is a stewardess and works in Frankfurt. She often stays at home in the evenings, but sometimes goes to the fitness centre. She plays the guitar and listens to music. (*Formal conversation*)

Grammatikübungen

1 der Orangensaft, die Kneipe, die Diskothek, der Lehrer, das Bier, der Kaffee, die Tasse, die E-Mail, der Abend, das Sportzentrum, der Fisch, das Glas, der Toast, die Studentin, das Käsebrot, die Deutschstunde

2 **a** beginnt **b** trinke **c** geht **d** liest **e** essen **f** gehe … aus, bleibe **g** Hast **h** steht … auf

3 **i** Eva geht nachmittags in die Bibliothek. / Nachmittags geht Eva in die Bibliothek. **ii** Ich esse manchmal Toast. / Manchmal esse ich Toast. **iii** Er sieht immer fern. / Immer sieht er fern. **iv** Ich gehe um 17 Uhr nach Hause. / Um 17 Uhr gehe ich nach Hause. **v** Sie spielt oft Tischtennis. / Oft spielt sie Tischtennis. **vi** Ich habe heute eine Deutschstunde. / Heute habe ich eine Deutschstunde.

UNIT 3

2 **a** **i** Stephanie ist 19 Jahre alt. **ii** Nein, sie ist ledig. **iii** Sie studiert Mathematik und Informatik. **iv** Ihre Mutter / Sie ist Architektin von Beruf. **v** Ihr Vater / Er arbeitet bei Siemens. **vi** Carolines Mann / Er heißt Heinz. **vii** Ja, Caroline hat zwei Kinder. **viii** Ja, er hat eine Freundin. Sie heißt Tina.

b *Your talk should be similar to the following*: Ich heiße Stephanie. Ich bin 19 Jahre alt. Meine Mutter heißt Martina und ist 51 Jahre alt. Mein Vater heißt Christian und er ist 53 Jahre alt. Meine Schwester Caroline ist 25 Jahre alt und sie ist verheiratet. Ihr Mann heißt Heinz und ist 29. Sie hat zwei Kinder, Jessica ist 3 und Michael ist 2. Mein Bruder Andreas ist 22 Jahre alt. Er ist ledig, aber er hat eine Freundin. Seine Freundin heißt Tina und ist 23. Mein Freund Alex ist 21 Jahre alt.

3 **a** ihr **b** Ihre **c** ihr **d** Ihr **e** Ihre **f** Ihr **g** Ihre **h** Seine **i** Seine **j** Sein **k** Sein **l** Seine

4 **a** **i** Mein **ii** 22 **iii** ledig **iv** Meine **v** 2 **vi** Ingenieur **vii** 51
b **i** Wie alt sind Sie? **ii** Sind Sie ledig? **iii** Wie heißt Ihr Mann? **iv** Haben Sie Kinder? **v** Wie alt ist Ihre Tochter?

vi Haben Sie Geschwister? **vii** Was ist Ihre Mutter von Beruf?

7 Stephanies Großvater hat ein Fahrrad, ein Radio, ein Telefon und eine Katze.

Er hat kein Auto, keinen Fernseher, keinen Computer und kein Handy.

8 **a/b** **1** Auto (n) **2** Fahrrad (n) **3** Kugelschreiber (m) **4** MP3-Player (m) **5** Brieftasche (f) **6** Handy (n) **7** Fernseher (m) **8** Radio (n) **9** Computer (m) **10** Handtasche (f) **11** Wörterbuch (n) **12** Kreditkarte (f) **13** Katze (f)

10 **a** f Sie wohnen in Mannheim. **b** r **c** r **d** f Sie essen viel Obst und Gemüse. **e** f Sie haben kein Auto. **f** f Beide sind 80 Jahre alt. **g** f Sie haben ein Auto. **h** r **i** r **j** f Sie gehen nie in das Sportzentrum.

11 *The inaccurate points:* **a** They often watch TV. **b** They sometimes drink wine.

Extra!

13 *Your key words should include several of the following:*
Annelie: ledig / zwei Brüder, Paul und Richard / Paul (23) studiert, Richard (19) arbeitet im Café / Annelies Freundin Marion wohnt in Kiel / Annelie und Marion gehen oft ins Sportzentrum / Annelie liest viel und hört Musik
Markus: seine Mutter ist Managerin, sein Vater Elektriker / seine Schwester Barbara (25) ist verheiratet und hat ein Kind (2 Jahre alt), ihr Mann ist Student / hat Freunde und geht ins Theater / fährt Rad und geht in die Kneipe
Hanna: ledig / hat eine Tochter (10) / Sekretärin, arbeitet vormittags / lernt abends (Abendschule) / wohnt mit Mutter / Freundin Vera / Kollegin / gehen manchmal ins Restaurant oder schwimmen / bleibt zu Hause und sieht fern

14 **a** **i** keine Überraschung **ii** Jugendliche **iii** besitzen **iv** (der) Zusammenhang / (die) Verbindung **v** (die) Untersuchung **vi** (die) Verfügbarkeit **vii** (die) Lesefähigkeit **viii** Noten **ix** profitieren von
b A study in England shows that children and young people are more likely to own a mobile phone than a book. There is a clear link between the availability of books in the home and reading ability. But does it matter? After all, you can learn to read on an iPhone or a computer too. What matters is learning to read and write, not how you do it.

Grammatikübungen

1 **a** eine **b** ein, ein **c** einen, kein **d** einen, eine **e** ein **f** eine, einen **g** keine

2 **a** das Land **b** der Student **c** die Mahlzeit **d** die Tochter **e** das Kind

3 **a** sind **b** wohnen (studieren) **c** haben **d** bleiben (sind) **e** essen **f** trinken

4 **a** Sie ist Sekretärin von Beruf. **b** Sein Bruder heißt Oliver. **c** Seine Freundin wohnt in Leipzig. **d** Ihre Katze heißt Minka. **e** Seine Mutter arbeitet (im Moment) nicht. **f** Ihre Schwester ist 12 Jahre alt. **g** Ihre beste Freundin heißt Hanna. **h** Sein Hund heißt Wolf. **i** Sein Vater ist Mathematikprofessor von Beruf. **j** Ihre Mutter ist 43 Jahre alt.

5 **1** f mein **2** d seinen **3** e ihr **4** c sein **5** a mein **6** b ihre

Answers

UNIT 4

1   **a** Felix **b** geht **c** Anna **d** raucht
   e gern **f** Auto

4   **a** t **b** t **c** t **d** f **e** f

5   **Gudrun trinkt** gern Tee / lieber Cola /
am liebsten Wein / nicht gern Bier.
Gudrun isst gern Käse / lieber Salat /
am liebsten Fisch / nicht gern Pizza.
Frank trinkt gern Wein / lieber Tee / am
liebsten Bier / nicht gern Cola.
Frank isst gern Salat / lieber Käse / am
liebsten Pizza / nicht gern Fisch.
Gabi trinkt gern Cola / lieber Wein / am
liebsten Tee / nicht gern Bier.
Gabi isst gern Pizza / lieber Fisch / am
liebsten Käse / nicht gern Salat.

7   **Astrid** likes going to the disco or for a
walk. She doesn't like going to the pub
because she neither smokes nor drinks
beer.
Christoph doesn't like dancing, he
prefers the pub. He too enjoys going
for a walk, but prefers to stay at home
and watch TV – especially football!

8   **b** **i** 5.45 **ii** 2.30 **iii** 9.15 **iv** 4.10 **v** 9.35

10 **a** They agree to meet for an Italian
meal at about 9 on Friday.
   b **i** Schade **ii** Ist das in Ordnung?
iii tut mir leid. **iv** Kommst du mit?
v das geht. **vi** vielleicht **vii** bis
Freitag. **viii** Wie geht's? **ix** Tschüss
x Wo treffen wir uns? **xi** fängt … an
xii leider
   c muss … arbeiten, will … essen
gehen, kann … ausgehen, können …
gehen, kannst … ausgehen, müssen
… gehen, muss … gehen

11 **a** Er muss in die Bibliothek gehen.
   b Sie will ins Sportzentrum gehen.
   c Nein, er hat am Mittwoch keine Zeit.
Er will mit Klaus nach München fahren.
   d Sie trifft ihre Freundinnen am

Donnerstag. **e** Sie können am Freitag
Tennis spielen. **f** Er will das
Fußballspiel sehen.

12 **a** **i** Öffnungszeiten **ii** Eintritt
iii italienische Küche **iv** ab 23 Uhr
v täglich **vi** Weinkarte
vii kinderfreundlich
   b **i** Man kann ins Restaurant / in die
altdeutsche Bierstube / ins Kino
gehen. **ii** Man kann in Charly's
Diskothek gehen. **iii** Man kann ins
Restaurant / ins Kino gehen. **iv** Man
kann um 15.30 oder um 19.30 ins
Kino gehen. **v** Man kann von 17 Uhr
bis 23 Uhr ins Restaurant gehen.
vi Man kann am Samstagabend um
20 Uhr ins Theater gehen.

Extra!

14 **Montag:** 10.00 Vorlesung (Philosophie) /
12.00 Mittagessen Kantine mit Markus /
13.30 Einkaufen / 16.00 Gitarrenstunde /
19.15 Fernsehen, kochen, lesen / 22.30
Bett
Donnerstag: 8.15 Schwimmen / 11.00
Vorlesung / 13.00 Spanischstunde / 15.45
Café mit Mutter / 17.00 Sportzentrum /
20.15 Kino / 22.30 Kneipe
Samstag: 11.00 Aufstehen /
Mittagessen mit Schwester und Freund
/ 16.00 Stadt (Einkaufen) / Musik hören
(zu Hause) / 20.15 Kneipe mit Anja /
21.30 Chinesisches Restaurant / 23.00
bis 2.00 Disko

15 **Sabine und Rolf können zusammen**
ins Kino gehen / in die Diskothek gehen
/ Apfelwein trinken / italienisch essen /
schwimmen gehen
Sie können nicht zusammen in die
Kneipe gehen / Fußball spielen / ins
Restaurant gehen / ins Sportzentrum
gehen

Grammatikübungen

1 **a** Ich trinke gern Mineralwasser / lieber Cola / am liebsten Orangensaft / nicht gern Bier. **b** Er isst gern Pasta / lieber Pizza / am liebsten Pommes frites / nicht gern Salat. **c** Ich lese gern / höre lieber Musik / spiele am liebsten Gitarre / gehe nicht gern spazieren. **d** Sie gehen gern ins Kino / lieber in die Stadt / am liebsten ins Sportzentrum / nicht gern in die Diskothek.

2 **a** Willst **b** gehen **c** kann **d** ausgehen **e** muss **f** bleiben **g** wollen **h** trinken **i** Können **j** sehen

3 *Your suggestions should include the following*: Man kann in Clubs und in die Diskothek gehen, und man kann in die Kneipe oder ins Kino gehen. Man kann ins Restaurant gehen / indisch essen gehen. Man kann ins Theater gehen oder einkaufen gehen. Man kann auch im Peak District spazieren gehen.

4 den Fernseher, das Radio, den DVD-Rekorder, den MP3-Player, das Handy, die Katze, den Hund, das Wörterbuch, die CDs (pl), das Moped, den Computer

UNIT 5

1 **i** Nein, sie ist unter der Dusche. **ii** Astrid ist im Unterricht. **iii** Sie arbeitet am Computer. **iv** Sie sitzt am Computer. / Sie ist in ihrem Zimmer. **v** Markus ist mit Anna und Jens im Eiscafé. **vi** Er ruft später an.

2 **a i** Sportzentrum **ii** Mensa **iii** Sportzentrum **iv** Kneipe

3 **das Wohnzimmer** – living room, **die Küche** – kitchen, **das Schlafzimmer** – bedroom, **das Badezimmer** – bathroom, **die Garage** – garage, **der Balkon** – balcony, **das Esszimmer** – dining room

4 **a i** Schlafzimmer **ii** Badezimmer/ Toilette (WC) **iii** Esszimmer **iv** Wohnzimmer **v** Küche

5 Es gibt einen Tisch und vier Stühle / ein Sofa / einen Sessel / ein Bücherregal / einen Fernseher / ein Radio.

7 **a i** unter dem Bett **ii** Bücher und Papiere **iii** auf dem Bett **iv** Tassen und Teller

8 1 hell 2 gemütlich 3 modern 4 wunderbar 5 dunkel 6 kalt 7 bequem 8 klein 9 kompakt 10 groß 11 toll 12 warm 13 neu 14 kitschig 15 altmodisch 16 exklusiv 17 teuer 18 köstlich

9 **a** *Your list should include some of the following*: Sie haben tolle Sessel / einen praktischen Balkon / moderne Stühle / wunderbare Kissen / ein kaltes, dunkles Schlafzimmer / ein neues (bequemes) Bett / ein großes Schlafzimmer / eine kitschige (altmodische/exklusive/teure) Lampe / eine kleine (kompakte/ gemütliche) Küche.

Extra!

10 *Your notes should include some of the following*:
Volker: wohnt in Berlin (Zentrum) mit Freundin Simone; ein Zimmer für Volker und ein Zimmer für Simone, ein Wohnzimmer, Küche und Badezimmer; Volker hat: ein großes Bett, einen CD-Spieler, einen Tisch und Computer, einen kleinen Schrank, ein Bücherregal, einen alten Tisch (vom Sperrmüll)
Silvia: wohnt in Dresden ; nicht zentral (hat ein Auto); hat eine große Wohnung; Wohnung hat einen großen Balkon, ein Schlafzimmer, Wohnzimmer, Esszimmer, Badezimmer (Dusche und Badewanne), Küche; Im Wohnzimmer hat Silvia ein Ledercouch und Sessel, einen Tisch,

moderne Bilder, ein kleines Bücherregal, einen CD-Player und Fernseher, eine Art Nouveau Lampe

Oliver: wohnt bei Ulm (kleine Stadt) mit Eltern; das Haus hat 5 Zimmer (Wohnzimmer, Esszimmer, Schlafzimmer, Olivers Zimmer, Zimmer für seine Schwester), 2 Badezimmer, Küche, Garage und Garten; großes Esszimmer, Esstisch und 6 Stühle, Schrank, eine altmodische Lampe

11 *Email should include*: Room: desk, office chair, lamp, bookcase, 2-seater sofa, bed and wardrobe. Communal area for 4: dining table, 4 chairs, cooker, fridge, wall cupboards. Bathroom: bath, shower, WC.

Grammatikübungen

1 ein Radio, einen Computer, eine Lampe, einen Fernseher, einen Schreibtisch, einen Kühlschrank, einen Elektroherd, einen Tisch, eine Waschmaschine, eine Mikrowelle

2 **a** der **b** ins **c** der **d** meinem **e** ins **f** im

3 **a** beim, in der **b** von einem **c** auf einem, im **d** mit seiner **e** zum

4 **a** schöne **b** neue, modern **c** kleines **d** elegant, bequem **e** kleinen **f** teure

5 **a** Wohnen Sie hier in Rostock? **b** Du backst köstliche Kuchen. **c** Haben Sie eine Wohnung mit Garage? **d** Habt ihr eine Dusche oder eine Badewanne?

UNIT 6

1 **a** **i** auf der linken Seite **ii** Geh über die Straße. **iii** Geh am Krankenhaus vorbei. **iv** wir sind um die Ecke. **v** an der Ecke **vi** die nächste Straße links **vii** direkt gegenüber der Schule

viii nicht weit von dem Krankenhaus **ix** in der Nähe **x** im ersten Stock

2 Ich nehme den Bus. Es gibt eine Haltestelle in der Humboldtstraße. Ich gehe über die Straße und dann rechts und die nächste Straße links. Ich gehe am Krankenhaus vorbei und nehme die zweite Straße rechts. Die Nummer 72 ist auf der linken Seite.

3 **a** **a** weit **b** rechts **c** Parkhaus **d** Seite **e** erste Straße **f** rechts **g** geradeaus **h** über

4 **a** Entschuldigen Sie bitte, wie komme ich zum Museum für Moderne Kunst? **b** Entschuldigen Sie, wie komme ich zum Parkhaus Bendergasse?

6 **1** d **2** g **3** a **4** j **5** m **6** l **7** k **8** f **9** b **10** e **11** c **12** h **13** i

7 **a** **a** rechts **b** zweite **c** Kreuzung **d** gegenüber **b** **e** links **f** rechts **g** rechten

9 **1** x **2** z **3** w

10 **b** **i** gegenüber einer, einem **ii** einem Blumengeschäft **iii** dem **iv** zwischen einer Kirche und einer Tankstelle **v** dem Parkhaus

c *Some possible answers*: **i** Die Bar ist gegenüber dem Hotel / gegenüber der Kirche / neben dem Schwimmbad. **ii** Das Kino ist neben dem Restaurant / gegenüber dem Krankenhaus. **iii** Die Schule ist gegenüber der Kneipe / neben der Mensa. **iv** Die Bibliothek ist zwischen der Universität und dem Museum / gegenüber der Mensa. **v** Der Park ist gegenüber der Universität/der Kneipe / neben der Mensa.

12 **a** Das Kleid ist zu lang. **b** Sie kauft einen Rock. **c** Sie will ein Hemd für Michael kaufen.

13 a i Dieses T-Shirt gefällt mir nicht.
ii Diese Jacke gefällt mir nicht.
iii Dieses Hemd gefällt mir nicht.
iv Dieser Pullover gefällt mir nicht.
v Diese Socken gefallen mir nicht.
vi Dieser Rock gefällt mir nicht.
vii Dieses Kleid gefällt mir nicht.
viii Dieses Jackett gefällt mir nicht.
ix Diese Schuhe gefallen mir nicht.

Extra!

15 a Brandenburger Tor **b** Berliner Dom
c Königliche Bibliothek

16 *You should mention three of the places below in your answer:*
Reichstag Germany's parliament; designed by British architect Sir Norman Foster; after WW2, the Reichstag was a ruin
Unter den Linden most famous street in Berlin
Staatsbibliothek 6 million books; lovely garden
Humboldt-Universität Berlin's first university; today it has 23,000 students, Karl Marx studied there
Deutsche Staatsoper destroyed twice in WW2; restored 1955; this week they are performing Mozart's "Marriage of Figaro"
(das) Deutsche Historische Museum oldest baroque building in Berlin; you can see 600 years of history
Museumsinsel cultural centre of Berlin; 5 buildings – museums and galleries

Grammatikübungen

1 i Trink **ii** Gehen Sie **iii** Kommt **iv** Bring **v** Geht **vi** Arbeite

2 i Gefällt dir dieses Kleid? – Ja, es gefällt mir sehr. **ii** Gefällt dir diese Jacke? – Nein, sie gefällt mir nicht. **iii** Gefällt dir dieser Rock? – Ja, er gefällt mir sehr.

iv Gefällt dir diese Krawatte? – Nein, sie gefällt mir nicht. **v** Gefallen dir diese Schuhe? – Nein, sie gefallen mir nicht. **vi** Gefällt dir dieser Pullover? – Ja, er gefällt mir sehr.

3 **1** f **2** e **3** d **4** h/c **5** g **6** a **7** b **8** c/h

UNIT 7

2 a im März **b** am neunzehnten **c** Tage **d** am einundzwanzigsten **e** am zweiundzwanzigsten **f** ab dem dreiundzwanzigsten

3 b i der vierundzwanzigste Januar **ii** der fünfzehnte April **iii** der neunte Juni **iv** der dritte Oktober **v** der zehnte Dezember
c i 5.11 **ii** 17.3 **iii** 22.8 **iv** 30.5 **v** 1.7

4 a Ich lerne seit sechs Monaten Deutsch. **b** Ich mache einen intensiven Sprachkurs. **c** Ich mache den Kurs, um mein Deutsch zu verbessern. **d** Er dauert zehn Tage. **e** Ich lerne Deutsch, weil ich im Ausland arbeiten möchte.

5 This letter confirms Vijay Basran's room booking for the students' hall of residence in Bonn. He has booked a single room with bath and shower, cable TV and telephone. There is a communal kitchen and a student refectory (open for lunch). The room is booked from 31 March till 9 April, price €21.00 a night without breakfast. The hall of residence is situated in the centre of Bonn, tram stop is 5 minutes away. Leisure activities include a sports centre, cinema and theatre, swimming pool and gym as well as bicycle hire.

6 b a Kiel **b** 15.04 **c** 14.23 **d** 3 **e** €48
c i Muss ich umsteigen? **ii** Wann kommt der Zug an? **iii** Was kostet eine

Rückfahrkarte? **iv** Einmal Bonn hin und zurück, bitte. **v** Zweimal einfach nach Kiel, bitte. **vi** der nächste Zug **vii** Wann fährt der Zug nach Kiel ab? **viii** von Gleis 3

7 **a** vom 4. bis zum 12. April / Zimmer Nummer 47, im vierten Stock / Johannes / Marion / die Vorlesungen

b Vijay arrives at reception and is handed the key to his room. There is no lift, but a porter can carry the suitcase upstairs. Vijay declines, as his suitcase is not heavy. He is introduced to Ms Schubert, the team leader.

9 **a** **i** The rapid choice option is for central destinations. You only need to press the appropriate button. **ii** You find your destination in the alphabetical list, which gives you a destination number. **iii** You press the rapid choice button and then choose the type of ticket you want. The machine will display the fare. Alternatively, you type in the destination number. **iv** Adult / child / day ticket **v** You can pay with coins or notes. The machine gives change.

Extra!

10 *Your grid should contain some of the information listed below*:
Paloma: *Personal*: comes from Madrid *Course*: is on a three-week course at university and has six hours of teaching a day / the course is interesting and the group is small / course very expensive; *Homework/duties*: a lot of homework (one to two hours per day) / likes talking, but finds writing difficult / exam at the end of the course: *Friends*: Italian friend Paola / they go shopping together (and to the disco and pubs) /

Paola hopes to visit her some time
Jean-Paul: *Personal*: comes from France; *Course*: six-week course in Munich / classes only in the morning / teachers a bit boring / enjoys the role-plays; *Homework*: not much homework, but projects on topics related to Munich / listens to cassettes to improve language; *Friends*: met nice French girl, Nathalie (speak French – bad for his German) / also made friends with a German, Manfred

11 *Suggested summary*: The hotel is only 1.5 km from the motorway. Rooms from €89, which includes breakfast, fitness centre and car park. All have a toilet and shower, cable TV, telephone and a mini-bar. It's on the river bank, with a terrace (beautiful view) and beer garden. There's also a restaurant and a cosy bar. It's located just a few minutes from the sights of Old Heidelberg.

Grammatikübungen

1 **a** Sie kann leider nicht kommen, weil sie am vierzehnten einen Test schreibt. **b** Ich weiß, dass er sehr gute Noten bekommt. **c** Wir haben keine Zeit, weil wir jeden Abend arbeiten. **d** Wenn das Wetter schlecht ist, komme ich schon am neunzehnten zurück. **e** Sie fahren nach Deutschland, um einen Deutschkurs zu machen. **f** Ich habe einen Job, um Geld für die Sommerferien zu verdienen.

2 **a** Seit drei Jahren wohnt Dieter mit seinen Freunden Uwe und Hans zusammen. **b** Seit November hilft er seinen Eltern im Büro.

3 **a** Klaus gibt ihm einen Brief. **b** Markus geht mit ihr ins Kino. **c** Ich kann Ihnen ein gutes Café zeigen. **d** Sagen Sie mir, wenn Sie Probleme haben. **e** Wie geht es dir? **f** Ali zeigt ihnen sein neues Auto.

4 a **i** der erste März **ii** der sechsundzwanzigste Juni **iii** der dritte Oktober **iv** der fünfzehnte Mai **v** der dreißigste Januar **vi** der siebte August **vii** der elfte November **viii** der siebenundzwanzigste Februar

b **i** Am ersten März fahre ich nach London. **ii** Am sechsundzwanzigsten Juni hat sie Geburtstag. **iii** Am dritten Oktober geht er zum Zahnarzt. **iv** Am fünfzehnten Mai ziehen wir um. **v** Am dreißigsten Januar schreibe ich einen Test. **vi** Am siebten August fahren wir zum Sprachkurs. **vii** Am elften November fängt der Sprachkurs an. **viii** Am siebenundzwanzigsten Februar gehen wir essen.

UNIT 8

1 a Und du, was hast du gestern gemacht? – Ich habe Fußball gespielt.

b **i** Sabine hat bei Aldi eingekauft. **ii** Sie hat Nudeln, Tomaten, Salat, Rotwein und Parmesan gekauft. **iii** Nach dem Essen haben die Freunde Musik gehört und ein bisschen getanzt. **iv** Sie haben Karten gespielt.

2 **Um Viertel nach acht** hat Verena **heute Toast** mit Marmelade gegessen, und dazu hat sie **ein Glas Mineralwasser** getrunken. Nach dem Frühstück hat sie einige E-Mails an ihre Freunde **in Norddeutschland** geschrieben. Sie hat **ein Buch** gelesen und dann **um 12 Uhr** im Café Bauer **ihre Schwester** getroffen. Sie haben beide **eine Cola** getrunken. Am Abend hat Verena **ihren Freund Andreas** angerufen, um **ihn** ins Kino einzuladen. **Der Film war langweilig**.

3 a bin aufgestanden – aufstehen / bin gefahren – fahren / bin geblieben – bleiben / ist gekommen – kommen / sind gegangen – gehen

b Harald got up too late and had no time for breakfast. It was raining, so he went to university by bus. There was no lecture because the professor was ill. Harald spent all afternoon in the library, looking for a book he needs for his dissertation – no luck. He went to the café with his friend Julius, then went home to watch TV all evening.

c *Your answer should read something like this*: Harald ist spät aufgestanden und mit dem Bus zur Uni gefahren, weil es geregnet hat. Der Professor war krank und Harald ist den ganzen Nachmittag in der Bibliothek geblieben. Er hat ein Buch gesucht, aber nicht gefunden. Sein Freund ist gekommen und sie sind ins Café gegangen. Am Abend hat Harald ferngesehen.

4 a Carima ist aufgestanden. **b** Sie hat gefrühstückt. **c** Sie ist mit dem Bus zur Uni gefahren. **d** Sie ist in die Bibliothek gegangen. **e** Sie hat mit einem Freund Kaffee getrunken. **f** Sie ist ins Kino gegangen. **g** Sie ist am Abend nach Hause gegangen. **h** Sie hat ferngesehen und hat eine Pizza gegessen.

5 a **i** Sie war krank und musste zu Hause bleiben. **ii** Sie hat eingekauft und ist ins Café am Marktplatz gegangen. **iii** Herr Schulz von ihrer Arbeit war auch im Café. **iv** Er ist sofort zurück zur Arbeit gegangen und hat allen Kollegen erzählt, dass er sie gesehen hat.

b **i** Horst hat eine Freundin in Bielefeld. **ii** Er hat sie in einer Vorlesung getroffen. **iii** Sie sind essen

Answers

gegangen. **iv** Sie ist schon fünf Jahre mit ihrem Freund zusammen.

7 a i Er war in der Bibliothek. **ii** Er war müde. **iii** Er ist in die Campus-Bar gegangen. **iv** Er hat mit Antje gesprochen und hat sie geküsst.

8 a i noch schlimmer **ii** hat erzählt **iii** die Wahrheit **iv** böse **v** liebt

9 a 1 i 2 g 3 e 4 l 5 b 6 k 7 j 8 n 9 f 10 d 11 h 12 m 13 a 14 c
b i glücklich (froh) **ii** gestresst (müde) **iii** krank (erkältet) **iv** optimistisch **v** verliebt **vi** gestresst

Extra!

10 a Sie ist drei Wochen in München geblieben. **b** Der Unterricht hat um halb neun (8.30) angefangen. **c** Sie ist zweimal jede Woche schwimmen gegangen, wenn es warm war. Sie ist auch ins Kino gegangen und hat ferngesehen. **d** Paola ist Palomas Freundin (aus Italien). Sie haben oft am Wochenende etwas gemacht. **e** Der Sprachkurs hat Jean-Paul nicht so gut gefallen, (weil die Lehrer langweilig waren.) **f** Er hatte nur morgens Unterricht und die Lehrer waren langweilig. **g** Er ist viel Rad gefahren und nach Regensburg gefahren. Er ist ins Museum und in den Park gegangen, und oft mit der U-Bahn gefahren.
h Nathalie ist Französin und sie ist sehr nett.

11 a Karin had a terrible weekend. She overslept and then went into town to buy herself a new dress. She tried on a lot of dresses, but couldn't find one that she liked. She was frustrated and it was raining, so she went home by bus. The ticket machine was broken, she had no change and the bus driver could not change her €10 note. Her boyfriend called and said he could not go to the cinema with her. She opened a bottle of wine and switched the TV on. The next day she had a terrible headache!

Kurt had a great weekend. His girlfriend got breakfast and they went on a trip to the mountains. They had lunch in a nice restaurant and the weather was brilliant. In the afternoon they had a glass of wine in the garden and then went to a party in the evening. They had a lovely time there, meeting old friends and dancing.

Grammatikübungen

1 a haben … gewohnt **b** haben … gekauft **c** hat … geküsst **d** Hast … geschlafen **e** Haben … geschrieben **f** habe … gefrühstückt **g** sind … gefahren **h** seid … gegangen **i** ist … gekommen; ist … geblieben **j** ist … aufgestanden

2 a i sie **ii** uns **iii** dich **iv** ihn **v** euch **vi** sie
b i ihn **ii** ihr **iii** ihm **iv** mich **v** dich **vi** sie **vii** mir **viii** sie

UNIT 9

1 a 1901 **b** 1945 **c** 1969 **d** 1989 **e** 2010
i neunzehnhundertneunundachtzig

2 a 1 Wolfgang Amadeus Mozart 2 Nelson Mandela **3** Robert De Niro 4 John Lennon
b 1 siebzehnhundertsechsundfünfzig 2 neunzehnhundertachtzehn 3 neunzehnhundertdreiundvierzig 4 neunzehnhundertvierzig

3 a C, B, A, E, D
b i Ich habe eine Stelle gefunden. **ii** Ich habe geheiratet. **iii** Ich bin in

Hamburg aufgewachsen. **iv** Ich habe meine Stelle aufgegeben. **v** Ich habe die Schule verlassen. **vi** Ich habe meinen Mann kennen gelernt. **vii** Meine Eltern sind umgezogen. **viii** Ich bin geboren. **ix** Ich habe immer gute Noten bekommen.

c i Nein, sie ist in Hamburg aufgewachsen. **ii** Ihre Eltern sind umgezogen. **iii** Das Studium hat sie nicht interessiert. **iv** Sie hat 1978 geheiratet. **v** Sie hat die Stelle aufgegeben, weil sie mehr Zeit mit den Kindern verbringen wollte. **vi** Sie arbeitet jetzt nicht mehr.

4 *Your version should read something like this*: Maria ist in Berlin geboren, aber ihre Eltern sind umgezogen und sie ist in Hamburg aufgewachsen. Sie hat immer gute Noten bekommen, aber sie hat mit 19 die Schule verlassen und eine Stelle gefunden. Sie hat ihren Mann im Sportverein kennen gelernt. Sie hat 1978 geheiratet. Sie hat die Stelle aufgegeben, weil sie drei Kinder hat.

6 **a** Von **b** Abitur **c** nach **d** angefangen **e** April **f** spreche **g** bisschen **h** Computerfirma **i** abends **j** gearbeitet **k** Computer **l** weil

7 **Hanna:** Viktoriaschule / Studium: Psychologie in Düsseldorf, jetzt in Heilbronn / Ferienjob in einem Reisebüro / würde gern als Psychologin im Krankenhaus arbeiten
Jens: Viktoriaschule, dann Bert-Brecht-Schule / studiert Sport / arbeitet im Supermarkt (Aldi) / möchte gern Sportlehrer werden

10 **c** *Your letter should be similar to the one below.*
Sehr geehrter …, / Sehr geehrte …,
ich habe Ihre Stellenanzeige mit Interesse gelesen und möchte mich um die Stelle als Kellner bewerben. Ich studiere Anglistik und Informatik an der FU und spreche fließend Englisch. Meine Französischkenntnisse sind gut. Ich habe Erfahrung im Restaurantmetier: Im September 2007 habe ich in einer Krankenhausküche gearbeitet, und in den Ferien hatte ich Jobs in einer Studentenbar und in einer Pizzeria. Dort habe ich im Team gearbeitet. Ich habe ein Auto und kann ab 17 Uhr arbeiten.
Mit freundlichen Grüßen,
Uwe Heimann

Extra!

11 **Alice:** studiert Politik und Literatur / wohnt mit zwei Frauen zusammen und will nach dem Studium ein Jahr in Afrika arbeiten / hat einen Freund, aber sie sind unabhängig und wohnen nicht zusammen / möchte weiter studieren / Thema: Frauen in der Dritten Welt
Barbara: hat gleich nach dem Abitur studiert – Mathematik / wohnt bei den Eltern, das ist billig / hat einen Freund (seit 2 Jahren) / sie wollen heiraten / will als Lehrerin arbeiten / hat sich um zwei Stellen beworben / will Kinder haben und nicht arbeiten, wenn die Kinder klein sind

12 **a** Er hat sich im Jahr 20.. entschieden, zur Universität zu gehen. **b** Er ist jetzt fünfundsechzig Jahre alt. Er ist 19.. geboren. **c** Ein typischer Student ist jung – kein Rentner! **d** Seine jüngste Tochter hat ihr Studium begonnen, und er wollte auch studieren. (… so was auch machen.) **f** sich entscheiden, sich informieren; the perfect tense

Grammatikübungen

1 sterben, **gestorben**, **sein**, **to die** / **enden**, geendet, **haben**, **to end** / **fallen**, **gefallen**, **sein**, to fall /

183

gewinnen, gewonnen, **haben**, **to win** / komponieren, **komponiert**, **haben**, **to compose** / **verbringen**, verbracht, haben, to spend (time) / **verstehen**, verstanden, **haben**, **to understand** / **interessieren**, **interessiert**, **haben**, to interest / finden, **gefunden**, **haben**, **to find** / **verdienen**, verdient, **haben**, **to earn** / **umziehen**, **umgezogen**, **sein**, to move house / aufwachsen, **aufgewachsen**, sein, **to grow up** / **heiraten**, **geheiratet**, **haben**, **to marry**

2   **a** Ich bewerbe mich um eine Stelle in London. **b** Sie interessiert sich für Sport. **c** Sie spezialisieren sich für Übersetzungen. **d** Er hat sich entschieden, eine Stelle zu finden.

3   **a** Sie würden gern in einem Team arbeiten. **b** Sie würde gern das Gymnasium besuchen. **c** Würdest du gern deine Sprachkenntnisse nutzen? **d** Wir würden gern eine Stelle finden. **e** Er würde gern umziehen.

4   **a** **i** Obwohl er viel Freizeit hat, geht er selten aus. **ii** Obwohl sie fließend Italienisch spricht, war sie noch nie in Italien. *oder* Obwohl sie noch nie in Italien war, spricht sie fließend Italienisch.
      b **i** Wann bist du geboren? **ii** Als ich letzte Woche in Berlin war, habe ich deinen Bruder gesehen. **iii** Wenn ich im Ausland arbeite, nutze ich meine Sprachkenntnisse.

UNIT 10

1   I don't know if I'll stay in this job for long. The work is rather monotonous and boring and I'd like to find a more interesting job – I need variety in life! I'd like to work abroad: perhaps in Britain or Italy. My English is better than my Italian but I'd really like to live and work in a hot country because the rainy weather here in the north makes me all gloomy. Have you ever been to Italy? Last year I spent almost a month in Verona. The climate, the people, the food – everything was fantastic. I'd like to spend more time there to get to know the life there better.

2   **a** weil es in der Buchhandlung (manchmal) (sehr) langweilig ist. **b** weil sein/der Boss nicht sehr nett ist. **c** weil er die Sprache fließend sprechen möchte / weil er im Ausland / in Italien arbeiten möchte. **d** weil die Leute freundlicher und kommunikativer sind. **e** weil es/das eine wichtige Erfahrung ist.

4   **a** Sinn für Humor, klein
      Sport – Schwimmen und Federball. Markus geht gern ins Kino: sie interessiert sich auch für Filme
      Politik – interessante Gespräche – modisch
      Musik – Pop und Jazz
      Freizeit – mit Freunden in der Kneipe oder in einem Restaurant. Manchmal tanzen.
      Reist gern – Italien, vielleicht im Ausland arbeiten.
      Nicht böse wenn ich mit Freunden weggehe, geht auch mit Freundinnen aus.

7   **a** Nein, sie ist (seit 30 Jahren) verheiratet. **b** Sie ist nach Westdeutschland gefahren, um Verwandte zu besuchen. **c** Es gibt mehr Freiheit zu reisen, mehr Auswahl beim Einkaufen und eine offenere Politik. **d** Ja, sie hat einen Telizeitjob in einem Supermarkt. **e** Jugendliche haben keine Arbeit und zu viel Zeit. **f** Sie hat gern gearbeitet, weil sie unabhängig war. **g** Die Kinder haben schlechtere Chancen, einen Job zu finden. **h** Tante

8 a *Your grid should contain several of the following*:

Damals: wenig Kriminalität / große, alte Wohnung / Man musste viel reparieren. / Miete war billig, aber keine Toilette in der Wohnung / Alle hatten eine Stelle. / Kinder hatten freie Kindergartenplätze. / Man konnte nur nach Ungarn fahren. / Kinder sind meistens in der gleichen Stadt geblieben. / Man konnte die Familie in Westdeutschland nicht sehen.

Jetzt: Kleine, aber moderne Wohnung / 20 Minuten mit dem Bus ins Stadtzentrum / teure Mieten / Viele Leute haben keine Arbeit, besonders Frauen. / Freiheit zu reisen / mehr Kriminalität, Drogen / Viele junge Leute gehen nach Westdeutschland. / Man kann die Familie in Westdeutschland besuchen.

11 a nach **b** wohin **c** Ausland **d** See **e** aufs **f** See

12 wandern, schwimmen, Rad fahren, lesen

Extra!

15 Helga S.: wanted to study architecture and share a big flat in Berlin / didn't want to get married / wanted to travel and be independent / had a baby and stopped studying / lives with boyfriend and baby and goes to evening classes / hopes to continue her studies

Benjamin B.: wanted to be a policeman and get married and have children / met his wife in South Africa / worked there in a hospital for 5 years / returned to Germany 2 years ago / now has a daughter and works in a hospital in Regensburg

Renate O.: left school at 16 to work in a florist's / wanted to marry, have children / got married at 21 and had 2 children / now divorced, children both at school / needs money and is working part-time / hopes to find a better job in the future

Dietmar L.: wanted to become a teacher / studied languages and went on exchange visit to France / met French girl but went back to Germany / his girlfriend came to Germany / he had job as a teacher, but his girlfriend wasn't very happy in Germany / he now teaches in France

16 There were two German states between 1949 and 1990. Communists built a wall between in 1961, to stop thousands of people leaving. East Germans weren't free to travel. In 1989 there were large demonstrations for the freedom to travel. The government understood that they had to reform the system. On 9 November 1989 they gave freedom to travel and the East Berliners went straight to the wall to see the west. That was the end of the wall and of East Germany. In March 1990 parties were elected that wanted to re-unify. In October five new Länder joined the Federal Republic.

Grammatikübungen

1 a Ein alter Freund **meiner Schwester b** Eine Freundin **seines Bruders c** Der Anfang **des Semesters d** Die Handtasche **unserer Lehrerin e** Die Bücher **der Studenten f** Das Schlafzimmer **meines Sohnes g** Der Parkplatz **des Sportzentrums h** Ein Foto **des Babys**

2 a interessanteren **b** besser **c** netter **d** schnelleren **e** größeres **f** schlechtere **g** billiger **h** glücklicher **i** angenehmeres

3 Sean darf keine Pommes frites essen – er muss Obst und Gemüse essen und Mineralwasser trinken. Er darf kein Bier

und keinen Wein trinken und er muss spazieren gehen. Er darf nicht rauchen.

WEITERE ÜBUNGEN

Unit 1

1 **b** Engländer/Engländerin **c** Franzose/Französin **d** Spanien **e** Italiener/Italienerin **f** Österreich **g** Schotte/Schottin **h** Ire/Irin **i** Belgien

2 Sie heißt Anne Jenkinson. Sie kommt aus England und sie wohnt in Oxford. Sie ist Sekretärin von Beruf.

4 **Anja** is German and she comes from Hamburg. She works as a teacher in Glasgow.
David is a student and he lives in Manchester, but he comes from Bristol.

5 **Alex** is a student from Russia. He is studying history and politics, but he also works behind the bar at *The Red Lion*. He lives in Redman Street and he is learning German. The teacher is German and is called Frau Wolters. Alex asks whether you are German or are learning German.

7 **a** kommt **b** in **c** arbeitet **d** Freundin **e** studiert **f** als

Unit 2

2 **a** 18.20 **b** 7.55 **c** 4.19 **d** 20.27 **e** 11.12 **f** 13.38

3 Anna gets up at 7.10 am and has breakfast at 7.30 am. At 7.50 am she goes to the university. At 8.35 am she goes to the library, and her lecture starts at 10 am. At 11.15 am she has coffee.

4 He has a lecture and a seminar in the morning, and in the afternoon he's going to the sports centre to play football. He has an English lesson at 5 pm. He seems to be free for coffee at 4 pm and after his English class.

6 *Note that different word order would also be acceptable.* Um 18 Uhr sieht Ralf fern. Um 20 Uhr geht er in die Stadt. Er geht um 20.30 Uhr in die Kneipe und trinkt ein Bier. Um 22.15 Uhr geht er in die Diskothek und tanzt. Er geht um 1 Uhr nach Hause und um 1.45 Uhr geht er ins Bett.

7 **a** Ich bleibe immer zu Hause. **b** Hörst du oft Musik? **c** Sie liest manchmal ein Buch. **d** Er sieht selten fern. **e** Gehen Sie nie aus?

8 der Kaffee, die Cola, das Bier, der Toast, der (das) Joghurt, das Käsebrot, das Schinkenbrot, die Nudeln (pl.), der Fisch, der Salat, der Orangensaft, die Pizza, der Wein, das Müsli

9 **a** um **b** Frühstück **c** trinkt **d** geht **e** Käsebrot (Schinkenbrot) **f** Hause **g** schreibt (liest) **h** spielt **i** bleibt **j** sieht **k** Universität **l** Mensa **m** lernt **n** beginnt **o** hört **p** liest **q** bleibt (ist) **r** Diskothek

Unit 3

1 **a** Sind Sie (Bist du) verheiratet? **b** Wie heißt Ihre (deine) Freundin? **c** Haben Sie (Hast du) Kinder? **d** Was sind Sie (bist du) von Beruf? **e** Was ist Ihre (deine) Mutter von Beruf? **f** Wie alt ist Ihr (dein) Großvater?

2 **a** richtig **b** falsch **c** falsch **d** falsch **e** richtig **f** richtig **g** falsch

3 **Dieter** (58), verheiratet mit **Clara** (57); **Dieter** (29) verheiratet mit **Ana** (25); **Carsten** (34) (ledig), **Silvia** (36), **Barbara** (9, Silvias Tochter)

4 **a** seine/ihre **b** mein **c** ihre/seine **d** unseren **e** dein

5 **a** **i** Schwimmbad **ii** E-Mail **iii** Tochter **iv** Film
b **i** das/das/das/das **ii** der/die/das/der **iii** die/der/der/der **iv** das/der/der/das

7 **a** Bruder **b** heißt **c** keine **d** Kinder **e** klein **f** Beruf **g** ledig **h** Hobbys **i** Geschwister **j** Eltern **k** Fahrrad **l** seinen (einen) **m** bleibt **n** wohnt **o** essen **p** gehen

Unit 4

1 **a** stehe … auf **b** bleibe **c** lese **d** höre **e** kochst **f** koche **g** bleibe **h** gehe **i** kaufe … ein **j** gehe … aus **k** fährt

2 *Your letter should look similar to the following*:
Liebe Karin,
ich gehe gern ins Kino, lese gern und ich kaufe auch gern ein. Ich gehe gern spazieren, aber ich fahre lieber Rad. Am Wochenende koche ich am liebsten. Ich rauche gern, aber ich trinke nicht gern Wein oder Bier. Kochst du auch gern?

3 **a** kann **b** ausgehen **c** muss **d** arbeiten **e** Mittwochs **f** keine **g** will **h** gehen **i** geht **j** ins **k** Eltern

4 Christian asks Anna if she would like to go with him to Munich on Saturday. She isn't sure because she has to revise for a test on Monday. Christian suggests that she can do that on Sunday, and Anna is easily persuaded to come along.

5 c, f, g, j, e, h, i, b, a, l, k, d

6 **a** Abend **b** gern **c** Viertel (zehn, …) **d** Tisch **e** Speisekarte **f** nimmt **g** lieber **h** trinken **i** den **j** fantastisch (sehr gut, …) **k** Zeit **l** will **m** Wein (Bier, …) **n** Hause **o** aufstehen **p** kann **q** beginnt

Unit 5

1 Herr und Frau Werner

2 **a** Wohnzimmer: großes Fenster, hell, Sofa, Tisch, Sessel, Balkon
b Küche: groß, großen Tisch, 4 Stühle, Elektroherd, Kühlschrank, Waschmaschine

3 **a** Sie will am Freitagabend grillen. **b** Sie grillt im Garten. **c** Er bringt eine Flasche Wein mit. **d** Sie braucht noch zwei große Baguettes. **e** Er muss beim Bäcker einkaufen. **f** Sie macht Nudelsalat und Reissalat. **g** Hanna, Ursula und vielleicht Martin kommen zum Barbecue. **h** Er will einen Film sehen. / Es gibt einen guten amerikanischen Film.

4 **a** Wir wohnen in **der Bismarckstraße** **b** Ich arbeite **am Schreibtisch** **c** Man kocht **in der Küche** **d** Sie essen **im Restaurant** **e** Er sitzt **auf einem Stuhl** **f** Das Auto ist **in der Garage** **g** Petra steht **unter der Dusche** **h** Ich tanze gern **in der Diskothek**

5 **a** Stadt **b** Wein **c** Wohnung **d** Essen **e** beginnt **f** großes (schönes) **g** gibt **h** klein (schön/groß) **i** Mutter (Großmutter/Schwester) **j** Lampe **k** im **l** gern **m** aufstehen **n** wir **o** auf **p** unter (auf) **q** auf (neben/unter) **r** will (kann)

Unit 6

1 Get off at the bus stop in Bismarckstraße. Go straight on, then first right. Go past the park – you then come to a big crossroads. Cross the road and go right. The hospital is on the left-hand side.

3 **a** **i** in front of the station **ii** at the station **iii** something/a detective novel for Fatma **iv** next to the bookshop
b der Blumenstrauß

4 **a** f **b** f **c** f **d** r **e** f

Answers

5 **a** She needs a summer skirt. **b** Ulrike already has 6 or 7 skirts, the skirt is too long, too colourful and too expensive. **c** He would rather buy 7 CDs with the money. **d** The skirt is size 38. **e** They will meet in the CD department.

6 **a** Stadt **b** Uhr **c** Auto **d** Bus **e** Nähe **f** Abend **g** Supermarkt **h** gehen **i** Ecke **j** der **k** trifft

Unit 7

1 **a i** Woher kommst du? **ii** Wie lange lernst du (schon) Deutsch? **iii** Warum lernst du Deutsch?
   b i Der Zug kommt in wenigen Minuten in Bonn an. **ii** Sie macht einen Sprachkurs. **iii** Sie will ihr Deutsch verbessern. **iv** Vijay hilft ihr mit den Koffern.

3 **a** Am **b** nach **c** machen **d** seit **e** verbessern **f** dauert **g** lernt **h** komme **i** mit **j** fahre **k** Universität

4 **a i** Er kann nicht mit ins Sportzentrum kommen, weil er eine Vorlesung hat. **ii** Er will am Samstag (zum Einkaufen) nach Köln fahren. **iii** Sie müssen mit dem Zug fahren. **iv** Er will nicht nach Köln fahren, weil er in Moment nicht so viel Geld hat. **v** Am Freitag will er die Wohnung aufräumen. **vi** Klaus will neue Schuhe und eine CD kaufen.

5 **a** f **b** f **c** r **d** f **e** r

6 **a** arbeiten **b** nach **c** können **d** schön **e** im **f** kann **g** spazieren gehen **h** Bus **i** müssen (können) **j** Fahrkartenschalter **k** Rückfahrkarten **l** können **m** weil **n** man **o** Wochenende (Samstag/Sonntag) **p** Hause

Unit 8

1 Er ist spät ins Bett gegangen und hat gut geschlafen. Heute Morgen ist er spät aufgestanden. Er hat nichts gegessen und nur ein Glas Wasser getrunken. Um 7.30 Uhr ist er an der Bushaltestelle angekommen, um ins Büro zu fahren. Er hat gesehen, dass er ganz allein war. „Es ist Samstag! Ich arbeite heute nicht!" hat er laut gesagt. Und dann hat er gelacht …

2 credit card was stolen / football team did not perform well / couldn't find books for essay / it rained for hours … Conclusion: will stay in bed next weekend.

3 1 f 2 c 3 a 4 d 5 b 6 e

4 **a** Ich habe bei Aldi eingekauft und (habe) für meine Freunde gekocht. Nach dem Essen haben wir Musik gehört und später haben wir Karten gespielt. **b** Sie hat Brot mit Marmelade gegessen und eine Tasse Tee getrunken. Sie hat E-Mails an ihre Freunde geschrieben. Dann hat sie die Zeitung gelesen. **c** Ich bin um sieben Uhr aufgestanden und (bin) mit dem Bus zur Uni gefahren. Ich bin den ganzen Nachmittag in der Bibliothek geblieben. Ich habe ein Buch für meine Dissertation gesucht, aber habe es nicht gefunden.

5 **a** sind **b** aufgestanden **c** gefrühstückt **d** Bahnhof **e** gesehen **f** angekommen **g** hatten **h** machen **i** können **j** sehen **k** gehst **l** treffen **m** vor **n** ist **o** angefangen

Unit 9

1 **a** neunzehnhundertsiebenundvierzig
   b neunzehnhunderteinundzwanzig
   c zweitausend(und)drei
   d neunzehnhundertzwölf
   e achtzehnhundertfünfzehn
   f neunzehnhundertdreiundneunzig
   g achtzehnhundertvierundsiebzig
   h zweitausend(und)fünf

2 **a** Meine Eltern haben mich nicht verstanden. **b** Seine Brüder haben in Frankfurt studiert. **c** Er ist nach dem Studium Lehrer geworden. **d** Haben Sie gute Noten erhalten? **e** Wir haben mit 16 die Schule verlassen.

3 **b** The interviewee was born in Stuttgart in 1973, but grew up in Hanover. He passed his **Abitur** with a good grade. He really wanted to find a job and get married. He didn't get married till 1999 and he now has a small daughter. They still live with his parents. He studied psychology and sociology and has found a job at a travel agent's. He would rather work abroad, though, because he is good at languages and doesn't enjoy his current job.

4 **Simon:** b; **Anja:** a

5 **a** **i** He did his **Abitur** five years ago, grade 3.9 (not very good). **ii** He worked for 18 months as an ambulance driver. **iii** He wasn't motivated. / He was bored. **iv** He eventually applied for a job in the library. **v** He worked on the computer a lot, but also with the public. **vi** He likes working in a team. / Speaks English quite well. **vii** He worked in a bar.

6 **1** , weil er gern anderen Menschen hilft. **2** , weil sie sich für Bilder interessiert. **3** , weil er sportlich ist. **4** , weil sie gern sehr spät ins Bett geht. **5** , weil er sich für Literatur interessiert.

7 **a** Geld **b** würden/möchten **c** liest **d** Stelle **e** kannst **f** wäschst **g** sucht **h** können **i** dich **j** bleiben

Unit 10

1 **a** **a** der **b** langweilig **c** würde **d** Ausland **e** Leben **f** Land **g** angenehmer **h** interessanter **i** will **j** Sprachkurs **k** Italienisch **l** ins **m** Erfahrungen **n** zurückkommt **o** verdient

b Markus finds his work in the bookshop boring. He would like to work abroad. Life in a southern European country is more pleasant and the culture is more interesting. Markus wants to do a language course to learn Italian. He's going abroad to gain new experiences. When he comes back he will hopefully earn more money.

2 **a** will **b** muss **c** darf **d** kann **e** muss

3 **a** die Fahrradtour, das Dorf, der Bauernhof, der Wald, der See, der Strand, der Hafen **See** (f.) = sea, but **See** (m.) = a lake

b Five (see section 3 of the Grammar Summary): Fahrradtour<u>en</u>, Dörfer/ W<u>ä</u>ld<u>er</u>, Bauernh<u>ö</u>fe/Strän<u>de</u>, See<u>n</u>, H<u>ä</u>fen

c malerische

4 **a** Job **b** können **c** gutes **d** mit **e** dem **f** teurer **g** Auto **h** fahren **i** zum **j** denn **k** das **l** sagt **m** gern

APPENDIX

Additional glossary lists

*Verb strong in present tense ▶**G14.2**

Unit 4 Am Wochenende

Aufgabe 13

bekommen	to get (here = to have)
die Tomatensuppe	tomato soup
das Huhn	chicken
die Sahnesauce	cream sauce
der Weißwein	white wine
die Nummer	number
sonst noch etwas?	anything else?
das ist alles	that's all
der Rotwein	red wine
das Vanilleeis	vanilla ice cream
das Schokoladeneis	chocolate ice cream

Extra!

zusammen	together
allein	alone
fast	almost
spät	late

Unit 5 Zu Hause

Aufgabe 8

das stimmt	that's right
kitschig	kitschy
altmodisch	old-fashioned
exklusiv	exclusive
teuer	expensive
kompakt	compact
der Kuchen (also *pl*)	cake
backen	to bake
köstlich	delicious
der Bäcker	baker
beim Bäcker	at the baker's
der Schokoladenkuchen	chocolate cake
die Idee	idea

Extra!/Grammatikübungen/Partnerarbeit

das Haus	house
schon	already

einladen* *sep*	to invite
die Toilette	toilet

Unit 6 In der Stadt

Aufgabe 12

tragen*	to wear
– er/sie trägt	wears/is wearing
der Anzug	suit
die Herrenabteilung	the men's dept
die Krawatte	tie
bunt	colourful

Aufgabe 13

langweilig	boring

Aufgabe 14

blau	blue
rot	red
grün	green
gelb	yellow
braun	brown
weiß	white
beige	beige

Unit 7 Fahren

Aufgabe 9

die Schnellwahl	rapid choice
das (Fahrt)ziel	destination
drücken	to press
entsprechend	appropriate
die Taste	button, key
erreichen	to get to
ein anderes Ziel	a different destination
das Verzeichnis	index
der Fahrpreis	fare
tippen	to type
wählen	to choose
gewünscht	desired
Erwachsene *pl*	adults
die Tageskarte	day ticket
der Automat	machine
die Zahlung	payment
Münzen *pl*	coins
Geldscheine *pl*	banknotes

zahlen	to pay
das Restgeld	change
zurückerhalten* *sep*	to get back

Unit 8 Gestern

Extra!/Weitere Übungen

gefunden	pp of finden
finden	to find
gestohlen	pp of stehlen
stehlen*	to steal

Unit 9 Lebensläufe

Aufgabe 7

das Reisebüro	travel agency

Aufgabe 9

motiviert	motivated
enthusiastisch	enthusiastic
selbständig	independent
teamorientiert	team-orientated
flexibel	flexible
freundlich	friendly
kommunikativ	communicative
pünktlich	punctual
zuverlässig	reliable
organisiert	organised
die Fähigkeit	ability, capability
mobil	mobile
fleißig	hard-working
Flugreisen *pl*	air travel
europaweit	throughout Europe
die Kundenberatung	advising customers
Läden *pl*	shops, branches
besitzen	to possess
der Geist	spirit
bieten	to offer
das Arbeitsfeld	area of work

Aufgabe 10

der/die Übersetzer(in) (n/nen)	translator (m/f)

sich spezialisieren auf	to specialise in
technisch	technical
das Gehalt	salary
ausgezeichnet	excellent
die Bewerbung	application
die Stellenanzeige	job advert
sich bewerben um*	to apply for
abgeschlossen	pp of abschließen
abschließen *sep*	to complete
Termine *pl*	deadlines
das Personal	personnel
das Metier	profession

Unit 10 Zukunftspläne

Aufgabe 11

noch nicht	not yet
die See	sea
aufs Land	to the country
die Nordsee	North Sea
die Ostsee	Baltic Sea
die Küste	coast
näher	nearer
bestimmt	definitely

Advert

die Vermietung	hire
Wanderungen	hikes, walks
Ausflüge *pl*	trips
Pensionen *pl*	boarding houses
Campingplätze *pl*	campsites

Aufgabe 12

Ski fahren	to ski
segeln	to sail
Kunstgalerien *pl*	art galleries
bergsteigen	to go mountain-climbing
wandern	to go on a hike, walk
die Vorbereitungszeit	preparation time

p. 112

wen	whom

INDEX